Playbook

Always cutting edge often prescient...

By J.M. Hamilton

To Jack

CONTENT:

Populism is Not the Problem....

By J.M. Hamilton (2-8-10)

Populism, as decried in the New Yorker article below, is not the problem.... Perhaps, populism is sometimes, a little misguided, yes, but in fact, it's the solution. As usual the instincts of the American people are, in fact, highly accurate. And any politician, who wants to survive and navigate these troubled times would do well to heed, get out in front of, and attempt to steer public opinion. Such is the calling of President Obama, the second coming of the Great Communicator, leading up to these mid-term elections!

As for the populist rallying cry of the Tea-Bag crowd, "cut taxes," this originates from the public's inherent fear of big government and rising fiscal deficits. Obama was elected on a platform of change, and what his administration gave the nation was not change, but a redux of the Clinton's first years in office. The bill that was about to be passed by congress, was NOT healthcare reform (or healthcare cost management), but rather, a serious power grab and an expansion of the welfare state.

And hence, the Massachusetts's miracle, or debacle, depending upon one's views!

What Mr. Obama really should have spent his first year doing, instead, was giving the nation real change, by addressing the public's need for jobs, and shearing Wall Street, and cutting it down to size, via the Volcker Rule and much, much more. In brief, the tax-payer owned banks should have already been broken up, which – allegedly (per the banks anyway) – creates diseconomies of scale, and hence, by definition, more jobs, via greater inefficiencies. Breaking up the banks into their core constituent parts would also go a very long way towards eliminating systematic risk; and breaking them up would help prevent the next financial melt-down.... A financial meltdown that this nation can ill afford.

President Obama would have been perceived as a real agent of change had he taken on Wall Street, and given government support to the people, instead of government support/welfare to Wall Street. Instead enormous piles of the President's political capital were wasted on millionaires and billionaires.

And what has it got the President?

The banks, are now lobbying against real reform, and they are planning Obama's overthrow, by biding their time, and NOT lending to small and mid-sized businesses.   As we read in today's NY Times, the banks are in fact getting ready to back the very same Republican party that ran this nation into the ground. That's right, the Republican Party that has ran record, annual, budget deficits, since Reagan, and unleashed today's financial crisis, via soft money policies and bank deregulation. Okay, the Democrats were not exactly absent for the last thirty years – but rarely were they in charge of the executive branch, except for Clinton – who actually ran budget surpluses.

In fairness to President Obama, Mr. Paulson, Goldman Sachs Alum, did set up the President, by attaching little or no strings to TARP lending.   But I digress…. It was Mr. Obama who brought Tim Geithner on board.

Had this administration spent its first year reining in Wall Street's worst tendencies, and had the President done more to stimulate the economy and create jobs (instead of giving hand outs, on top of hand outs, to the banks)…. One wonders if the Tea-Bag movement would have ever gotten off the ground? But what we got instead was not change, but business as usual in Washington: finger pointing, half measures, and stale mate.   Exactly, what the Republican Party delivered for the last eight years.

As for the populist….it's important for all of us to remember that tax cuts are always nice, but unless they are coupled with reductions in government spending, they are no better than government spending that is not supported by tax revenue.   In short, tax cuts w/out corresponding reductions in government spending (Republicans) are no better than increased government spending which is unsupported by an increase in government tax receipts (Democrats), because they both lead to …What?…. greater government borrowing, greater dependence upon our enemy, China, and an ever rising national debt to GDP ratio.

It would be grand to emulate the great supply-siders of the 20th Century:

Kennedy and Reagan!

However, our National Debt no longer allows such extravagances. Instead, it is this President's challenge, to create jobs and spur economic growth through means other than government spending. And what better way to create jobs than to break up the banks, and insist that any foreign banks – operating on U.S. soil – also adhere to U.S. bank law (Volcker Rule, Et Al.), and also be cut

down to their proper size. Otherwise, foreign banks who do not adhere –
good-bye.

President Obama was very wise to embrace Messrs. Volcker and King' counsel,
post Massachusetts.   Healthcare reform – real cost containment – can wait for
another day, like when unemployment is below 6% again (for two consecutive
quarters), and the banks are made to heel!

The President has to do this with both governmental arms tied behind his back,
that would be the House of Representatives and the Senate.   Let us all pray for
President Obama's success! Obama's success is our country's success.   Given
the incompetence of the U.S. Congress, the President truly will need divine
intervention, and truly deserves our best wishes.   Time for Obama to channel,
not only Reagan optimism, but the trust busting courage of Teddy Roosevelt.

The Sovereign Debt Crisis is Sucking the Wind out of the Global Economy…. The "Can" Just Got Punted Down the Road!

By J.M. Hamilton 5-10-2010

Wow, what a difference a weekend makes. Do you ever notice how central banks do their "wild and craziest" maneuvers on the weekends: whether it's letting Lehman Bros slide into oblivion, or deciding to bailout AIG (or was that a weekday?), or in the case of Europe, bailing out PIIGS!   Looking into the future when it comes to bailing out the world's fiat currency, one might imagine that happening on the weekend, too.

One of the words we heard thrown around Europe's second bailout of the banks is "sterilization" of the expansion of money supply.   Simply put, "sterilization" means as money is pumped into the European central banks, if I have this correct, the banks will give up their toxic PIIGS debt in exchange for European or Euro debt, so that money supply is not increased. What a relief!

Either way you look at it folks, the Euro just got a little bit weaker with one trillion Euros magically appearing from no where, and toxic assets being moved on to yet another central bank's balance sheet.

Why this special emphasis, by our European brethren, on money supply "sterilization?"

Well, because the Europeans remember very well (unlike some Americans) the Weimar Republic and how hyper inflation lead to the rise of a paper hanger/would-be artist, named Adolph Hitler, and the global calamity called World War II. Europeans remember, all too well, particularly Germans, the whirring of the printing presses and currency created out of thin air, and the resulting madness.   And the German's just to show the world that they remember their history voted resoundingly against Chancellor Merkel's Christian Democrats… and as of Sunday, her party is no longer holding down upper house of German Parliament, due to Merkel's real or perceived support of the bailout that transpired this weekend.

Sure, this time, the world is a little more sophisticated… The major banks – which are beholding to the politicians for their bailouts – have agreed, in their Japanese-Zombie state, to leverage up the free money they receive from their respective governments, and "hoover-up" the ever expanding national debt. Heh, why not… after all, taxpayer funded rates of return trump the vagaries of lending to the private sector any day. Right?

Except there's one problem: The crowding out effect is coming to fruition, as government borrowing takes precedence over providing credit to businesses in the private sector, which has a stifling effect on jobs creation and tax revenue.

What we are in right now, citizens of the world, is a vicious economic cycle, perhaps globally – certainly in the U.S. and Europe, where governments, who depend upon the private sector for jobs creation and a tax base, are literally destroying private sector opportunity – through the crowding out effect in the credit markets. Check out the Shadow Banking web site, and the contraction of M3 or the money supply (http://www.shadowstats.com/charts/monetary-base-money-supply).

The cycle continues in that governments in turn have to borrow higher and higher amounts of money to provide benefits for the ever growing ranks of the unemployed, which leads to even greater private sector crowding out of the credit markets. If we review our history further, the last country to crowd out the private sector, totally, this time at the barrel of a gun, was the former U.S.S.R. And many of us remember how that story ended.

The Wall Street Banks, and their European Peers, were bailed out in 2008…. For making wild bets on speculative real estate, and real estate CDO's and derivative products. But now we can already see that European banks are being bailed out, less than two years later, for holding junk sovereign debt. The worry of the major powers in Europe has not been avoided by this weekend's events, that a chain of sovereign dominoes would fall (as the stronger nations attempted to bailout their weaker sister states); but rather, the thesis has been confirmed.

And now, the PIIG's must anti-up with politically unpopular social benefit reductions, and tax increases – all contractionary economic policies – or dissolve in chaos, as governments are overrun and are overturned by their upset citizens. We saw hints of social unrest in Greece just last week. More than likely, those same citizens will be hitting the streets again, very soon. Either that, or the Greek government will not enact the spending and tax reforms necessary, so that they will be back at the E.U., yet again, looking for additional bailouts.

Moral hazard affirmed once again... this time, among sovereigns and the banks that lend to them.

Unfortunately, few politicians have the political will to address these issues. There's always an excuse to kick the can down the road a little further: say political expediency, an election around the corner, an economy that isn't quite back on its feet, or wars to be fought and wars to be won.

The cold hard reality however, is that when a currency is weakened by over expansion, or inflation, subsequent bailouts become increasingly more expensive, and, possibly, more frequent, until such time as the currency is no longer viewed as holding any value. World banks steeped in the U.S. dollar and euro holdings, in the long run, may be no better off than they were going into this weekend holding PIIGS' debt.

Our banks and governments ability to handle the next economic catastrophe, or geo-political crisis, is now in question. The hope is that these successive bailouts will give the economy time to heal, and that we can grow our way out of our problems, or take on contractionary fiscal policies – during better economic times; but increasingly, one wonders if the bailouts are just a means of kicking the "can" just a little further down the road, and only serving to aggravate the inevitable day of reckoning?

Monopolies & Double Standards....

By J.M. Hamilton 6-19-2010

A little over thirty years ago, Jeane Kirkpatrick, the first women U.S. ambassador to the U.N., wrote her master work, *Dictatorships and Double Standards*. The work was brilliant, and she soon became a key member of the Reagan foreign policy establishment, and her analysis from *Dictatorships and Double Standards* became a cornerstone in Reagan's foreign policy. In it, Doctor Kirkpatrick posited that the Carter administration, and indeed members of the Democratic establishment, were prone to coddle leftist dictatorships (who were anti-American), while castigating right-wing dictatorships (who were often neutral to American interests). Ms. Kirkpatrick went on to argue that left wing dictatorships were prone to, marching towards, or already socialist in nature, and therefore, far more oppressive to their citizens, than most right wing dictatorships. Remember this was written during the crucible on the cold war, when it was feared that Communism's stated goal of global hegemony, still might be achieved. Republican's and the political right rallied around Mr. Reagan, and his new found apostle, Doctor Kirkpatrick, and the rest is history.

Republican's were right to oppose both communism and left wing dictatorship, and history would seem to support their assertions that private enterprise and freedom produce greater amounts of prosperity, per capita, than the economic misery created under, say a socialist regime. Even China, the last of the communist hold outs, appears on board with this notion.

This begs the question: Why then have Republicans turned their back on their march against socialism, by embracing democracy's equivalent, or the private sector equivalent to socialism, monopoly?

Anyone who has taken Econ 101 knows the inherent evils of socialism and monopoly, and indeed, if we review what those evils are, they are not dissimilar: they include, but are not limited to, inefficiencies in production and the utilization of scarce resources; services and products tend to be shoddy, as there is no competition; and creativity, innovation and merit are not rewarded and are stifled, as there is only one game in town. Consumers, employees, and society suffer under both socialism and monopoly. Socialism by definition, and its cousin monopoly, also lead to, or are a product of, outsized political control over the citizens of the state.

Therefore, Americans, correctly enough, has been taught to abhor socialism; but on monopoly, rarely discussed, the conversation in democracies goes rather quiet.

During the Reagan, and Thatcher revolutions, and over the last thirty years, we have been fed an ideological diet expressing the virtues of the free market, private enterprise and laisezz faire doctrine. Rightfully so, but again, little is said against the evils of monopoly.

If we look closely at the writings of Adam Smith, we discover that he abhorred monopolies, probably for the very reason Mr. Smith would have disdained socialism. Even Mr. Hayek, founder of the Austrian and Chicago school's of economics (and a Free Market deity), had his concerns and issues with laissez faire capitalism.

Why(?), because laissez faire unchecked leads to the jungle, and the elimination of competition, and hence, monopoly.

In a nation governed under the rule of law, and as we do not operate in the jungle, monopolies do not occur naturally. The referee of the private sector, government, allows monopolies to occur and allows them to operate. And there are legitimate/societal reasons for monopolies to exist. The classic example is utility services and power companies, because of the massive infrastructure involved, there is merit and societal value in monopoly, in this instance. But what about other sectors of the economy where monopolies operate for no good societal reason? What we find is that combination has been allowed to occur for the enrichment of a few, the ruling class, and the private citizens in whose hands the grant of monopoly has been placed, all to the detriment of society.

So if socialism is bad, and monopoly is bad, why have the last thirty years seen an increase in the concentration of economic power, and a record number of mergers and acquisition, all granted and authorized by the U.S. and Western European governments?

One rationalization for the combinations authorized by democracies is economies of scale, efficiencies in production, and synergies in supporting departments and management. However, we also know that too much concentration leads to diseconomies of scale, that is the organization is so big that management loses control, risk management falls apart, and chaos ensues.

But this is rarely discussed, or written about, and that is because in this country anyone who speaks out against corporate combination is immediately branded a communist, socialist or worse. The reality, however, is one can be pro- capitalist, pro- democracy, and pro-free enterprise and have a complete disdain for monopoly and oligopoly for the very same reasons one would oppose socialism.

If we look very closely at the situation, we discover that monopoly is socialism by private proxy.

Corporate endeavor has become synonymous with free enterprise, and in many instances, it is an absolute truism; but when corporations pass the Rubicon, and by government sanction, become monopolies or oligopolies, it is then that citizens of a democracy should exercise their duties, query their elected leaders, and vote accordingly – as it is those elected leaders who are trusted to protect society from the deprivations of socialism and monopoly.

Americans witnessed both the subservience to untrammeled economic power, and the inefficiencies of combination this week, as the drama between Representative Barton and B.P. continues to unfold. By now, nearly all Americans, and indeed much of the world, are well aware of the total lack of risk management and corporate control executive management (to hear the CEO tell it) exerted over B.P. B.P. is the classic example of a corporation growing so big that it no longer operates in the interest of society, or itself, but rather, to the complete and absolute detriment of society, its shareholders and partners. Rep. Barton is tragically confused, apparently, between allegiance to the citizens he serves, free enterprise that benefits his constituents, and absolute subservience to the B.P. corporation. The latter is not alligned with the former!

As we witness diseconomies of scale play out in the gulf, and the abdication of responsibility – and the failure of sound risk management principles – by B.P.'s management, it's important to remember the systematic risk and catastrophe imposed on the citizens of the world by another oligopoly, and that would be the Wall Street banks. The economies of the world are still reeling from the total lack of accountability by the biggest concentration of power known in the Western world, and that is by the banking sector. Unfortunately, democracies have done little to rein in the worst tendencies of the banking cartels they have created; and if a government does attempt to do something, say in the case of the Obama administration, said government is immediately branded as socialist or anti-business.

Let's be clear on this issue: monopolies, cartels and oligopolies are not pro-business or even capitalist structures, but are the antithesis of the same. They are by their very natures anti-competitive, predatory and government authorized or created. Monopolies play out the economic double standard by wrapping themselves in the cloak of the free market, while doing everything in their power to eliminate competition and obtain extraordinary profits.

Corporations are but one of many vehicles/organizations for democracies to achieve their economic hopes and dreams, and great good can come from corporations (for society, management, stockholders, governments and employees); but blind subservience to the worst tendencies of corporations (e.g. combination for the elimination of competition) are something that prudent and responsible governments must hold in check, manage, supervise, and guard against. And if government does allow monopolies and oligopolies to exist, the price that those entities should pay for economic concentration is government oversight, regulation, and vigilance, all the better to guard against socialism by private proxy!

Jeane Kirkpatrick, on the international stage, was noted to have said, **"Russia is playing chess, while we are playing Monopoly. The only question is whether they will checkmate us before we bankrupt them."**

Such irony that multi-national monopolies, in the form of too big to fail banks, and the oil industry (through its diseconomies of scale playing out it the Gulf), may do what the Soviets never could do, and that is bankrupt the great Western democracies. Both oligopolies operate behind the facade of the free market.

Thinking the Unthinkable

J.M. Hamilton (7-5-10)

As stocks continue their downward decent (the S&P 500 is down 8.3% for the year), and unemployment remains recalcitrant (Shadow Government puts the U.S. unemployment/under-employment figure in excess of 20%), Keynesians, lead by Mr. Krugman, and Fiscal Conservatives, presently embodied by Mr. Paulson, are at war with one another.

Mr. Krugman is a Nobel Laureate, and a Princeton economist, and a long time advocate of the poor and the down trodden. His primary pulpit is the N.Y. Times editorial pages.

Mr.Paulson's notoriety derives through that "market maker" institution – Goldman Sachs; Mr. Paulson, allegedly, hand-picked the deck in a CDO issuance, and walked away with extraordinary profits. A civil complaint has been filed against Goldman Sachs by the SEC, over this very same transaction. No similar filing, by the SEC, has been made against Mr. Paulson or his hedge fund.

The Keynesian Argument

Mr. Krugman is hammering for greater government spending to spur economic activity and to get Americans through the great recession. Mr. Krugman argues that we are not out this recession by a long shot; and only government spending can make up for, in terms of job creation and economic activity, the contraction in private sector spending and growth.

Keynesians argue that in the short run deficit's don't matter (as opposed to former Vice President Dick Cheney, who – when it's politically convenient – is said to argue that deficits do not matter at all), and that deficit spending is a valid policy response to a down turn in the economy. They further argue that when times are good, government should rein in spending, and put money away for the next, inevitable, downturn.

Generally, many Americans would side with Mr. Krugman, were it not for the monstrous national debt visited upon this nation, by every administration from Reagan forward (the sole exception would be President Clinton, who actually ran budget surpluses). In fairness to President Obama, he inherited this fiscal nightmare, and gets a pass on deficit creation, at least in the short run.

Bottom line: There are two problems with the Keynesian argument: One, the second half of the Keynesian thesis simply falls apart in reality; that is to say, seemingly, no politician on earth, or all too few, has the self control to rein in government spending during the good times, and create budget surpluses. If the alleged keepers of the faith of fiscal conservatism, the Republicans, cannot rein in federal spending during prosperous time (e.g. witness Bush – Cheney, who actually expanded Big Government, with Entitlement D of Medicare), then how can U.S. citizens expect well meaning liberals to act accordingly? And two, the U.S. debt to GDP ratio is hovering around 90%… the servicing of such debt, and magnification of that debt, presents a huge fiscal drag on the U.S. economy, and other sovereign nations facing similar circumstances (witness the PIIGS in the E.U., and the fiscally "healthy" sovereigns propping up same).

Additional budget deficits at this point, although well meaning, may actually have a reverse effect, as businesses spend their time on alternative non-core pursuits, such as hoarding cash (to pay for inevitable higher taxes and worse economic times yet to come), hedging currencies, and loading up on gold. *Moreover, governments with sky high debt cannot continue to borrow forever to finance the Keynesian model, just ask Greece?*

If the debt to GDP ratio wasn't in the stratosphere, with the CBO and the OMB predicting trillion dollar deficits – seemingly in perpetuity, Mr. Krugman's policy prescriptions would seem to make sense, in the short run.

The Fiscal Conservative Argument, or Let Them Eat Cake!

If one absolutely did not give a damn about the unemployed in this country, nearly 1/5 of all Americans, Mr. Paulson's argument would be the way to go: simply rein in government spending, and cut social services – in order to get our fiscal act together . If one had a huge financial stake, in perpetuation of the status quo – unemployed be damned – then Mr. Paulson's "Pollyanna/rose colored glasses approach" would make perfect sense.

Who said Herbert Hoover is dead, why his spirit is alive and well in Mr. Paulson!

Mr. Paulson seems to be thinking (while not speaking it), if I may **paraphrase** and cut to the chase, *'Heh, the economy is growing. The government largess, joy, and love showered upon the nation's banking sector, seems to be a rising tide for me and my hedge fund, so why rock the freaking boat???'*

The problem is the "voodoo economic theory" (read: laissez faire) that has been passed down for over a generation now, appears a bit tired and worn. *Main Street is not profiting from the unprecedented bailout of Wall*

Street. And in fact the only parties that appear to be profiting from government intervention into the market place (TARP, TLGP, Fed Funds rate at Zero, Et Al.) are, ironically, the Wall Street banks, and their close associates.

The rising tide is not lifting all ships, thank you Mr. Paulson, nor can the 1/5 of American's presently unemployed wait for crumbs to come trickling down. Mr. Paulson seems to have forgotten, conveniently enough, that the manner in which he's made his extraordinary fortune, via an unregulated derivatives market and Goldman Sachs (now being pursued by the SEC), in short laissez faire capitalism run amok, are both primary contributors to the mayhem visited upon both the U.S. and world economies.

Mr. Paulson's position, if allowed to play out, could lead to problems with the social fabric. For some reason, Americans have come to believe in the semi-egalitarian social construct of a middle class.

Monetary Policy

Another approach to our economic Hiroshima is through monetary policy, which posits that massive inflows of liquidity into the economy should stimulate growth and prosperity.

Note to readers, I am on my roof, nightly, feverishly scanning the horizon for Ben Bernanke and his helicopter to come to the rescue, and dump that load of cash right into my waiting arms. But alas, no Ben - only pigeons dumping an entirely different load.

Here again, a liberal monetary policy would work quite well if the nation had healthy banks and some semblance of a normal fiscal policy, but this perfect storm of a financial nightmare appears to have left monetary policy face down in the water.

That is to say, while Mr. Bernanke is busily printing money at the Fed, he appears to be "pushing on a rope," in terms of stimulating the economy. Try as the Fed might, M3 is actually contracting at an alarming pace. The banks aren't lending, at least not to small or mid-sized businesses, or individual consumers – the life blood of U.S. job creation and the engine of economic growth.

Instead, the Wall Street banks appear to have entered into a symbiotic relationship with the federal government, whereby the government provides them with free liquidity through the Fed Funds window, and severely watered down bank reform legislation, and in return the banks finance ever growing government debt.

Many banks balance sheets are still a wreck. And globally banks are so leveraged up with government debt that – going forward – when we talk about governments bailing out "the banks," we really are talking about bailing out the international order or world governments, themselves. Governments and banks are more interconnected than ever, but I digress.

Thinking the Unthinkable: A Global Restructuring of Debt

So if all the economic answers (Keynesian, Fiscal Conservatism, and Monetary policy) are shot, dulled, or worse yet, may actually aggravate the situation, what then? What is left?

Here's a hint: South and Central American countries have been known to do it from time to time, and some have done quite well, economically, after the fact.

Centrals bankers meet some weekend, ask the creditor nations to take a "haircut," and abracadabra a new currency is born, Monday morning.

Of course, this could upset the international order of things. On the "con" side: Creditor nations might demand that in exchange for "haircuts" on debt, that the western democracies surrender the ability to print fiat currencies? Fiscal order might be pushed by creditor nations, and profligate government spending might be banished (e.g. the end of politicians making spending promises that have to be financed), but is that really a bad thing? After seeing the chaos within the E.U. and the lack of centralized political power over the euro, a real world bank might be created to control, monitor, and oversee a new world currency. The monetization of debt might no longer be available to many sovereign nations. The truly American value of living within one's means, thrift and frugality, might be imposed, where our politicians have failed us.

On the "pro" side: The crushing debt with which western democracies are presently faced with might be wiped out, or eliminated to a large degree. The government deficits, and debt, that are such a drag on the world economy, could be eliminated. Governments, no longer faced with catastrophic debt, would no longer have to deploy contractionary fiscal policies during the ongoing economic crisis, such as tax increases and reductions in public spending and social services, so that debt loads could be serviced. The social order could be preserved. Governments – no longer dependent upon banks to buy their debt – could, in turn, install mark to market accounting and let the chips fall where they may among banks. In short, no more propping up banks so that they can finance sovereign debt, the mess that we are presently in. Banks that survive mark to market accounting would be free to lend to the private sector, again, instead of being tied up financing government debt. With bad banks washed away, and healthy banks free to lend, a floor could be established in the real estate market, a huge driver of economic activity, job creation, and wealth creation. As real estate makes a comeback, government, the Fed, Freddie/Fannies, and the banks may actually make a buck off of what is presently referred to as toxic assets.

Protectionist forces might be held at bay.

Basically, we are talking about clearing the decks for global economic activity. The global economy may enjoy a renaissance, and economic growth could be explosive! Today's creditor nations, post restructuring, could be primary beneficiaries of rapid worldwide economic growth, especially the export lead Pacific Rim (i.e. China). Multi-national business would flourish, having to worry less about hedging currencies and escalating taxes. Global banking could be significantly simplified. Business could expand globally, as they would no longer have to worry about market instability and problematic currencies.

Main Street could return to a preeminent position of economic activity, and Wall Street could return to its secondary position of supporting Main Street. The "pros" of a global restructuring, at the end of the day, could overwhelmingly outweigh the "cons."

Reactionary Forces

To be sure, there would enormous political pressure not to engage in such an enterprise, much of the pressure deriving from the banking sector, hedge funds, politicians, and some sovereign nations (admittedly, a fierce crowd). The old international order of nation states might come under fire, to some degree, as they surrender some economic power to a global bank; but many nations/states have already surrendered banking authority to some centralized power, such as: all 50 states that make up the United States, or members of the E.U.

The need for many disparate powerful private banking enterprises, and the incumbent global systematic risk and moral hazard, might also come to an end – or be mitigated; and with it, the tremendous sway the banks hold over the political and economic processes, particularly within democracies.

There would be many intended and unintended consequences from such a proposal, but if we are truly honest with ourselves, isn't this what the world is headed towards anyway, a global financial restructuring? The only question is will it happen sooner rather than later, after considerable economic suffering and hardship.   Is it more advantageous for the U.S. to engage in restructuring negotiations now, while the dollar is still strong, or to wait until such time as there is a global run on the dollar?

Apparently, the only reason the dollar is strong is due to the collapse of the euro – the catalyst for the euro down fall occurred when Goldman Sachs sold Greece derivative products, all the better to obscure Greek financials for E.U. admittance. Up until the fall of the euro, presumably more than one hedge fund and more than one Wall Street bank (and perhaps some U.S. politicians) were gambling that the dollar was in the decline, and in the long run, they, unfortunately, are correct.

The point at which nations can no longer finance their debt load is near for many countries around the world. And how will each country handle their respective crisis(?), by printing paper! Either that, or wealthier nations will have to come to the table to bailout nations with problematic financials, but in doing so, the financially stronger nations will only weaken themselves (German citizens appear well aware of what is happening in the E.U. and many are perfectly prepared to walk away from the Euro). And we wonder why corporations are hoarding cash!

And the alternative to a global restructuring? Well, read the press, take a walk in your local mall, look at the stock market, stagnation and decay are appearing everywhere, as is substandard economic growth, except in the golden halls where Mr. Paulson operates.

The Fourth of July is all about Freedoms: Economic, Political and Spiritual. A global restructuring may serve to better preserve those freedoms, as well as greater economic opportunity, for the many rather than a few! The real question is will politicians surrender power, the ability to monetize debt, and global economic hardship, so that the world economy can take off again? World-wide economic recovery is being held up by crushing sovereign debt and an exceptionally nasty private sector debt hangover, in the incarnation of banks and the real estate bubble. A world economy deserves a global banking system.

The Exceptionally Nasty Politics of Unemployment… And the Most Fiscally Conservative President in the Last Thirty Years

By J.M. Hamilton 7-7-10

Here's a hint, it sure wasn't Reagan…

This week President Obama named a new budget director to replace Peter Orszag. The President was quoted as saying: "If there was a hall of fame for budget directors, then Jack Lew surely would have earned a place for his service in that role under President Clinton when he helped balance the federal budget after years of deficits," and "Jack is the only budget director in history to preside over a budget surplus for three consecutive years."

It's been awhile, what does a budget surplus look like, and for that matter, how does an unemployment rate of less than 5% appear?   Both, the budget surpluses, Mr. Obama wistfully commented on, and an unemployment rate of less than 5% occurred under President Clinton's watch. These highly enviable economic results didn't come easy to President Clinton, and they occurred during a personally painful time for the President, his second term.

The nation's unemployment rate during the '90s:

Year	Rate		
1992	7.49		Bush H.W.
1993	6.91		Clinton
1994	6.10		
1995	5.59		
1996	5.41		
1997	4.94		
1998	4.50		
1999	4.22		
2000	3.97		

Source: http://www.miseryindex.us/urbyyear.asp

Hind sight is 20/20, and we now know that Clinton was not a favorite in the business community and of many ultra wealthy investors, in either of his terms in office. The nation's top income tax rate was 39% under Clinton, up from 28 and 31% under H.W. Bush (interestingly enough, this same tax bracket was 50% for much of Reagan's two terms in office). So here's Clinton jacking up the tax rate on the rich, the wealthy, the investor class (stealing the punch bowl at the great capitalist party), and he's an absolute pariah among Republicans; in short, Clinton was viewed very much in the same manner President Obama is viewed by the rich, today, for threatening to snatch away the Bush (W) tax cuts (who lowered Clinton's top tax rate to 35%).

Boy, talk about your economic buzz kill! All manner of conservative economist, republican politicians, and many CEO's, will tell you that a tax increase in the middle of a recession is a sure way to derail the economy, and will make matters worse. But after Clinton was reelected exactly the opposite happened, the economy jumped and hard: U.S. GDP grew from approximately 7.5 trillion in '93, to nearly 10.0 trillion in 2000, almost 2.0 trillion of that growth, the lion's share, came during Clinton's second term.

So what happened? Well, I don't have a crystal ball, and it's beyond my skill set to be able to peer into the hearts and minds of the business/corporate elite, but here's my hypothesis: the plutocracy, possibly, held up on their investment plans in the hopes that Clinton was a one term wonder.   Maybe, just maybe, corporate American and the banks slowed up on hiring and loans, so as to run the Arkansas *wunderkind* out of office?   After all, CEO's are people too, and we know that the many of them are Republican. Gee, wouldn't it be human nature to make things tough on the political opposition and take a wait and see mentality (particularly if you are wealthy), slow down on the spending/investments a little? Meanwhile the economy is tough; the public – who's also experiencing the financial pain of an early '90s recession, albeit more painfully – could conceivably empathize with the business community, if investment and jobs weren't exactly forthcoming.

Back at the White House, Clinton hooked up with a campaign advisor, Dick Morris (former advisor to the most right wing Senator to enter the halls of U.S. Senate, in the modern era – Jesse Helms); and Clinton turned right of center before his second term, at least in terms of taking on a more "pro-business" stance.   In '96, Clinton, with some help from Perot, ran over Bob Dole, smoking him by nearly 10 million votes. Clinton, who had also signed NAFTA and presided over a considerable amount of banking deregulation, was not just watching the revenue side of the ledger with his tax increase, but like any good accountants, Jack Lew and the President were also watching the spending side.   Clinton, keeping an eye on government expenditures, signed: the Personal Responsibility and Work Opportunity Act, or simply put welfare reform.

Following through on my hypothesis then, the business community, seeing that their efforts to unseat the President had come to naught, may have decided that sitting on the sidelines for the balance of the '90s was not fun and costing them money; and hence, cranked up the show. The banking and business elites learned to live with the Clinton tax increase, and a Democrat in the White House.   The economy, the Street, and profits roared to life - reaching the pinnacle for that era with the Dot.com boom and the Dow's 10,000 benchmark.

Messrs. Clinton and Lew went on to hand the Texas usurper three years of budget surpluses, which he promptly wasted on two wars, irresponsible tax cuts, and profligate government spending and deficits (but that's a story that is still firmly burned in the nation's collective memory).

Are we, as a nation, revisiting circa '94-'95 all over?   Again, we have a Democrat in the White House, who's had to take – through no fault of his own – some tough stances with the business community and is about to enact very modest bank regulatory reform.   We know many corporations are flush with cash, holding on to that cash very tightly, and not investing said cash in CAPEX or new hires; we know that some very large banks, having received the mother of all bailouts, are also flush with liquidity, enjoying a Fed Funds rate at or near zero percent.

Key question: Could some members of the business elite be waiting or biding their time? Waiting out this administration, in the hopes that Obama is a one trick pony?   Maybe. Perhaps?   Afterall, if the economy continues to perform poorly, and unemployment remains high enough, Americans just might vote the President and his party out of office, or so the reasoning goes.

To be sure, there are exogenous and endogenous economic variables today that make the early 90's recession not entirely analogous, like the financial Armageddon unleashed on an unsuspecting citizenry by firms such as Goldman Sachs, Countrywide S&L, and AIG.   The inherited debt to GDP ratio is definitely higher for this sitting President.   And unlike Clinton, Obama did see some semblance of "healthcare reform" signed into law.

That said, the shrill cries that Clinton faced are not dissimilar to the anger faced by Obama…. Complaints that Obama is a socialist and anti business, by the

Chamber of Commerce set, were also faced by Mr. Clinton in the '90s. Could it be that some part of our nation's present economic misery is by calculated political design then, from some elites keeping too tight a grasp on the purse strings, and what would cause them to spend, or loan, again? If these same elites (banking and business) are indeed, biding their time, then we can only hope that a good showing by the Democrats in November 2010 will quite possibly hasten their desire to accept both bank reform and the possible end of the Bush era tax cuts, and partake of the great capitalist party once again.

Who knows? With increased business expansion and a resulting increase in government receipts might President Obama and Mr. Lew be incited to enact some Clintonian cuts in federal spending?

If the Clinton years are indeed analogous to the Obama years, let's hope that the midterm elections in 2010, and Obama's reelection in 2012, sets off an economic renaissance.

NO MORE AFGHANISTANS

By J.M. Hamilton 7-31-2010

Those who do not learn from history will not survive! Afghanistan: The very definition of "insanity."

This week's editorial was going to address our soaring debt to GDP ratios and the political party that is largely responsible, the Republicans; but there is much time, an ever growing cascade of bad news to exploit in that endeavor, and the political season in on the horizon, so we'll save that gem for later.

Instead, we depart from economic matters and discuss something very close to my heart: foreign policy and in particular, the war in Afghanistan. It appears that things are not going so well in Afghanistan, not as well anyway, as we had been lead to believe. In fact, if we compare this war with another war without end that the U.S. was engaged in forty to fifty years ago, the parallels are remarkably similar, almost frightening. And while the outcome of the Afghanistan war is not preordained, we can almost predict the outcome, if the prior war is any example: a mighty superpower proclaiming victory but severely humbled, walking off the world stage, and learning, hopefully (for a generation anyway), the limits of military power. For war, as Mr. Clausewitz has told us, is an extension of politics, and therefore, war is not a means to an end. It is but a tool in our political arsenal.

The problem with our present war, like the war the U.S. was engaged in some forty years ago, is that the U.S. is using conventional forces to fight a guerilla insurgency. Like the war in Indochina, the benefactor of the insurgency against the U.S. is a nuclear power(s); and while the indigenous populations in both wars disliked the guerilla forces, they grew to have an even greater disdain for U.S. military operations over time. This week saw the release of a substantial body of secret military information in the form of the Wikileaks documents, illustrating that the American people have been deceived about the realities of the Afghan war. And like the papers released this week, the New York Times published similar documents in the form of the "Pentagon Papers" in 1971, revealing the same information about that war. Meanwhile, the American people's appetite for the war in Afghanistan is eroding over time, and patience is wearing thin as the body count grows. History repeats.

In both wars military and political goals have been nebulous and changing over time. Towards the end of the earlier war, President Nixon set the goal of "vietnamization," so that South Vietnam would learn to care for and defend itself. Sound familiar? Nixon also set time tables for troop withdrawals, as has our current President. For entirely different reasons, both wars lead its respective military commanders to go home in shame and defeat: Westmoreland and McChrystal.   What the U.S. came to find out at the end of the Vietnam War was that the world went on for America; the enemy did not take over the world, and in fact collapsed upon itself over time, in the form of the Soviet Union. In a similar fashion, if America pulled out of Afghanistan tomorrow, would America crumble and implode?   Probably quite the opposite.

So who do we turn to then for some expert guidance on our present predicament? Well that would be none other than the master statesmen himself, the sly one, Richard M. Nixon. *Hold on, hold on,* before you shut down your computer or toggle onto the next site, hear me out.   Mr. Nixon, despite personal failings, was a brilliant foreign policy expert. Some would say President Nixon was deeply paranoid, but you'd be paranoid too, if the Kennedy clan stole your 1960 presidential bid.   Besides, given the economic events that have unfolded in the U.S. and world economy over the last five years, what is paranoid? Not even your worst nightmares can compare to this Kafkaesque economic dreamscape America presently exists in, brought to us all by the fine folks at Goldman Sachs, the FED, the U.S. Treasury, and AIG, Et Al. But I digress.

Back to the man, the war, and the lessons not learned.   Upon leaving the White House under less than auspicious circumstances, Mr. Nixon set about cleaning up his image and he wrote several books. Quite possibly one of the more obscure books Mr. Nixon wrote was called: *No More Vietnams*. And within it, Mr. Nixon laid down some very salient advice and counsel in conducting U.S. foreign policy, and in particular, the manner in which the U.S. military is to be utilized to further America's political aims and goals. Let's cut to the chase, shall we. Former President Nixon wrote, and I paraphrase:

1)   Wars must only be engaged in with the support of the American people and the Congress of the United States.

2)   Military force should only be utilized as a last resort, and it must be used sparingly.

3)   The President must be highly selective in the use of force.

4)   Military goals and objectives should be clearly defined and achievable, and the objectives vital to our national interest.

5)   There should be only one overriding goal for the U.S. military and that is: Absolute Victory!

Funny, Mr. Nixon didn't put "nation building" on the list, which apparently was one of Mr. Bush's goals, or came to be one of his goals over time, in Afghanistan. To hear Mr. Holbrook (special ambassador to Afghanistan and Pakistan) state it: the Bush administration's "mission statement" for Afghanistan had been much more ambitious than the goal set by the Obama White House.

"It was creating a modern state, a modern democracy in Afghanistan with limited resources," Holbrooke said of President George W. Bush's goals.

Sounds like nation building then, shouldn't be the job of a single nation, or the U.S. military for that matter, but rather the duty of an international body, with International support and funding.

The bottom line is politicians do the U.S. military, and the United States overall, a tremendous disservice when we assign irrational goals and objectives to the men and women in uniform.   The first President Bush (H.W.) recognized all of President's Nixon's objectives, laid out above, in the first Gulf War. **In the first Gulf War it was:** *Veni, vidi, vici !!!* And then you pull the military out, and let the politicians and diplomats set the parameters, hopefully, of a lasting, or at least well monitored, peace.

Based upon our lessons in Vietnam and with" vietnamization," our activities in Afghanistan appear "irrational," and nearly meet the definition of "insanity."   And this is meant as no insult to the Afghan people, but attempting to turn people – with a rudimentary culture, education (if any) and economy – into democrats, overnight, would appear to meet that definition.   The U.S. military, the most effective military the world has ever seen, could spend four decades in Afghanistan and might never achieve the Bush mission statement. Mr. Bush then, maybe with the best of intentions, set up our troops to fail with his goal of nation building; the former president might as well as told the U.S. military to capture and defeat the wind.

As for vital U.S. interests, the military goal was clear after 9-11, and the U.S. military achieved that goal in a matter of weeks, when Osama Bin Ladin was last seen running from Tora Bora and heading into Pakistan. Done. From that point on, the U.S. should have held its so-called ally, Pakistan, personally responsible for any and all terrorist activities against the U.S. or its citizens. Because, as the leaks revealed this week, and as we all have known for some time, Pakistan plays a large role in providing safe haven, intelligence, support, and initiating the actions of destabilizing/terrorist forces in the region. The problematic forces all receive support inside Pakistan, within the state of Warizstan.

In 1985, Mr. Nixon, a man ahead of his time, said it best: *"Terrorism today is an international challenge to an international order, and it requires an international response."*

Terrorism is not a war, in the conventional sense, but a cancer that has to be treated at multiple levels, on an on-going basis, within a society in turmoil: politically, diplomatically, economically, spiritually, educationally, and culturally.   And yes, terrorism must be addressed when called upon, through the proxy arm of God herself, via U.S. military or NATO forces. How do terrorist gain a foothold in a society(?), by responding to a vacuum, by providing the humanitarian and basic services that any decent government should be providing, to any group of people in a state of malaise or chaos.   Hamas in Gaza is a case study in point.

Based upon Mr. Nixon's good guidance then, the U.S. military had already achieved victory in Afghanistan. Nation building, and policing up the region, should be taken up by the U.N. and financed by the world.   Mr. Bush's goal, in its present form, of building a modern democracy within Afghanistan is an abject failure, and a reflection on him, Dick Cheney, and his cohorts, the Republican Party.   The Second Bush administration, unlike his father before him, had no exit strategy in the region, and the same, probably, could be said of his administration's goals and aims in Iraq. (By the way, this dichotomy, Nixon/Elder Bush versus Cheney/Younger Bush, establishment Republican versus the Neo-cons, is the clearest example of what is wrong with the Republican Party today, and the reason why so many members have fled and independents are turned off.)

It goes without saying that the U.S. owes this man a debt, but Mr. Bush, in particular, as does the Republican Party, owes General Patraeus an everlasting debt of gratitude.   *However, at a time of record federal debt, unemployment/underemployment in excess of 20% (per Shadow Government), the time and place for nation building is now, and right here at home, in America.* A long and sustained parting shot inside Waziristan by the U.S. Air Force, as the U.S. military pulls up tent stakes in Afghanistan, just might deliver the message that Pakistan needs.   And that is Pakistan will be held accountable for any and all terrorist activities within the region, or that initiate from its borders, globally.

If Pakistan wants to play big boy politics with proxy forces and nukes, then they need to join the international order, and stop acting like some third world thug – dictatorship. President Nixon was right, the last thing the U.S. needs is anymore Vietnams, but unfortunately, President Bush set the U.S. up with a beauty of a Vietnam in Afghanistan!

Bubba Called

By J.M. Hamilton (8-17-10)

A very good friend phoned the other day to rant about Obama. "Obama is a one termer, for sure," he said. And then Bubba went on to gloat about the resiliency of the Texas economy, and how there's no state income tax. I had heard much of this before. "He's out... watch the midterms."

Bubba dates back to my youth, those days when you feel nearly invincible, and you just might live forever. Bubba, in those days, could charge an offensive line with the best of high school line backers, rend it, and stack it up like so much beef. Bubba always felt that high school football was the closest he'd ever get to have a legal license to maim, and he was right.   He was the kind of guy that you'd shot gun a six pack with on a Friday night, just to set the tone: simpler and more prosperous times, indeed.

"You (carpetbaggers) are going to *looose*," Bubba, again, on the shifting political winds. (In the interest of full disclosure, Bubba actually used a different phrase, but this is a family oriented blog.)

Unfortunately, Bubba, like many of my Republican friends, I would argue, is out of touch with the present realities of the Republican Party. Simply put the Republican Party of Reagan, and the eighties, is about as far removed from the present day Republican Party, as well, let's say "night and day?" In fact, one could argue that Reagan's rhetoric was out of touch with the Republican Party of his era, but we'll sort this out in a few more paragraphs. Bubba sums up the current administration with one word: "socialist."

Ah Bubba, I knew you when.   I knew you when your future wife came hauling across the cow pasture, locked up the brakes in front of the pick-up that we quietly sat drinking beer in, *our après water ski ritual*, slammed the car door, and glaring at you, all 110 pounds of her stalked into the trailer and slammed the trailer door, a metaphorical exclamation point to her intense rage. The trailer shuddered, and the glass rattled. Bubba quietly put down his beer, and w/out so much as word followed his future bride into the cave. The screaming and shouting was tremendous – barely muffled by the thin walls of the trailer, which contained 38 caliber bullet holes, created by firing a weapon from the inside. Don't ask. Sally (name changed to protect my best friend's wife), soon departed, slammed the trailer door behind her, and sped back out across the pasture, leaving a blinding dust cloud. I didn't even merit so much as a withering look from the angriest blond I'd ever seen.   It was late afternoon, but near the century mark. I considered the dust rude, as it threatened the liquid refreshment.

As the dust began to settle, Bubba opened the trailer door and emotionless, sauntered over to the pickup, cracked open the cooler, and grabbed a cold one. Bubba popped the can, and reclining back into the bed of truck, offered up the following immortal words:

"If I told her once, I've told her a hundred times, she's going out with the drunk and she's just going to have to get use to it."

Some may consider those words sad coming from a young man in his early twenties, but I appreciated, greatly, the honesty and the life lesson.   Bubba, this one is for you!

Socialist Defined

For fiscal conservatives, the Reagan Revolution started out promising enough, after all this is the President who, in his first inaugural address said the following: "In this present crisis, government is not the solution to our problem; government is the problem."

But there was a disconnect between the rhetoric of Reagan and the dramatic growth in government under his watch. That is to say, the debt to GDP ratio soared, as government spending picked up and tax cuts were installed.

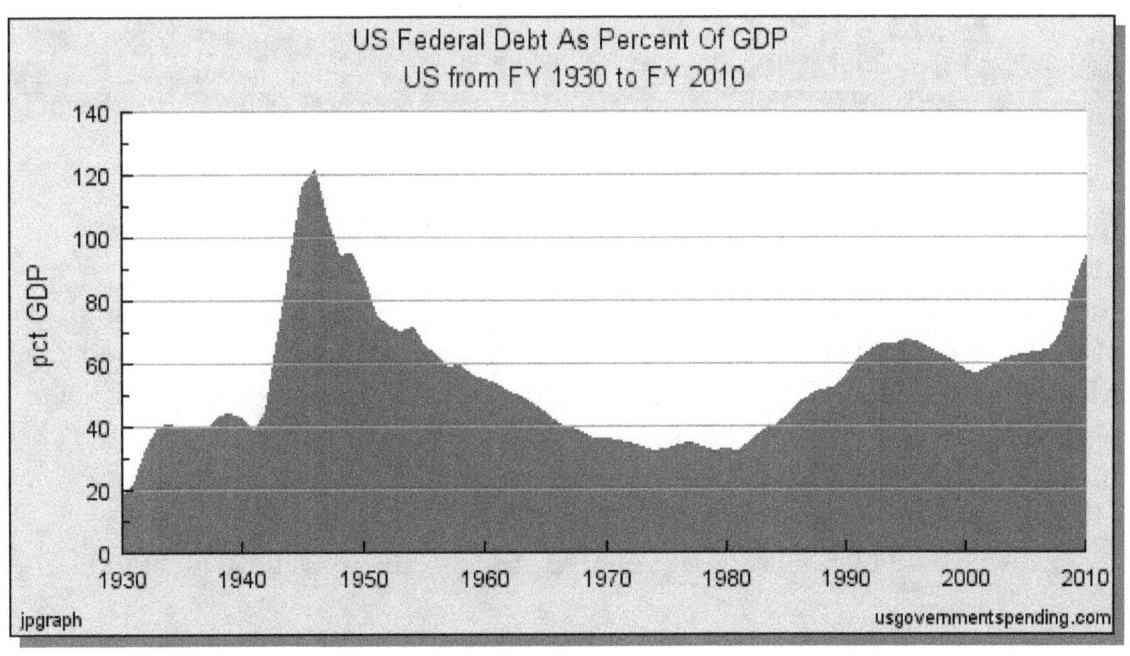

Debt to GDP doubled under Reagan and his successor, George (H.W.) Bush, who when he tried to rein in the debt with a tax increase was turned upon by the more reactionary party members. H.W. did not believe in "VooDoo economics" or the fiscal irresponsibility of deficit spending; and since the party of Reagan had no appetite to cut social programs, military spending or corporate entitlements, there was no other solution but to raise taxes; but this is anathema to Republicans, as exemplified by Reagan's line: "I have only one thing to say to the tax increasers: Go ahead, make my day."

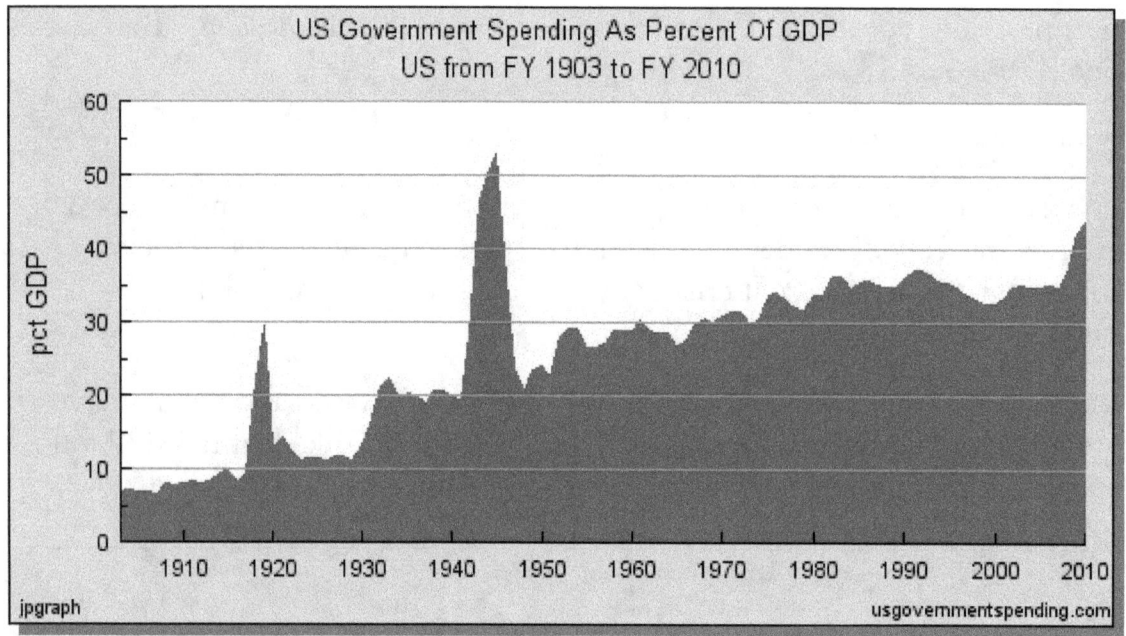

Of course, allowing government spending to increase without a matching increase in tax revenue is the height of fiscal irresponsibility. Basically, America has been living on a credit card economy, since the 80's. And in the last decade Republican's eschewed the fiscal responsibility rhetoric altogether, when Vice President Cheney stated: that deficits do not matter. VP Cheney, however, as a former CEO, knows that deficits do matter, and in fact if a business's expenditures are greater than its revenue - it will soon go out of business; unless of course you are a patron of the Republican party and a recipient of Republican bailouts, as in the case of AIG and the Wall Street Banks!

For Republicans now to cry foul when a Democratic administration runs a deficit is the epitome of hypocrisy, almost like a drunken sailor, or drunken

Bubba, howling at the wind! It appears that deficits do matter after all, particularly when you are out of power and cannot dispense fiscal largess on your core constituencies.

Monopoly's Economic Drag

So what's with the double standard? It appears that when the Republicans are in power, it's perfectly okay to run catastrophic deficits as long as the money is going to Wall Street Bank bailouts, the military industrial complex (via two wars, in Afghanistan and Iraq), or to support monopolistic genesis.

The Reagan 80's and the Bush 2000's saw a record number of business mergers and consolidations in the American economy, fueled by private equity and the Fed's easy money policies. Of course, this frenzy of consolidation often leads to monopolistic, or oligopolistic, powers, and the ability to make extraordinary profits. Look no further than Exxon, who, in the heart of economic down turn, with a glut of supply and a fall in demand, continues to take record money.

Of course, as this blog has written about (see: *Monopolies and Double Standards*) monopolies don't occur in a vacuum; but rather, occur via government sanction and authorization. *Since these mega corporations are the creation of government, the unchecked profits earned by these industry leviathans represent a form of taxation on the U.S. citizen, and this taxation represents a tremendous drag on the overall economy.*

But it's okay if the crony capitalism makes record profits – while unemployment and underemployment is in excess of twenty percent - because our friends, the Republicans, have taught us through a steady diet of laissez faire indoctrination that if corporate America , or business, does it, it's gotta be wholesome, righteous and in the public interest.

So not only are the Republicans in favor of deficit spending, but they also favor the covert taxation that monopolies impose on ordinary Americans every day. Except the toll taken by Republican authorized monopolies doesn't go to pay down the Republican created deficits, it goes straight into the pockets of the plutocracy!

Like the Bubba of yesteryear, the Republican Party is drunk. Drunk on the power of big government, deficit spending, and the exorbitant profits of the monopolies they have created and authorized while in power.

Command Economy & Capital Strike

Republican's on the campaign trail, spurred on by the Tea Bag community, like to take on the present administration over its effort to bailout the Detroit auto makers. And of course, they did not like this administration's forays into Healthcare; but where were their objections when Bush/Paulson spent trillions bailing on the Wall Street banks and AIG, or when Bush expanded Medicare to include prescription drugs?

If we are honest with ourselves, Americans have to recognize that we have been living under a command economy for years. Eisenhower, in his farewell address to the nation, warned of the military industrial complex. Energy, Big Pharma, High-tech, the Agricultural oligopoly: are all examples where the government has created, and encouraged, massive incentives for these industries to concentrate and accrue massive wealth and power.

In authorizing this concentration, Republicans have ignored the deleterious impact on the American public and the citizens of the world. The hubris surrounding today's Republican Party is nothing short of amazing, where the ends always justify the means, as long as the ends align with Republican interests.

So that today's business man, and capital, is literally on strike, in protest over the Obama administration's policies, as they represent a deviation from the thought that to say "no" to business, or attempt to regulate same, is a direct threat to business itself. Corporations are hoarding cash, and banks – despite gigantic bailouts – are not lending, both in protest over the current administration; but who brought the uncertainty and the instability that big business is protesting, more specifically, what political party aided and abetted the greatest financial meltdown in the history of man? Agreed, Democrats share in the blame, but more importantly - who lead the charge?

Political dogma is a dangerous thing. It has to be continually evaluated and dissected. Are the assumptions of yesterday, or the claims of a political party truthful and accurate, or just hollowed out rhetoric? How did the Republican party stray so far from the path, from at least talking the talk, under Reagan, to neither talking the talk or walking the walk, under "W" (or in the case of Cheney, outright apostasy and a cynical manipulation of core beliefs and values)?

Perhaps over time Republicans will reform; but right now their rejection of government (except when it can be used to spread financial cheer among friends), their pandering to the baser instincts in the population, their idolatry of money and profits before all, will not serve Americans or business. The present Republican path is nihilistic, which appears to wish for, and embrace, government insolvency.

Bubba and Sally, my readers will be happy to know, grew up, married, and had two wonderful children. They still like to tip a couple on the weekend, but he's responsible, usually - well mannered, and makes a contribution to society.

I wish the same could be said of the Republican Party. Then again, perhaps Republican constituents have been going out with a fiscal drunk, and we just need to get used to it.

One Can Love Our Fighting Men and Women, and Appreciate the Techie Tech of the Defense Industry, but Also Glance at the MIC, and Recognize that It is FUBAR!

War is our Profession

By J.M. Hamilton (9-5-10)

Apparently, peace is no longer our profession…

In 1961, in a career noted for stability, sobriety, and not prone to embellishment, Eisenhower gave his farewell address to the nation, and an unprecedented warning. President Eisenhower stated:

"This conjunction of an immense military establishment and a large arms industry is new in the American experience. The total influence – economic, political, even spiritual – is felt in every city, every Statehouse, every office of the Federal government. We recognize the imperative need for this development. Yet we must not fail to comprehend its grave implications. Our toil, resources and livelihood are all involved; so is the very structure of our society.

In the councils of government, we must guard against the acquisition of unwarranted influence, whether sought or unsought, by the military-industrial complex (MIC). The potential for the disastrous rise of misplaced power exists and will persist.

We must never let the weight of this combination endanger our liberties or democratic processes. We should take nothing for granted. Only an alert and knowledgeable citizenry can compel the proper meshing of the huge industrial and military machinery of defense with our peaceful methods and goals, so that security and liberty may prosper together."

Merchants of Death

The President's warning was highly prescient. Observe, the following facts and figures generated, approximately, fifty years later:

* Depending upon whose figures one believes, the U.S. spends more on defense, annually, than all the other nations in the world combined, and certainly more than the G-20.

* The top ten U.S. government contractors in the nation, by revenue, are all defense contractors.

* The military industrial complex now makes up 5.6% of GDP, a sizable figure in the world's largest economy.

* In terms of arms export, the U.S. leads the world with a 40% market share, that's a whole lot of hell being peddled around the world. (How much ends up, directly or indirectly, in enemy hands?)

With concentration of wealth comes political power. In order to keep the war-machine humming, and to better justify government defense expenditures, and prevent "peace dividends," America's defense industry must have an enemy, and a never ending arms race among nations, as the technology, dedicated to controlling and killing man, continually improves.

Presently, the U.S. finds itself in two hot wars, and covert operations throughout the globe, while running deficits and national debt that are precarious. Military spending and war was a significant driver of the sudden and sharp uptick in national debt that accrued over the last decade, with trillions in debt raised to pay for the war effort.

Much of U.S. military activity, today, was derived by 9-11, and knowing what we know now, quite possibly, the military outreach/over reach was a complete overreaction to a gang of third world terrorist, many of whom Ronald Reagan formerly employed in successful efforts to bring down the Soviet Union. Say what one will about President Reagan, he was intelligent enough to topple the Soviet Union without utilizing the U.S. military in a hot war; instead, Mr. Reagan smartly employed proxy/indigenous/guerrilla forces to aid that campaign. The very same forces the U.S. is fighting in Afghanistan, today, were formerly called the mujahedeen (or freedom fighters), when they were America's ally and shed their blood willingly to aid in bringing down the Soviet empire; and today, these same mujahedeen are labeled the Taliban or America's enemy.

Mr. Reagan's success, however, was not good for MIC financial statements.

Having gone through the 80's and the 90's without a major war, and with all kinds of happy talk about "peace dividends" and the "end of history," our friends in the MIC weren't having it. Enter Vice President Dick Cheney, former Defense Secretary and CEO of Halliburton, and of course, the 9-11 crew that brought down the World Trade Center. And with the success of the first Gulf War (presided over by the highly competent George H.W. Bush) largely washing way fears, lessons, and any objection created by a less successful war in Indochina, fought a couple of decades earlier, the U.S. entered into the graveyard of empires, and a cycle of endless war.

Profits for the MIC soared!

Graveyard of Empires

After nearly a decade of war in Afghanistan none of the grievances of Mesopotamia's vox populi have been addressed, which leaves America more deeply in debt, winded, more cynical about military power, and less able, financially or militarily, to handle the next crisis –which may truly, require a military campaign.

After slugging it out in Iraq, and continuing to do so in Afghanistan, the root causes of the evil visited upon innocents in NY and in Washington D.C. in 2001 are still on full display: world dependence upon middle east oil; the U.S. propping up oppressive dictatorships throughout the middle east with petrol dollars and free military support; and those same dollars going to finance the grinding injustice executed upon middle east citizenry by their respective governments, which only serves to create more terrorist and anger at America (a vicious circle).

The vacuum in government service created by the corrupt and ineffectual regimes (e.g. Karzai) is filled all too willingly by the order imposed by terrorist regimes; no matter how back ward the societal structure imposed. Witness the recent return of "stoning" in Afghanistan. No, not as a means to get "high" in this narco-terrorist state, but as a means to meet out justice.

As the departing U.S. commander of military operations in Afghanistan recently observed in the pages of Rolling Stone: for every innocent civilian killed in Afghanistan ten terrorists are created.

Of course, thanks to the defense industry, the arms merchants have gotten better at their task… the ratio of dead enemy combatant (and collateral damage)to deceased coalition forces only improves with each war; which is supposed to make the mayhem and carnage more palatable, or better yet, something to be forgotten and ignored.

But, did I tell you MIC profits are up?

Killing is our Business… Business is Good.

Today, with the terrorist fear factor largely played out and deficits ever spiraling, the writing in red ink is somewhat on the wall. Secretary of Defense Robert Gates has put the Pentagon on notice that cut backs are on the horizon, not due to a peace dividend this administration is careful to emphasize, but to better bring about efficiencies and to better prepare for the next war.

Would that be the next world war to lead us out of our current Great Recession?

Mr. Gates, with expertise in military matters unsurpassed, has even targeted a few military spending programs for the chopping block, such as extra C-17 Cargo planes, redundant engines for the F-35 fighter, and a Joint Forces Command Center in Virginia. Such is the power and sway of the MIC that politicians are already lining up to defeat Mr. Gates efforts… Deficits and debt be damned.

Despite the enormous drag the MIC puts on American finances and the taxpayer, the distortions it creates in the economy and in the labor market, and chiefly, the crowding out effect the MIC creates in the credit markets (as government borrows to pay for MIC products and services and finance wars), the MIC roars on, unquestioned and under- analyzed. And as long as the MIC remains the 800 pound gorilla in the room, almost certainly aligned with such powerful interests as Wall Street Banks (who receive commissions and fees for financing war debt) and Big Oil (whose products and interests are protected by the MIC), there is possible incentive to invent enemies, and exaggerate the power of real enemies, that spawn war. As a result, America today, finds itself on a permanent war footing, and because "wolf" has been cried so many times, ill prepared and too distracted to fight our real enemies.

As soon as there is a lull in the next quarterly MIC financial statement, one might expect the arrival of a new enemy or a resurgent boogeyman. Of course, there is that mother of all endless wars that the MIC can rely upon, the forty year old war on drugs, the lessons of Prohibition America having been entirely lost upon our elected officials.

And the historical lessons? Well, America was not always the biggest kid on the block... we once were a small but proud nation, and our founding fathers, correctly, led us to believe the following: be weary of foreign entanglements; and dread the infringement upon freedoms (social, political and economic) that a standing army may create.

Lessons not lost upon many of our, alleged, allies in the G-20.

"Of all the enemies to public liberty war is, perhaps, the most to be dreaded because it comprises and develops the germ of every other. War is the parent of armies; from these proceed debts and taxes ... known instruments for bringing the many under the domination of the few.... No nation could preserve its freedom in the midst of continual warfare."

—*James Madison, Fourth President of the U.S.*

To the military men and women who serve, this nation owes an eternal debt. Whether the war or battle fought was necessary, or a political contrivance, many of the men and women who wear the uniform for this nation should be canonized. But to the bloated MIC, moral hazard defined, and the politicians who vote largess for same, we owe vigilant and constant scrutiny. Mr. Madison knew his topic well.

Ultimately, one wonders if the market place has a role in reining in the MIC, since our politicians have failed. If the true costs of running the MIC were transferred from the American tax payer to the true beneficiaries of America's exercise of martial power… would corporations, multi-nationals and the G-20 insist upon a greater say in how America's military prowess is utilized and how that monolithic budget is spent? Absolutely! Blood and war are a tremendous expense.

The Plutocracy Paradox and Remember the 70's, When the Democrats were the Fringe Party?

By J.M. Hamilton (9-19-10)

The Republican Party has become the party of nuts, and the crazed... As things stand now, I'll take a "tax and spend liberal" over a "borrow, spend, and wish, conservative," any day.

Frustration with the Obama administration may have peaked last week, at least in the short run, with the Tea Party takeover of the Republican Party. A quick read of the situation may suggest that more mainstream Republicans, of the Ike and H.W. Bush variety, may flee to the Democratic Party, as the Tea Party continues its coup. That's not to say the Obama administration has not fallen in stature, and admittedly a great deal of political capital, and good will, have been spent. It does appear that Republicans may make some gains in November, although that could be mitigated if the schism within the party continues to widen and grow.

The Koch brothers created and nurtured this beast, and now the GOP has to live it (I call it the Plutocracy Paradox). Who knows – longer term, perhaps the party will be torn in two?

None of this meant to deflect some of the anger and frustration directed towards this administration by the opposition, and by members of the Democratic Party.   It seems that to some degree, Obama has upset everyone. Many of us are very quick to judge, but before we do so, we would all be wise to remember what exactly this man inherited.

*Thirty years of financial deregulation, which culminated in the largest global financial crisis known to man, a crisis that is still with us today?

*Institutions, such as banking and big oil, that have been allowed to grow so large and powerful, that their failure poses systematic risk to the world economy.

*Government regulators who failed to act, or were outright captured by the very businesses they were supposed to monitor and control. And in the extreme example of the Minerals Management Service outright banged and drugged by the oil industry.

*A Congress that is the epitome of dysfunction, and makes the corruption and graft of ancient Rome look like shoplifting by comparison. The "For Sale" sign was posted right in front of the halls of power with the Supreme Court's ruling in Citizens United v. <u>Federal Election Commission</u>.

*Accounting rules and standards that do more to obscure financial information than reveal results, like Repo 105s and 108s.

*Derivatives and Hybrid financial products that have contributed to the casino atmosphere of Wall Street, and that facilitated the hyper leveraged environment that precipitated the crisis. This market is totally rogue, unregulated, hidden, and worth trillions in notional value.

*Record Federal and State debt, as well as global government debt, so that the next crisis is not unlikely to be a sovereign debt crisis.

*Skyrocketing unemployment and underemployment that may be as high as 20%, or greater, and a spike in poverty not seen in this country in decades.

While President Obama's lot in life, as President, maybe akin to Moses…. Last we checked, President Obama is not God, which is the only known entity powerful enough to address the aforementioned mess, in 21 months or less, particularly when Republicans and the plutocracy are doing everything in their power to throw sand in the gears of government.

Not for the faint of heart, indeed. Many of these problems are intractable, given our special interest dominated government culture. And this administration inherited a bailout that was already set in motion by the Bush administration, TARP, TLGP, 0% interest at the Fed Funds window, etc. A bailout, which has, in all probability, consigned the American economy to a lost decade, or greater. Moreover, as a result of Bush/Paulson's commitment to Goldman Sachs, Wall Street banks, and AIG, the focus of fiscal and monetary policy has and will be on propping up the banks for many years to come, and ameliorating the effects of the economic crimes perpetrated on the American people by same. Look no further than the Fed's efforts at quantitative easing, and the holding down of interest rates: great for the banks, but bad for retirees, who depend upon fixed income investment results to meet their monthly obligations.

And to be sure there are things not to like about the administrations first 21 months.

*The focus on healthcare, when the focus should have been on on jobs.

*The President's outreach to a jaded, anti-government, and recalcitrant, post-modern, Republican Party, best personfied by Mitch McConnell.

*The Dodd-Frank legislation, which offers too many passes to Wall Street banks, delays reform that is needed now, and places too much reliance on the very same government bodies and regulators what were supposed to keep us out of our present, and on-going, financial crisis.

**Some of President Obama's appointees left a great deal to be desired, and actually were participants and contributors to the Great Recession: Larry Summers and Tim Geithner, immediately come to mind.

There have been some bright spots however, like the President's handling of BP and the creation of the 20 billion dollar fund for the BP victims (depending upon how future litigation goes, BP shareholders may actually thank the President for the fund creation). The six month moratorium on offshore drilling. The very recent appointment of the New Consumer Financial Protection Chief, Elizabeth Warren, was a positive development, which showed that the promise of "change" was more than a campaign slogan. The strong Administration push to aid and assist small business, which the Republicans walked away from. Finally, just the fact that this administration didn't attempt to white wash the entire financial crisis, as surely a Republican Administration would have, was a breath of fresh air.

So the rhetorical question stands: Given the aforementioned problems, and obstructionism, is now the time to turn the car keys over to the Republican Party?

This blog offers a quick "no" in response. And here's why: probably in an effort to keep the political dialogue open and civil, the President understates the case against the Republican Party with the car/car keys metaphor. Updating and offering a more truthful paradigm for the state of economic and political affairs left by the Bush administration, we get the following.

If we peruse the economic/political police report produced by the fiscal cops on the scene, we find the following:

"1-20-2009: Crime Scene: the Potomac River.

Bush, Cheney, Greenspan and a dealer/ pusher (commonly known as "Big Oil") were last seen fleeing a burning vehicle, the Econo 2000. At the scene was found a known prostitute (aka W.S. Banks), who was incapacitated, and in severe need of medical attention. Pulse was weak. Ms. Banks appeared under the influence of any number of substances. Paramedics indicate Ms. Banks was suffering from easy money (more powerful than crack), and the sudden with drawl of liquidity. After the vehicle fire was brought under control, schedule one drugs, drug paraphernalia, and liquor, were found throughout the car, along with a large cache of firearms and ammunition. Billions of unmarked taxpayer dollars were found in the trunk of the car.

The events leading up to the crash into the Potomac are as follows: The Econo 2000 was originally "jacked" in January of 2001, and was reported stolen by the co-owners, Messrs. Gore and Clinton. At that time, the Econo 2000 was in mint condition, with a full tank of gas. Also reported stolen, and contained within the vehicle, was an ATM card with a surplus balance. It is reported that after the economy, I mean car (the Econo 2000), was stolen, the ATM card was liquidated and ran debit balances, before the card was shut off.

While driving at high rates of speed, Bush/Cheney engaged in several gun battles (wars); and it is rumored that during these gun battles, Mr. Greenspan pushed the acceleration of the Econo 2000 to new limits.

Before abandoning the car, the Econo 2000, under the command of Mr. Bush, caused a 20 car pileup (G-20) at the intersection of Goldman and AIG. Messrs. Bush and Cheney have also been charged with moral hazard, reckless endangerment of a global economic system, and encouraging and promoting systematic risk.

The vehicle appears totaled."

Bottom line: Not only should the car keys not be returned to the GOP, but the Republicans should have their license revoked.

What might the President Obama do, post midterms, to enhance his odds of re-election in 2012? Tune into this blog next weekend.

A Nation of Whiners!

By J.M. Hamilton (9-26-10)

"Thank God the economy is not as bad as you read in the newspaper every day." – Former Senator Phil Gramm, Republican, UBS Bank Executive, and former campaign advisor to John McCain

The free market guru and economist, Hayek, recognized the importance of government in establishing the rules of the road for capitalism. In fact, one almost gets the feeling from the following passage, from *The Road to Serfdom,* that he's annoyed that the topic must be addressed. It's a given.

"Of course, every state must act and every action of the state interferes with something or other. But that is not the point. The important question is whether the individual can foresee the action of the state and make use of this knowledge as a datum in forming his own plans, with the result that the state cannot control the use made of its machinery and that the individual knows precisely how far he will be protected against interference from others, or whether the state is in a position to frustrate individual efforts."

The central point is: Are the rules of the road firmly established, so that businesses are willing to invest in, and hire for, the future? Unfortunately, after 30 years of financial deregulation, and the subsequent Great Recession caused by Wall Street banks, it was the Obama administrations responsibility to re-establish the rules of the road. After thirty years of hearing "yes," from government, to every request made by Wall Street, the new rules (Dodd-Frank) were not well received, even if the legislation was essentially Pro-Wall Street. The result: a Republican party attacking Democrats as anti- business, and socialist, for what Hayek acknowledges is a fundamental responsibility of government, that is establishing the rules of capitalism. Political opportunism, timing, combined with high unemployment, means that the Republicans more than likely will take over the house.

So how does Obama turn the tide, post November elections? Plan A: Nationalizing the banks, globally, and hitting the reset button on global debt, via restructuring, and establishing a global currency for a global economy, is not in the cards just yet. That will have to wait for the next financial Hiroshima, which, according to Mr. Jamie Dimon and financial history, should be just around the corner (Hints of QE2 by the Fed suggests that the financial health of our nation's banks is in question). The failings of Dodd-Frank, and Basel III, will insure the next global financial meltdown, as sure as the sun will rise tomorrow.

Until then, this leaves the Democrats with Plan B, which is not news to anyone; Plan B having already been well established by the last great fiscal conservative, President Bill Clinton.

When life gives you Republicans, it's best to co-opt the bastards! And just as a Clinton did before him, President Obama should steal the thunder from the Republican herd by adopting an extremely pro-business stance, effective immediately.   The recent legislation supporting small business, awaiting the President's signature, shows that the administration may already be headed in that direction, as does the recently announced departure of Larry Summers.

To kick it up a notch, and to confirm that the rules of the road are firmly set, might the administration, but for two notable caveats, commit to the following: A two year moratorium on further government regulation of business and industry; a two year moratorium on increases in government spending; and a two year moratorium on tax increases?

The two notable caveats are the Bush tax cuts, created by the most fiscally intemperate President, should be allowed to expire; and secondly, in terms of regulation, Elizabeth Warren must be allowed to work out on Wall Street banks. Let's all hope that accounting transparency is a part of Ms. Warren's portfolio.

Why the exception for Elizabeth Warren and further bank regulation? Contrary to what Senator Shelby (R- AL) suggests, banking interests, and the business community's interests are seldom aligned; this is best exemplified by Goldman Sachs, who would short sell family members, let alone clients, if there was a buck to be made. A laissez faire Wall Street is bad for top line growth, and bottom line profits for many of the world's businesses; okay, admittedly Wall Street does appear to be good for businesses that service bankruptcies, and foreclose on commercial and private real estate. My guess is that both the American people and American business clearly understand this nuanced dichotomy.

The second part of Plan B, also from the Clinton play book, is to roll back government.   Just as President Clinton had his Personal Responsibility and Work Opportunity Reconciliation Act of 1996 (Welfare Reform), President

Obama has the entire "ginormous" federal government with which to whack at. And just as it took Nixon to embrace Red-China, it takes a Democrat to successfully roll back big government. As an aperitif, Sarbanes Oxley (SOX), accounting standards created post-Enron, was supposed to protect the American people from the financial apocalypse we are presently facing, and yet, it failed. Why not give ol' SOX the boot? Surely there are other regulatory mandates that are either obsolete or fatally flawed, why not jettison them? And while we are on the topic of rolling back government, just as business must consolidate and trim costs during trying economic times, why not look at consolidating the various services provided by local, county, state and federal government? The MIC, too, would appear ripe for, at the minimum, a freeze in entitlements, and winding down the war in Afghanistan would also help trim deficit spending.

So far Plan B is designed to create jobs, give the President fiscal credibility, and marginalize the Republican Party, all worthy goals. That said, with the fiscal and monetary tool kit worn thin, how might the President facilitate the creation of jobs in this country and tax base expansion? Here, the President should look no further than the Pacific Rim, and the *unfair trade practices* aligned against the United States. It's time to return manufacturing to U.S. shores.

While Republican orthodoxy demands strict adherences to "free trade" dogma, most educated American know that there is no such thing as "free trade," just as we all know there is no Santa Claus. In short, "free trade" is nothing more than some form of arbitrage, whether it is labor, regulatory, or avoidance of tax, which often benefits some multi-nationals at U.S. expense. Here, the Obama administration can turn to none other than Ronald Reagan, who despite a great deal of "free trade" rhetoric, was actually, one of the great protectionist Presidents of the 20th century.

"Treasury Secretary James A. Baker has boasted about the protectionist record: Reagan 'has granted more import relief to U.S. industry than any of his predecessors in more than half a century.'"

Rather than start an ever escalating trade war with the Pacific Rim, via tariffs and quotas, the U.S. should leverage its supremacy as a world market, and create economic incentives for Asia to set up shop in America and hire U.S. labor.   Honda and Toyota never had to be told to establish manufacturing facilities in America, they pre-empted future tariffs and taxes on Japanese exports to America, by setting up shop within our borders. China may want to follow in a like path, in order to prevent imports from stacking up on Shanghai docks. By hiring American labor, China allows the U.S. to thin the ranks of the unemployed, lower unemployment spending, and cut deficit spending. Also as a result, the U.S. becomes a more stable market for China, the dollar becomes a more stable currency, and America is less reliant upon China to finance U.S. debt.

China would gain by setting up shop in the U.S. by purchasing less U.S. debt to sustain the purchase of China's imports, and by gaining a stronger foothold in the world's largest economy. It avoids a nasty trade war, and social upheaval, if Chinese exports were to suddenly to stop flowing to America. In fact, **IF** America and China coordinate this well, the rise in China's hiring on U.S. shores, and the cutting back of exports to America, could also rise with an increased standard of living in China (an appreciation of the Yuan), and the rise of a Chinese market place parallel to, if not ultimately exceeding, its U.S. rival.

"Plan B" then, assists in addressing U.S. job creation, the size of government, fiscal matters, and some foreign policy issues, which leaves the political component.

In economics the goal of predatory pricing is monopoly; and likewise, between the two parties, the goal of predatory politics is hegemony. Since Messer. Bush and Cheney had their way with the U.S., the Republican Party has been on the verge of a political, philosophical, and social crack up. Why not push them over the edge?

Therefore, Plan B must also contain a political component designed to gain maximum advantage over the schism currently breaking the GOP apart at the seams. Fortunately for Democrats, the Republican Party appears to be taking themselves out of the picture. Witness the following:

McCain's top economic adviser Phil Gramm tells America to suck it up and stop complaining about the economy:

"You've heard of mental depression; this is a mental recession," he said, noting that growth has held up at about 1 percent despite all the publicity over losing jobs to India, China, illegal immigration, housing and credit problems and record oil prices. "We may have a recession; we haven't had one yet." And, "We have sort of become a nation of whiners," he said. "You just hear this constant whining, complaining about a loss of competitiveness, America in decline."

Phil Gramm was a U.S. Senator from Texas, who, as head of the Senate Banking Committee, was responsible for much of the banking deregulation that directly contributed to our current crisis. After finishing his Senate career, Mr. Gramm went to work for UBS.

House Minority Leader John Boehner compared the Dodd-Frank legislation to "killing an ant with a nuclear weapon."

"This is killing an ant with a nuclear weapon," Boehner said of the bill. "There are faults in our regulatory system, some in terms of transparency, most as a result of ineffective enforcement by the bureaucracy, who have no idea what these financial products look like today. That could've been fixed, but that's not what we have here."

Mr. Boehner, a perennially tanned chain smoker, will likely be the next Speaker of the House; Mr. Boehner's insensitivity to the ever growing ranks of unemployed, and those citizens who make up the recently reported spike in poverty (welcome to Mr. Boehner's ant hill), may only be exceeded by the poster boy for the Republican Party, Joe Barton.

"I'm speaking totally for myself, I'm not speaking for the Republican Party ... but I'm ashamed of what happened in the White House yesterday," Barton told Mr. Hayward (CEO of BP), shortly after the Gulf Oil Disaster, and right after President Obama demanded that BP set up a 20 billion dollar fund for its victims.

Of course, Mr. Barton looks almost normal, compared to the Tea Bag candidate, Christine O'Donnell.

So how might the DNC capitalize on this gang in 2010 and beyond? Well for starters Democrats may want to steal a page right out of the Republican play book, and utilizing the Supreme Court's ruling in Citizen United V. The Federal Election Commission, actually – in select instances – crossover and support the Extreme Right/Tea Baggers in their bid to hijack the Republican Party and invade government. The more extreme the candidate, possibly, the greater the financial support deployed. The more rabid, nonsensical, and polarizing the Republican Party becomes, the easier it will be for Democrats to make their case against the GOP, post-election and headed into 2012.

Separately, as the President's Chief of Staff heads for Chicago, President Obama will want to channel his inner Rahm and go after the RNC for the sins committed over the last thirty years: from policies of deficits don't matter, to starting two wars, to embracing Big Oil and Wall Street banks – contrary to the business interests of the nation. The Republican party has left itself wide open. Even today, the Republican Party is married to the very ideas that brought this nation to its knees. Best of all, if the GOP regains control on the House, Republicans are going to have to do far more than say they favor tax cuts; they will actually have to govern, and explain which government programs they want to cut.

Perhaps Republicans could start with President Bush's greatest expansion of big government, Plan D of Medicare, or what I like to call, The Big-Pharma Entitlement Act. Note to Republicans: Abdication of responsibility to the social contract, and blind adherence to Laissez Faire doctrine is not governing.

Like Clinton before him, President Obama may actually thrive with a Republican controlled House of Representatives.

After all, a nation of whiners needs all the help it can get!

The True Axis of Evil (Part I)

By J.M. Hamilton (10-10-10)

"... the Reagan administration has failed to promote free trade. Ronald Reagan by his actions has become the most protectionist president since Herbert Hoover, the heavyweight champion of protectionists."

- *The Reagan Record on Trade, Rhetoric versus Reality*, **by Sheldon L. Richman – Published by the Cato Institute.**

George Bush first used "axis of evil" on January 29, 2002, during a State of the Union address, to describe the primary threats to U.S. and world stability: Iraq, Iran, and North Korea. We now know that Iraq was not a threat (nobody is looking for WMDs, anymore). And North Korea's Kim Jong-Il, dictator of death's twilight kingdom, when he's feeling fine, only pokes his head up long enough to extort aid and financial assistance from the West. For the moment, Iran's nuclear ambitions are being sidetracked by a computer virus named Esther (who needs standing armies, the U.S., probably, has computer geeks writing malware code). So much for the threat to the West poised by President Bush's axis, instead we have two very serious threats to U.S. national security and world stability, and J.M.H. aims to take them both on.

The threats identified in this two part piece are, possibly, far more frightening than Islamic fundamentalist bent of global jihad, or rogue petrol states seeking nukes…. For the threats offered up cut to the core of the American economy, and have already begun to carry out the American dream.

A Slam Dunk for Bipartisan Support

Of the two threats, by the far the easiest one to target, politically, is China. For Democrats, attacking this job draining succubus appeals directly to its core constituency, unions and labor.   By pegging the Yuan to the U.S. dollar and exploiting a limitless labor pool of impoverished Chinese, China literally exports its demographic problems and political unrest right onto America's shores; and it holds with an iron fist the U.S. dollars, utilized to purchase China's products. Otherwise, the Yuan, if allowed to float, would naturally rise in value, making American products more affordable in the global market.   Therefore, the pegged Yuan, and the vast stores of U.S. dollars retained, gives China an unfair trade advantage over U.S. products.

For Republicans, taking on the People's Republic of China harkens back to the days when the G.O.P. nearly ruled the known U.S. political universe. For inspiration, think of the glorious commie bashing days of Eisenhower, Nixon, and Reagan! What could invigorate the Republican base more than resurrecting the arch-nemesis of God, country, mom and apple pie? Who said Reagan's evil empire was defeated? Why it's alive and well, and kicking our economic ass; but not because of any superiority over American labor or American ingenuity, but rather, because of unfair trade practices and a U.S. government that has allowed this to happen.

Together, Democrats and Republicans can unite to defeat an economic foe, for entirely different political and ideological reasons.

Trade-o-lanche

In making our case, the U.S. Bureau of Economic Analysis provides us with some cold hard facts:

Period	Balance		
	Total	Goods	Services
Annual			
1992	-39,212	-96,897	57,685
1993	-70,311	-132,451	62,141
1994	-98,493	-165,831	67,338
1995	-96,384	-174,170	77,786
1996	-104,065	-191,000	86,935
1997	-108,273	-198,428	90,155
1998	-166,140	-248,221	82,081
1999	-264,239	-336,310	72,072
2000	-378,780	-446,233	67,453
2001	-364,393	-421,980	57,586
2002	-420,524	-475,345	54,821
2003	-494,183	-541,544	47,361
2004	-609,345	-665,631	56,286
2005	-714,176	-783,801	69,625
2006	-759,240	-839,456	80,216
2007	-702,099	-823,192	121,093
2008	-698,802	-834,652	135,850
2009	-374,908	-506,944	132,036

From the table: U.S. International Trade in Goods and Services: Exports, Imports and Balances

We can project from this table that the advocates of "free trade" have provided America with trade deficits that, if left unchecked, could ramp up to a trillion dollars, annually, very soon.

One sees from the BEA's figures that a whole lot of jobs are being exported outside the United States.

We now know there is nothing free about "free trade," when it costs Americans jobs, erodes the U.S. tax base, and leads to tremendous drain on our government, in the form of social payments and unemployment insurance. "Free trade" also directly feeds our national debt – by cutting America's taxable income base and increasing the aforementioned social service expenditures; and "free trade" further feeds the U.S. *jones* for easy debt financing, both private and public, as net Exporter countries send some U.S. dollars back to America in the form of debt financing.

And the single largest contributing nation to the U.S. trade deficit (?), well this very same Bureau of Economics will tell you that would be China.

Slave Trade

To fight this true force of evil, the U.S. should leverage its preeminence as a world market to assist China in bringing about necessary societal reforms, so that China can become a global market that aids America in driving the world economy. As it stands now, an elite cadre of communist party leadership, and a handful of crony capitalists, surfs a massive wave of Chinese humanity that is exploited daily as inexpensive labor; moreover, this leadership employs all, or nearly all, of the tools designed to curtail U.S. exports to China: from tariffs and taxes to insisting that American business, wishing to operate on China's shores, partner with Chinese business.

In the worker's paradise, Chinese labor does not enjoy the basic social services or safety net that Western democracies provide for its citizens; instead, the average Chinese worker, operating in an economic gulag, is paid a fraction of his American counterpart, and must save to provide for catastrophic medical care, and retirement. So that by allowing China to carry on like this, we not only do America and American labor a tremendous disservice, but we allow Chinese leadership to continue to exploit nearly 20% of world's population for communist elite enrichment.

If the Chinese government had any sense of morality at all, it would take some of its profits, and foreign reserves, and invest them in setting up a social safety net that would allow Chinese workers some semblance of dignity and discretionary income. The result: a Chinese consumer society, and a self sustaining market for China's massive productive capacity, and a rising middle class; of equal importance, it would take the monkey off America's back to be the engine of global economic consumption, help prevent global currency and trade wars, and give the world's exporters a new market with exceptional potential.

The Fear Card

China's Red Leadership is no hurry to adopt these reforms, for they like things the way they are – with an elite fraction of society on top, reaping incredible profits, and more than a billion citizens beneath them, operating at a near sustenance level. Setting up a safety net for China's population will, undoubtedly, prove expensive in the short to intermediate run, as the cost of China's labor rises; but in the long run profits should soar, as China transforms into a consumer society, and, ultimately, a preeminent world market.

To be sure some Western multi-nationals, of a manufacturing focus, may not like such an economic and social transformation, as the rising cost of labor increases the costs of goods sold, or erodes fat and rich profit margins on consumer electronics and other products. Not to pick on Apple, whose products we all know and love, but does this company really need to enjoy a greater than 50% profit margin on iPhone, courtesy of suicidal Chinese labor and the predatory Chinese company, Foxconn?

No, unfortunately, in order to assist China's Red Aristocracy to move forward, America is going to have to pull out every stop in the economic and political play book to leverage China into doing the right thing. Trade sanctions and taxes on Chinese imports are a great beginning. Labeling China a currency manipulator is another step. Or worst case, by simply freezing China's imports out of the U.S. market, we tap into the communist party leadership's greatest fear: political and societal unrest.

If you think the fat cats in Beijing and Hong Kong are tough, just think what hundreds of millions of angry and hungry Chinese workers looks like moving en-masse.

And will China actually dump its massive stockpiles of U.S. currency reserves, the scenario U.S. leadership fears most? Not likely, for such an act will only serve to devalue China's own holdings, remove their leverage card, and make American goods and services that much more competitive, globally.

The Long March!

A myth has sprung over the last couple of decades that China and the Chinese government are this warm cuddly capitalist bear, who means the world no harm. Mr. Alan Abelson, of *Barron's*, a financial weekly, over the course of many Saturdays, has eviscerated this fantasy that China is some sort of free market Disneyland, when nothing could be further from the truth. Mr. Abelson's weekly editorial, *Up & Down Wall Street*, gives us a clearer picture (e.g. IPOs and stock market to the contrary, the majority of China's largest businesses remain under the control and watchful eye of the state; the economic planning of this command economy, and the infusion of funds into these large Chinese companies, is directed by technocrats within the big red machine; and the captains of Chinese industry who run these large companies work side by side with communist party cadres).

Chairmen Mao wrote in 1935: *"The Long March is a manifesto. It has proclaimed to the world that the Red Army is an army of heroes, while the imperialists and their running dogs, Chiang Kai-shek and his like, are impotent. It has proclaimed their utter failure to encircle, pursue, obstruct and intercept us. The Long March is also a propaganda force. It has announced to some 200 million people in eleven provinces that the road of the Red Army is their only road to liberation."*

Chinese leadership today, under threat from few if any countries, seems to have chosen a different path to "liberation," one of crony capitalism and command economy; but the world should make no mistake that China's leadership remains on that long march, even if it means a short run detour into faux capitalism. American leadership has nothing to fear from an exploited and humble Chinese people, but should be highly weary of the goals, ambitions and designs of China's communist party leadership, who appear bent on economic and political hegemony. Perhaps a less sinister, but ultimately naïve read of the situation is: This same leadership is just trying to stay one step ahead of 20% of the world's population?

This blog's greatest concern is that China has, for the last couple of decades, lulled America into a sense of economic calm and a consumer opiate haze, as U.S. jobs have been shipped overseas, and America and the American government has become addicted to cheap debt financing. Meanwhile, Federal deficits spiral out of control, from over consumption, lack of national savings, and a shrinking tax base, and the need for ever increasing unemployment benefits. And to what end (?): A weakened, declining and debilitated United State of America.

Who also benefits by a diminished manufacturing base within America? Why that would be U.S. banks and the shadow banking industry, who have become one of the larger employers in America, and who can in turn leverage this fact against our own government to pay for Wall Street's financial disasters.

"You will never find a more wretched hive of scum and villainy. We must be cautious."

Without firing a shot, China, and in this country a band for free market zealots (like some fifth column working it's evil from within), has done more to harm and damage America, economically, than the Red Army ever could have done. Why merely check out this nations unemployment and underemployment rate of 20% or greater. Look no further than Federal and State budgets and a government debt that is spiraling out of control; and glance at the last gasps of Federal Reserve policy, with yet another round of bank bailouts under the auspices of QE2, wearing the mask of monetary stimulus.

To be sure righting the balance of trade is not the answer to all of America's economic ills, but it's a good start; and to be sure, China is not the only nation who has exploited America's "free trade" dogma for their economic betterment.

But what is absolutely sickening are the elites at the Chicago school of economics who still tout this faded catechism as some absolute, when they are surrounded by the decay "free trade" has wrought, in Cleveland, Pittsburgh and Detroit. There is no such thing as utopian "free trade," only wealthy industrialist and manufacturers seeking out labor, tax and regulatory arbitrage, in order to maximize profits (and governments who in turn profit, or lose, but nearly always – at the expense of its people).

America's share of the world economy has shrunk over time, but approximately 24% of global GDP still resides within U.S. borders, and we must leverage this fact in establishing U.S. trade policy. We owe it to ourselves, and ultimately for the betterment of the citizens of the world, to insist upon fair trade and U.S. trade policies that mitigate the advantages of labor, regulatory and tax arbitrage. It's good for America and it forces some developing countries to catch up with the American economy, by creating their own, internal, markets to rely upon. Once these self sustaining markets are established globally, in the so-called BRIC nations, and when the differences in tax codes, regulation and the cost of labor are mitigated, then fair trade and the global economy can take off as never before.

But until then, the U.S. should insist upon fair and equitable trade from its global partners, all the better to protect against predatory trade policies.

The True Axis of Evil (Part II)

By J.M. Hamilton (10-25-10)

The Business of America is Business, and NOT Banking!

At his 1964 coronation ceremony within the Cow Palace, Barry Goldwater, perhaps, offered up the most regrettable line in American politics, when he said: "I would remind you that extremism in the defense of liberty is no vice!" Of course "extremism" can be analogous to the old saw, "the ends justify the means." Extremism, in the hands of the wrong leader, can be rationalized and deployed against nearly anything or anybody, even the extinguishing of freedom, itself (Witness President Bush's Orwellian named Patriot Act. The beginning of a slippery slope, possibly?). And in these desperate times extremism is everywhere. We can see it in the Koch Brother's Tea Party movement. One senses extremism in a combative Chamber of Commerce, who apparently, believes that to seek redress against Faustian Wall Street Banking community is an assault against American Business; the Chamber's strategy is not unlike the strategy deployed by, what some would call, an extreme group, the NRA, who argues that any roll back or rules in fire arm ownership, even assault rifles, is an attack upon gun ownership.

And that's what today's "Axis of Evil" is… it is the extremes: from Communist China, with its billion or more of enslaved citizens, to the West's laissez faire capitalism (LFC), and the Wall Street banks that are, or were, LFC's present incarnation.

In nature, the extremes (black swans) tend to be weeded out, as flukes or freaks, in the long run; but, in the short run, the extremes can have cataclysmic impact, and should be guarded against or tempered. As for Mr. Goldwater, history tells us that while he was, arguably, a great U.S. Senator (especially in his later years), the American people, astutely, recognized possibly something extreme in Mr. Goldwater, and rejected him as a candidate for this nation's highest office.

A virulent and extreme form of capitalist doctrine is laissez faire or quite simply, anything goes, from dynamiting your competitor's rail road to Wall Street banks issuing, what Mr. Buffet refers to as, "financial weapons of mass destruction." We all know that capitalism is an incredible engine, or vehicle, capable of many great things: lifting nations out of poverty to increasing the standard of living of citizens to name but two. But like any powerful engine, or vehicle, the world requires safety features, or rules and regs. Take away these safety features, say the brakes, and instead of a capitalist car of growth and opportunity, the world is left with a killing machine.

LFC may have reached its pinnacle as doctrine in the last thirty years, culminating in 2008 financial crisis. Let us hope. But there are still fanatics who believe that government has no place to play in the market place. To hear the Chamber of Commerce tell it, government has created a great deal of uncertainty in the business community, and as a consequence the means of production is hoarding cash as never before (observe Apple with over $50 billion in cash sitting on its balance sheet), rather than invest in CAPEX, growth and labor.

Unfortunately, the Chamber's anger would appear misdirected.

While government does bear some responsibility for our current predicament, it was the adherents of LFC that advocated, lobbied, and supported the removal of the brakes from capitalism's car. This is best illustrated by the Wall Street banks, which made billions of dollars short selling America, the American people, American business, and an engine of economic growth, the housing sector. So when the Chamber's members look at shrinking top line growth, and the prospect of tax increases to pay for rising government unemployment benefits, they should look no further than LFC and Wall Street banks as the root cause. After all, our politicians only did what they were paid to do, service LFC and the banks!

For the high priests of LFC, as best exemplified by the Wall Street banks, the world is one big fatted calf, to be exploited, sacrificed and consumed. In the LFC religion, there is no allegiance to God and Country, only blind idolatry of profits, all in the name of furthering stockholder interests. Funny thing about "stock holder interests," however, if we take a close look at how the Wall Street bank stockholders have fared in recent years, we can see that, if anything, blind faith in LFC has led to diminished stockholders returns, in equity and dividends. Meanwhile, bank management seems to get richer and wealthier, even while on the government dole.

It was not always this way, Wall Street banks were not always this nihilistic. If we read Ron Chernow's House of Morgan, we know that, *not without self interest*, Morgan financed some of the adversaries of Germany in WWI, and we know that Morgan bailed out numerous banks, and assisted a foreign government, or two, during and after the crash of '29. Siegmund Warburg is another example of banker from another era, who never lost sight of his ethical compass, wrote that the most important element of private banking was "moral standing."

Compare that to Goldman Sachs today, who having been bailed out by the full faith and credit of the U.S. taxpayer in 2008, had bet against the U.S. dollar. A position Goldman later unwound, when dollar unexpectedly strengthened in the face of a collapsing Euro, an event Goldman played no small role in when it sold Greece CDS to help obscure debt from its financial statements.

http://blog.jmhamiltonpublishing.com/2010/03/29/goldman-ends-bet-against-the-dollar-dollar-appreciates-in-value-against-the-euro.aspx

What's so frustrating for most Americans is double standard that we live with daily. In other words, majorities of Americans pay their bills, and live by the laws of the land, or suffer the consequences, bankruptcy, loss of home, and/or job. Apparently, unlike the Chamber/LFC crowd, and the U.S. Banks, we cannot call upon the Federal government for bailouts for egregious behavior. Which points to the entire LFC fallacy, the Chamber/Banks want LFC when there are profits to be had, but want to socialize the losses incurred in the event of a financial catastrophe: Too Big to Fail and Moral Hazard in action!

Many of these same TARP recipients are under fire, yet again. Bank of America (BOA) is a case in point. Having purchased Countrywide S&L, and having made some residential bets itself, BOA is being hammered by: a large volume of underperforming assets; lawsuits stemming from its failure to properly service residential mortgages; lawsuits from mortgagors, as BOA attempted to foreclose with shoddy paper work; and now Freddie and Fannie and Institutional investors are attempting to return CDO products, due to lousy underwriting standards.

Could yet another bailout be around the corner?

We know a back door bailout in the form of QE2 will soon, more than likely, be launched by the Fed, under the guise of monetary stimulus, all to better to keep the banking industry on morphine drip, and the U.S. economy on ice. Not coincidentally, business failures continue to rise (tens of thousands per annum), and unemployment rises, as the Fed and Treasury desperately attempt to keep these zombie banking institutions alive.

Our entire economic system is being held back, held hostage, so that we can keep these banking behemoths from failing.

Meanwhile, back at the White House, Treasury Secretary Tim Geithner assures the President and America people that TARP was a smashing success, having played no small role in its genesis as President of the Federal Reserve Bank of N.Y. Whether or not the debt to society will ultimately be paid back by the banks and AIG, no small amount having been converted from debt to equity, remains to be seen, but that' s not the point. The repatriation of TARP monies back to the Fed was insignificant compared to the business and social costs, the resulting increase government deficit spending, and the loss of business revenue, as a result of the banking crisis. And yet, Mr. Geithner assures us that the American taxpayer has been paid back. By who's stretch of the imagination?

Recent press suggests that Mr. Geithner may also be an advocate of another fiction perpetrated by the LFC/Chamber crowd, free trade!

And what about all those Goldman traders, including the likes of Fabulous Fab Tourre, who brought this crisis upon America and the world? Well fear not … Reuters reported recently that many of those traders have landed on their feet at that other bastion of LFC, private equity's KKR!

With the Republicans and Chamber of Commerce set to take over the House, and possibly the Senate, how long before the extremist wrap the car, economy, around a tree?

http://blog.jmhamiltonpublishing.com/2010/10/09/the-true-axis-of-evil-part-i.aspx

MRSA and Private Equity

For both there is a cure!

By J.M. Hamilton (11-7-10)

Several interesting titles came to mind for this week's editorial, among them: *Private Equity, the Killer Whales of Capitalism*, or *Private Equity & Saturated Fat, Clogging the Arteries of Commerce and the Economic Recovery*.   But hey, I have nothing against Killer Whales, who are only acting out their role in nature by culling out the weak and infirm from the seal population. And saturated fat is absolutely benign compared to private equity.   At least with a little will power we can avoid saturated fat. Private equity, on the other hand, is more pernicious, insidious and prevalent in our society; that is to say, private equity is much more analogous to the super-bug, MRSA or *methicillin-resistant staphylococcus aureus*. Besides, the government's concern about MRSA, and required intervention into market place, nearly completes the hook, and allows this piece to run full circle.

Government Intervention into the Market Place: Democrats, Republicans and Bears! Oh My!

The *Times* ran a story this week, *Looking for a Superbug Killer*, where for once, we may actually have both Democrats and Republicans coming to agreement that government intervention into the market place might be a positive thing. Its seems as though MRSA, and assorted superbugs, are overthrowing and growing beyond the reach of medicine; and Big Pharma has more profitable endeavors to pursue (like adding vitamins to medicines, so that patents and monopolistic profits can be extended), than developing new antibiotics to fight MRSA and his deadly friends. Funny how the most ardent Laissez Faire Capitalist becomes all "lovey" about government, when the market falls on its ass, and there's a life threatening crisis at hand.

Seems as though both Democrats and Republicans want to throw all kinds of financial incentives, tax breaks, and other assorted financial goodies, Big Pharma's way (on top of the multitude of breaks Big Pharma already receives), so what would transpire in a more perfectly capitalist system, can now happen through government intervention into a oligopolistic market place. Unfortunately, as usual, government is attacking the symptom of the problem (Big Pharma intransigence and greed), instead of the problem (Monopolies authorized by our government), essentially applying a band aid to the boil on the skin instead of addressing and attacking the MRSA that lurks beneath the boil.

Adam Smith and an "Absurd Tax"

We'll eventually get to private equity, but first a quick visit to our friend Adam Smith. Mr. Smith warned about the pernicious tendency of capitalism to metastasize into monopoly, when he wrote:

(The interests)... "in any particular branch of trade or manufactures, is always in some respects different from, and even opposite to, that of the public. To widen the market and narrow the competition, is always in the interests of the dealers... and can serve only to enable dealers, by raising their profits above what they would naturally be, to levy, for their own benefit, an absurd tax upon the rest of their fellow citizens. The proposal of any new law or regulation of commerce which comes from this order (Merchants, Dealers, Monopolies), ought always to be listened to with great precaution, and ought never be adopted till after having been long and carefully examined, not only with the most scrupulous, but with the most suspicious attention."

No way. Adam Smith, a free market deity, nearly 235 years ago warned that monopolistic profits are a tax on society, and warned about capitalism's tendency toward combination? And as this blog has written about (see Monopolies and Double Standards, Et Al.) monopoly can only occur by the grant and authority of the government. And hence, the market place failure we are now witnessing: Having created the oligopoly, Big Pharma, the government now has to go begging this oppressive power for core and fundamental medicine. Had the government not allowed Big Pharma to consolidate and grow so powerful, there would be many varied entities and entrants in the pharmaceutical market place, each seeking out their own niche, presumably one of these would have been antibiotics to keep up with superbugs. Instead, we have a few powerful actors, Big Pharma, who can hold out for compounded government largess, at the expense of the tax payer and general welfare of society, before developing drugs that would otherwise, most likely, be developed in a less monopolistic market sector.

"This is market place failure," states California Democrat Mr. Waxman in the *Times* article. Indeed, Mr. Waxman, but rather than throw yet more tax payer money at Big Pharma (in the form of financial incentives and tax breaks), perhaps the real solution is the break up the pharmaceutical cartel, so that there are more players to address life threatening disease and illness?

How the Game is Played

Enter private equity…. Shadow banking's co-evil twin. Private Equity makes its money by acquiring, merging, leveraging up perfectly healthy companies and corporations with colossal amounts of debt, front loading profits, extracting huge management fees, of course taking a portion of the profits (if any) from the targeted company, tax deductibility on the massive debt, and even enjoys the kicker of special tax break, under the guise of "carry forward." Private equity further guarantees profitability by sealing itself off from loss by creating LLC funds and holding companies; hence, profits can flow up, but losses and bankruptcy may stay below with the LLC. But the really big pay off occurs when the private equity company takes the acquired firm and flips it, by taking it public (IPO), merging it with another company (M&A), or tossing said company to another private equity firm (to be leveraged up and "debted up" all the more), much as a pack of Orcas does with baby seals. Of course, private equity, like MRSA, goes barely unnoticed when things are going along swimmingly; but when the economy heads south or the bubble bursts, all that leverage, and the debt service load, tends to tear a company apart at the seams, to the detriment of: society, management, investors, employees, bond or debt holders, vendors of the bankrupt company, and the tax base.

Witness a record number of business failures in this country in the last couple of years, possibly half of them pushed over the edge by their recent, or present liaison, with private equity. From the NY Times story, *Profits for Buyout Firms as Company Debt Soared (10-5-09)*, we get the following:

"A disproportionate number of the companies that were acquired during that frenzy are now struggling with the enormous debts. More than half the roughly 220 companies that have defaulted on their debt in some form this year were either owned at one time or are still controlled by private equity firms, according to analysts at Standard & Poor's. Among them are household names like Harrah's Entertainment and Six Flags, the theme park operator."

http://blog.jmhamiltonpublishing.com/2010/11/06/retro-blog-private-equitys-brave-new-world.aspx

Gee… all those tax breaks and special considerations, do you think private equity has some ties to the Federal Government? You bet. Why look no further than the occupations of our recent Treasury Secretaries:

*Mr. Henry Paulson (Bush Administration) former Goldman Sachs, CEO and creator of TARP. Say no more.

*John W. Snow (Bush Administration) now a member of Cerberus Capital Management Groups, private equity, and the fine folks who helped bring Chrysler down.

*Larry Summers (Clinton Administration), lieutenant of Robert Rubin, and a key player in the deregulation of the derivatives industry. The derivatives industry will and does, undoubtedly, play a significant role in private equity, and yet another round of M&A activity to come.

*Robert Rubin (Clinton Administration): Goldman Sachs, Citigroup, both of which ran and supported private equity operations.

Alone, of our recent Treasury Secretaries, Paul O'Neill (Bush Administration) stands out as a man of fiscal integrity, a man who bucked the Bush tax cuts and the neo-cons, and a man who did not come from, or return to, investing banking and private equity. Perhaps that's why Mr. O'Neill was let go? As for Mr. Summers, the derivatives he has championed over the years play a unique role in private equity, by allowing investments banks, and private equity, itself, to hedge their bets against targets for acquisition. Derivates can secure profits for debt holders, if a takeover target fails, so that, depending upon the deal, and the subsequent financial results, the investors, private equity, banks and bondholder, may actually have an incentive to see the target fail or enter into bankruptcy. As we can see in our on-going financial crisis, Wall Street makes money coming and going (lose, win or draw), and if the system blows up, well there's always Uncle Sam ready to offer a bailout.

Fed Reserve and QE2:

The mother's milk of private equity is cheap liquidity. We are talking tons of money sloshing around, like the kind we see right now under QE 1 and QE2. Private Equity has enjoyed peak periods, during bubbles, and massive monetary easing, like that seen in the mid to late eighties courtesy of Fed Chairman Alan Greenspan, and the earlier part of this decade, again under the auspices of the Fed, commanded yet again, by Mr. Alan Greenspan. During these periods private equity awash with easy money, courtesy of investors and friends in the banking industry, runs around preying upon companies, leveraging them, merging them, and most stock analyst's favorite, creating "synergy" and "economies of scale".... All code for down-sizing, layoffs, and organizational restructuring.

At a macro level, as companies merge or fall prey to their massive debt load, private equity plays a critical role in the consolidation of industry and markets, that is to say, the creation of monopolies and oligopolies, not unlike what we see with Big Pharma, and problems associated with Big Pharma, like MRSA.

Of course these monolithic business entities have tremendous problems with risk management, as we saw with B.P. earlier this year, and often end up performing poorly for their stockholders and society.

And the Fed's and Treasury's role in all this? Well presently, the Treasury finds itself in the ownership of a car company, and several financial institutions. What better way for the Fed and Treasury to divest themselves of these entities, than to print money, flood the market with cheap liquidity, drive down bond yields and treasury yields, and drive unwilling participants back into the stock market…. So that the Fed can exit, stage left, from its forays into the private sector. TARP might, officially, then be proclaimed an economic/government success, and the preeminence of "Too Big to Fail," as a government policy, upheld.

Of course, an intended or unintended consequence of massive liquidity, and lower bond yields, is to drive investors into junk bonds, and riskier investment vehicles, such as hedge and private equity funds. Again, all the mother milk of private equity….so that at a time of record unemployment in this country, and with the Fed printed money so fast that the printing presses are beginning to smoke, we can reasonably expect more job killing raids by private equity in the market place. Merger and acquisition activity should soar.

The Bottom Line:

Merger and acquisition activity, as well as, the taxation and regulation of private equity, like monopolies themselves, all fall under government purview. One quick way for government to arrest rising unemployment is to slow merger and acquisition activity (via Justice, SEC and the FTC), and tax private equity at the appropriate rate all businesses face, and eliminate the tax deductibility of debt; all the better the for government to address unemployment, MRSA and intransigent industries, such as Big Pharma, who are literally holding public health hostage, so that they can, possibly, extract further financial concessions from our government.

Private equity, too, has a role to play. Perhaps instead of becoming a contractionary force in our economy, it can be a force for good, by deploying its capital toward new ventures and start-ups that create jobs and opportunity, instead of the elimination of same.

At the end of the day, MRSA is a growing life taker and a threat to the nation's health; likewise, private equity, in its present incarnation, is a threat to society, business, the consumer, management and employees, and our nation's economic health. For both there is a cure.

Reap the Wind...

Inter-generational wealth larceny and other Fed voodoo... Stagflation anyone?

By J.M. Hamilton (12-4-10)

Is your head spinning yet? The financial news is coming in so fast and furious that it's almost the perfect storm of economic sensory overload, but, unfortunately, this storm appears to be winding up. Bankers are working weekends and, perhaps, holidays to save the Euro, and justify QE2. As mentioned in a prior blog, one knows it's serious when bankers meet on weekends, and the on-going financial crisis appears to be a never ending case in point. One thing is for sure, the trend of banks being bailed out, at the expense of the proletariat (that would be about 99% of us), continues unabated. The policy mistakes that were made in Japan in the 90's are still the rage in Europe and America.

Heh, at least the bankers are happy. Everybody else... pound sand!

The Politicization of the Fed

The recent exchange between Republicans and Dems was pretty interesting. Some Republicans are calling for the Feds mandate to be clipped to just insuring the stability of the dollar, that is to say:

Dear Chairmen Bernanke, please stop this nonsense about looking out for the unemployed, we have wealth to protect.

In other words, one in five Americans out there will just have to find their own cake and pudding. And the Treasury's response was we can't politicize the Fed... QE2 is a righteous policy, and a wonderful thing to behold. Unfortunately for Americans, corporate interests, and the world, the Fed was politicized long ago and the last time we had somebody in the chair with the *cojones* (please excuse the vulgarity) to chart an independent course was June 2, 1987.

This picture is worth more than a thousand words.

http://blog.jmhamiltonpublishing.com/2010/03/12/if-volcker-remained-in-power-instead-of-the-maestro-would-america-and-the-world-be-in-the-mess-its-in-today–assuredly-not.aspx

That's right, after Volker, essentially, saved the Reagan presidency, and helped us forget all those zany WIN buttons from the seventies, the administraton threw their savior overboard in favor of someone who was a little suppler.

Intended and Unintended Consequences

Enter the new chairmen, presently known as Mr. Greenspan, formally known as the maestro, and very easy money. The result: a Fed more willing to acquiesce to the political desires and needs of the Executive branch, who appoints the Fed chairmen (after all, what's a President to do with this messy thing called "democracy," and the Senate and the House?); and liberal Fed policies that played no small role in the bubble that blew up the world economy, and in particular the Western economies, in 2008. Entre Chairmen Bernanke, and to borrow a verse from *the Who*: "here's to the new boss… same as the old boss!" Yes, indeed, it appears that the easy money policies, that helped create our economic Hiroshima, are here to stay.

And the stated aim of QE2? Per Mr. Dudley, Chairmen of the Federal Reserve Bank of NY, we get the following:

"We have no goal in terms of pushing the dollar up or down," Mr. Dudley said. "Our goal is to ease financial conditions and to stimulate a stronger economic expansion and more rapid employment growth."

Okay. But as we all know the Fed is a body of extremely bright men and women… surely, there are other explicit, and tacit, goals and objectives at play here, besides "stronger economic expansion" is quite vague. Let's examine some of the repercussions of easy money, or QE2:

$$$ Well we know from Shadow Government Statistics that M3 is still contracting, and the dollar multiplier is also exceptionally low… that is, there is a below normal money velocity in the economy. Gee, that couldn't be because banks and corporations are hoarding cash, and in the case of the former, due to highly impaired balance sheets? The Fed knows, fully, that the banks are not suffering from liquidity issues, but impaired assets and earnings on their balance sheet and income statements, respectively. All QE2 does is buy the banks more time to clean up their financials. QE2 does little to address the true crisis, which is the finding a floor in the housing market, and restoring jobs to Americans.

$$$ The Fed, as does the Executive Branch/Treasury, very much has a vested interest in seeing the policies of the last two years (i.e. the Bank Bailouts and

the continuation of Too Big to Fail) succeed. By any economic measurement and in terms of mitigating human suffering, it would appear that TARP, and the myriad other Treasury and Fed policies since 2008, are a colossal failure. Rather than admit failure, the Fed continues to throw good money after bad, and give the banks yet another round bailouts, via QE2. (By the way, if the 50 state attorney generals don't succeed, in what Bush/Paulson should have done when this crisis first erupted — i.e. SHUT DOWN THE BANKS — then, perhaps, the investor class, who purchased all those toxic debt securitization products from the banking industry, will.)

$$$ The government also owns, or has partial ownership, in several prominent corporations. By holding interest rates low, it forces American people and corporations to look at riskier means to earn a reasonable rate of return – think stock market. One very wise economist on Tom Keene's Bloomberg radio program, called this "inter-generational wealth transfer, or larceny," in short the Fed is giving the depositors, and saving class in this country, nothing, so that the banks can have depositor money for free to further prop up impaired bank financial statements and create greater margins on earnings for same. So what's grandma to do (?)… What with flash trading and sharks on the Street, and asset bubbles galore, well she can just take her 2% at BOA and party hearty!

$$$ There's also a geo- political angle in all this, too… which reminds me of *God Father III*, where the Vatican's banker, in that movie, stated: "Finance is a gun… politics is knowing when to pull the trigger." And it appears that Bernanke and Co., have pulled the trigger on the Pacific Rim, and in particular, a currency manipulator named China. Here, the Fed is attempting to combat the Yuan's peg to the dollar, which makes China's goods and services more affordable, at the expense of American goods, services and labor; but the Fed's policies also has the impact of destabilizing the Renmenbi, since China's printing presses have to work overtime printing Yuan to purchase the flood of U.S. dollars, in order to make the currency peg hold. Add to this the flood of U.S. dollars entering the Pacific Rim, in the form of investments, and you have a bunch of communists leaders suffering night sweats and inflation fears.

I never said QE2 was all bad.

$$$ And, the future unintended consequence from QE2 ???: Well that would be stagflation… a scenario, whereby interest rates and inflation are high, and unemployment is also high, and you are not high. In fact, many of us will be feeling quite low. Remember the misery index? There will be no inflation as a result of QE2, QE3 and QE4, in the immediate future, because there is high

unemployment and week demand; but inflation is around the corner because as the Fed sprays the world with paper, commodity prices rise in the face of a devalued currency, and because our friends the bond vigilantes, presently kicking serious butt in the E.U., will soon happen upon future Treasury auctions. And you think the gloom and malaise shrouding the country right now is tough… just wait. Time to duct tape your wrists, boys and girls.

Right now, the Fed enjoys a unique position in history of controlling the world's fiat currency, and watching its primary currency competitor, the Euro, dissolve into thin air. The dollar is the only game in town, and will remain the defacto haven of wealth for the immediate future. Unless the E.U. unites, politically and fiscally, instead of merely monetarily, it is extremely doubtful that Germany and France are going to want to bailout the rest of Europe for their profligate ways, and perpetuate sovereign moral hazard. Hence, we all may very well be witnessing the death rattle of the Euro…. This allows the Fed to continue lobbing trillions of dollars in liquidity around the world, and here in the U.S., without threat of immediate repercussions. The Renmenbi has its own inflationary problems, and is not quite ready for prime time (courtesy of the Fed and global investments); plus China does not appear ready to take on the currency mechanizations of Wall Street, hedge funds, private equity, and the flash trading crowd.

If America's political class, both Democrats and Republicans, could get their act together and govern in a united fashion, instead of endless internecine political warfare, then maybe the Fed wouldn't have to attempt to address fiscal, monetary and foreign policy issues, simultaneously. The Fed is ill equipped to do so, and does not enjoy the mandate of the American people. But what's a President to do?

A Posthumous Nobel Award for Dr. Suess in Economics?

By J.M. Hamilton

One can imagine the tykes Blankfein and Diamon reading "The Sneetches," hungrily…

On one level Dr. Suess' children's books have always been a bit of a Technicolor trip, providing an alternate universe with fantastic creatures, and always hugely entertaining. Then there's the deeper meaning behind the stories, quite often providing social or political commentary. One of the many great things about being an uncle is you get to go back and read some of these fine stories, and in the process, one can pick up on a whole different set of meaning.

The good doctor, apparently, was quite the economist, among his many varied gifts and talents. In one particular story he presaged our own economic crisis by nearly fifty years, and Japan's economic problems by nearly thirty years; and in the same book also wrote of financial hedging more than a decade before Black & Scholes offered up "*The Pricing of Options and Corporate Liabilities*," a cornerstone of modern day derivatives trading.

Within this mini-novella, Mr. Suess writes of an economic meltdown, and an asset bubble in stars. It's all here: greed, avarice, social-climbing, wild mania and speculation. And at the center of the story is a unique figure, who appealing to the vanity of the masses, sells them exactly what they want, stars.   But what makes Mr. McBean so unique is that he foresees the inevitable crash in stars, and hedges his bet by offering star removal (in essence a financial move against his own product), which only fuels the extraordinary delusion even further. *Hence, Mr. McBean makes money coming and going, while leaving the multitude penniless, deeply depressed, and in a state of economic collapse.*

One can imagine the tykes Blankfein and Diamon reading *The Sneetches*, hungrily, with wide-eyed amazement and wonder. Could that story, published in 1961, have lodged in many a future banker's subconscious, and what did it do to their young and malleable minds? Either way, clearly Mr. Suess was quite cutting edge in matters concerning banking and commerce, and perhaps should be awarded a Nobel Prize in Economics, posthumously?

Derivatives Trading

Today, Mr. McBean is best exemplified by the Wall Street banks, which make money coming and going, and quite often bet against their own product offerings. And the vehicle of choice for Wall Street banks to bet against the public, their own clients, and hedge their own bets, is the derivative or credit default swap (C.D.S.), the very same financial instrument that played a hugely important role in our present economic collapse. The derivative is what the esteemed Mr. Buffet referred to as "financial weapons of mass destruction," that is to say, when one of his many storied companies isn't buying and selling derivative products, themselves.

For despite the best efforts of Dodd-Frank, this product worth hundreds of trillions in notional value remains largely hidden from public view, opaque, and under the absolute control of the Wall Street Banking cartel. As such, the world is primed, yet again, for another financial Armageddon. Louise Story, in a **New York Times** piece, "*A Secretive Banking Elite Rules Trading in Derivatives*," writes of how the major Wall Street Banks collude to fight full disclosure, an options board/clearing house, and additional entrants into the swaps markets place, at every turn.

http://blog.jmhamiltonpublishing.com/2010/12/12/the-banks-in-this-group-which-is-affiliated-with-a-new-derivatives-clearinghouse-have-fought-to-block-other-banks-from-entering-the-market-and-they-are-also-trying-to-thwart-efforts-to-make-full-information-on-prices-and-fees-freely-available.aspx

Why? Answer: Per the banks to protect the public, but also to secure their own profits.

The implications for the public, business, and governments are staggering. A clearing house would make the CDS/derivatives market transparent to all, the pricing of this commodity would become far more competitive for businesses and investors, and the capital or equity backing these bets would, presumably, be held by the exchange or clearing house, and not left in the hands of the banks. Society, and the consumers of such products, would benefit immensely from the proposed controls, since the pricing of the product is there for all the world to see, capital is put up to secure these bets (helping to avoid future bank bailouts), and wild swings in the market (including those initiated by short sellers, hedge funds and banks) can be observed in advance by watching the trade In C.D.S. All of which would serve to limit some of the speculation in these products, and cut into bank profits.

Hence, the fight, if you can call it that. For despite the role these instruments played in the crash we are all living through today, and that basically insured the wild speculative fever in stars, I mean real estate in Europe and the U.S., the banks remain in control.

What's even more frightening is that these same products serve, primarily, to insure banking, business, and government debt issuance. And as predicted by this blog, and by others, our next source of economic crisis is likely to be from sovereign debt.

Haircut Time for the E.U. Bond Holders... NOT Yet!

The McBeans of the world, and an opaque derivates market, play a key and crucial role in why the problems of international finance are placed upon the taxpayers of the E.U. and the United States, instead by the perpetrators of our present economic crisis, the banks themselves.

Politicians have over promised their citizens more services and largess than states can possibly provide, which leads to the issuance debt. In many instances, the sovereign debt problem has become so acute that many private and institutional investors in state, muni and E.U. bonds will not purchase government debt without the insurance protection provided by a derivative and C.D.S. contract (which provides payment in the event of a default by a sovereign). Add to this salient fact that the vast majority of CDS contracts are purely speculative, as opposed to being purchased by the relevant counterparties (the debtor and debtee), by exponential ratios, and that the notional values of these instruments is worth hundreds of trillion in value, and we have yet another economic time bomb just waiting to go off.

All of which explains why governments are so eager to bailout banks, and each other, at the expense of its citizens and taxpayers. For if our elected officials attempted to hold the banks, or their own governments accountable for financial malfeasance, and went into bankruptcy, which would require a debt restructuring (i.e. "haircut" among bond holders), the entire banking system would collapse, and possibly a global currency or two, with it. That is to say, as governments and banks went into default, it would trigger payment from these wildly speculatively, hidden, and more than likely under-collateralized instruments, known as derivatives/CDS.

But heh, these instruments are incredibly profitable for banks to trade.

Meanwhile instead of forcing the plutocracy to take a financial hit on their holdings of bank bonds and sovereign debt, the costs of a never ending stream of bank and sovereign bailouts are carried by debt monetization and taxpayers.... All so that the banks don't have to close up shop. This scenario is a never ending economic fugue, headed in the wrong direction, as many sovereigns have absolutely no hope whatsoever of paying their debt, and wealthy nations, such as Germany, end up bailing out fiscally irresponsible nations, such as the PIIGS. As a result, the human suffering and hardship, created by rising taxes, reductions in social services (such as education), commodity inflation, and austerity measures, is no longer being taken with equanimity among the citizens of the world.

A House of Cards, or a Chain of Dominos, Choose your Metaphor!

Even as I write this bond vigilantes, many of them undoubtedly hedged with C.D.S. products, are testing E.U. sovereign bond issuance and interest rates spreads. The bond vigilantes know that if they can make a sovereign default they will be handsomely paid via their own speculative C.D.S. contracts, and what better way to tear a fiscally impaired sovereign budget apart than with higher interest payments, a cost that will undoubtedly be carried by the taxpayers of a target country, if not cause outright default.

The problem is that sovereign debt, and C.D.S. issuance, is so interconnected throughout the globe, that if one sovereign defaults it could set off a chain of sovereign dominos, as stronger countries continue to throw good money after bad in the hopes of staying one foot ahead of the contagion. Strong countries, in essence, becoming and joining the ranks of the weak, through successive bank and sovereign bail outs.

Fiscal policy and monetary policy, in the U.S., is well on its way to becoming impotent; as pointed out by Mr. Randall Forsythe in his column, *Current Yield*, in **Barron's**, the recent continuation Bush era tax policies, combined with the monetary policy of QE2, was met with rising treasury yields: expansionary fiscal and monetary policy runs into reality and higher yield, a contractionary force.

Ultimately, the ability to print money to fund a never ending stream of bailouts is going implode, and politicians are grasping at straws with the limits of fiscal and monetary policy; and ultimately, the only way out is going to be some sort sovereign and bank restructuring program, and in the process all those speculative holders of C.D.S. and derivatives contracts are going to have to be told that their contracts are worthless, or worth a great deal less than there notional value, as is a C.D.S. holder's perfected interest in assets in the event of a bankruptcy.

As for our friends the Republicans(?), the party in charge when the current financial crisis erupted, well they want to delay implementation of a watered down Dodd - Frank legislation, because they believe it needs further study on the impact of bank profits; and the banks themselves, particularly the international Wall Street banks, well they are fighting Basel III, international bank regulation, at every turn.

Doctor Suess hit the nail on the head at the end of his book, *The Sneetches*. We have the jaded view of Mr. McBean (aka Bankers) that the public won't learn, and we have the reality that the Sneetchs (aka the Public) will eventually catch up on the scam, and not repeat the mistakes of the past:

"Then, when every last cent of their money was spent,
The Fix-It-Up Chappie packed up. And he went.
And he laughed as he drove In his car up the beach,
"They never will learn. No. You can't Teach a Sneetch!"

But McBean was quite wrong. I'm quite happy to say.
That the Sneetches got really quite smart on that day.
The day they decided that Sneetches are Sneetches.
And no kind of Sneetch is the best on the beaches.
That day, all the Sneetches forgot about stars and whether
They had one, or not, upon thars".

Ultimately, my bet is on the Sneetches!

Why Progressives should take a Second look at the Good Doctor!

By J.M. Hamilton (1-16-11)

"Concentrated power has always been the enemy of liberty."
- Ronald Wilson Reagan

He's an iconoclast, a Texan, a lightning rod, and the third rail of American politics, personified. He's upsetting to Republicans and Democrats, alike. He stands for freedom *in extremis*. He's a throwback, a political freak, and he reminds us of what the Republican Party was over a half century ago when it *was*, for the most part, grand. He's old and crusty. And for all these reasons Ron Paul holds some appeal for this author. Anybody who can upset the established order of things, and yet, attract American youth to politics is worth paying attention too.

It is the intellectual side of Mr. Paul, and his embrace of freedom that this blog finds most attractive. And if we, as individuals, are often defined by both, our friends and our enemies, then politicians are often defined by both the positions they take and the resulting reaction. As progressives are, increasingly, feeling left out in the cold by this administration, a second look at Mr. Paul's core positions on several key issues is worth reviewing, and of equal importance, the reaction Mr. Paul's positions ignite. Let's take a look:

1)   **Mr. Paul appears to be in favor of the decriminalization of marijuana and greater civil liberties.**   And who does this upset? I don't know… possibly, Big Pharma, police unions, and the state authorized beer, wine and liquor distribution monopolies. Oh, and did I mention the South and Central American drug cartels, they too, would not be in favor of the end of Prohibition (aka President Nixon's War of Drugs), and the black markets and obscene profits Prohibition creates for said cartels.

2)   **The good Doctor is not a fan of American jingoism, and the, endless, wars in both Iraq and Afghanistan.** The upset parties: Well that would by the MIC, primarily, who depends upon a constant enemy, or threat, to insure a never ending stream of government largess directed at its financial statements. As this blog has argued, foreign governments and some corporations, enjoying the protections of the U.S. military and NATO, seemingly without cost, also would not be fan of Mr. Paul's position. Make no mistake about it, this blog is a huge fan of the men and women in uniform who *defend* this country, and the industries that

arm and protect these men and women; but "nation building" in the narco-terrorist country of Afghanistan, arguably, should not be a part of their mission, particularly when our government and Western democracies provide financial aid in the billions, and petrol dollars in the billions, to our enemies in the region, the Pakistani and Saudi governments, respectively.

3)   **Mr. Paul has a great disdain for the Fed, and the "Bankocracy," that exercises outsized influence on this country and the governments of Western and Central Europe.** In a recent *Bloomberg Surveillance Broadcast with Ken Prewitt and Tom Keene*, Lew Rockwell of the **Mises Institute**, and a former chief of staff to Mr. Paul, notes just how damaging the Federal Reserve is to Main Street and the average person, while throwing off money to the banking cartel, and aiding and abetting the Wall Street bank's all consuming and nihilistic worship of the quick and leveraged buck. This blog, and others, have written extensively about the destabilizing effects to the economy, the huge fiscal drag, and the burden placed upon the American worker and business, that government sanctioned monopolies create. The solution Mr. Rockwell argues is bankruptcy and restructuring. Upon hearing Mr. Rockwell speak, one almost hopes that the Republican Party's efforts to overturn the fatally flawed Dodd-Frank legislation do succeed. All the better to bring about more rapidly the next, inevitable, financial crisis, and the much needed break-up of the "bankocracy." Until then, look no further at the Japanese economy, over the last two decades, as to what awaits this country and Europe.

If you're a liberal, or a progressive, or otherwise sentient member of society, you've got to be scratching your head. Let's see, we now have had the Bush administration, and, by way of comparison, for the last two years, the Obama administration, and what has changed? We still have two full blown wars, not including a forty year old war on drugs and the resulting hot war just South of our border - in Mexico, and after the banks nearly destroy the known civilized world, the Wall Street cartel is still calling the shots in Washington. (Granted, President Obama has made some strides and improvements, in a very difficult situation.)

At this point, Mr. Paul is sounding pretty damn rational! The problem is Mr. Paul, and the citizens who formed the Tea Party movement, have been co-opted, subsumed, muzzled, and triangulated by Republican Party pros, like Dick Armey, and the billionaire Koche brothers. And for evidence of this look no further then the recent coronation of the 112th U.S. Congress, where the

Republican party is already reneging on its pledge to cut $100 billion from this year's federal budget (roughly 2 to 3% of Federal outlays for 2011, per OMB). The darling of the Republican Party, and "*uber*-fiscal hawk," Rep. Ryan, appears to be back sliding. And while we are talking about the disingenuous and irrational, look no further than the Republican' party's move to declare tax cuts as fiscally neutral, when we all know that tax cuts, not supported by spending reductions, add up to deficit spending and greater government borrowing. But the Republican's don't have the heart to cut spending, nor do they have the chops to govern, especially when it comes time to educate the public and make the really tough decisions.

Instead of joining with Democrats to address the crucial problems of the day, the Republicans in the House intend to engage in political masturbation by rejecting the Obama Healthcare plan, only to see this exercise rejected in the Senate or face a veto on the President's desk. Great! Run down the clock to 2012, and score political points, while Washington's balance sheets run red and Americans suffer. On the other hand, bankers, hedge funds, and private equity are happy because the heats off!

Politics, indeed, makes for strange bed fellows! Admittedly, Mr. Paul would not pass the "Robert Reich litmus test," as a doctrinaire liberal; and that's all right too, because Mr. Paul's greatest contribution, ultimately, is providing competition to the political oligopoly that runs our nation. And the sooner Mr. Paul, and his followers, realize that they have not been taken seriously, but rather, used and abused by the Republican party once again, the sooner they may get on with the business of creating a third party that will provide a direct counter point to the Democrats and Republicans.

As President Reagan noted, concentration of power truly is a direct threat to our liberty, and I would add a threat to our well being and to the nation's financial health. And just as government sanctioned monopoly and oligopoly are bad for the private sector, political monopoly and oligopoly are even worse within the public sector. There is a lack of honest dialogue coming out of Washington, and when there is some adult-like candor, it almost inevitably comes from Mr. Paul. Disagree with Mr. Paul's proposed solutions, sure, debate is always welcome, as are alternative ideas and solutions, but at least this man is highlighting the problems of the day, and has been for years. Mr. Paul and the Tea Party movement do not have all the answers to address the nation's ills, and some of their proposed solutions are unacceptable to many, but they can make legitimate contributions to the solution. The sooner they part company with the big government elite within the Republican Party, the better for our nation.

Both Democrats and Republicans politicians can use a little competition.

Lombardi, Exceptionalism, and the Rule of Law…

By J.M. Hamilton   (2-3-11)

Before there was AMC's *Mad Men*, there was a true man of the sixties named Vince Lombardi. One gets the feeling that Lombardi would have flossed his teeth with Mr. David Draper. As hard as Lambeau field in January, Lombardi burned brightly throughout the sixties, and lead the Green Bay Packers to win the first two Super Bowl games every played. His passion, dedication and commitment to the game of football made Lombardi a winner, and an American icon. His name graces the Super Bowl trophy awarded to the champion ship team, year after year. As with any genius he would drive some of his players "nuts," and many others would have a "love/hate" relationship with the man, long after they stopped playing for the Packers, Giants or Redskins. We get a snap shot of Lombardi by reading David Maraniss' book, *When Pride Still Mattered*. Note the following passage after the 1967 New Years Eve win over the Dallas Cowboys, in the fabled Ice Bowl:

"The Locker Room was a jangle of cameras and lights when Lombardi got there after the game. He evicted the press and talked to his men alone, telling them how proud he was: for running to win, for persevering and meeting their greatest challenge, winning three straight championships. He barely stifled the tears that came so easily to him, then fell to his knees and lead the team in the Lord's Prayer."

Now, by way of comparison, can you imagine Lloyd Blankfein, CEO of Goldman Sachs, dropping to his knees to lead a board room in prayer, after hitting quarterly financial targets? Both men, Lombardi and Blankfein, are brilliant in their respective fields of football and banking, and both men are fully engaged, and extremely focused. Both men are razors.

But what makes one man loved and adored by many, while the other man is despised and reviled by many? I have thought about this question long and hard, and have concluded it is one thing: it is the rules that these respective men play by.

It is said that there is a thin line between madness and genius, and my guess is the dichotomy centers around whether or not society is the beneficiary of the singular individual's talent and achievements, or whether it is the victim. Robert Downey Jr., in the movie *Rodney Dangerfield - Back to School*, once identified football as a "crypto fascist metaphor for nuclear warfare." Now, I don't believe Mr. Downey's comedic line for a moment, but if football devolved, by a change in the rules, into some sort of barbaric blood sport during Mr. Lombardi's time, complete with knives, guns, and collateral damage into the stands, then my guess is society would not view Mr. Lombardi and football in such a favorable light. Conversely, the rules of banking have become so heinous and so detrimental to society, that the genius Blankfein is not viewed by many as a prince of a man, but rather, a villain. Why? Quite simply Mr. Blankfein's reputations, and that of his Wall Street brethren, are victims of their own rules.

Take Dodd Frank bank reform legislation for instance. These rules, on the heels of the worst banking crisis known to man, were stripped down and were basically written behind closed doors, in large part, by members of, or lobbyist for, the Wall Street banking cartel. **"Financial weapons of mass destruction,"** Mr. Buffet's phrase to describe derivatives and credit default swaps, remain, for the most part, beyond the reach of regulators, and hidden from public view. These derivative instruments with hundreds of trillions in notional value played a very large role in our last global financial crisis, and undoubtedly will play an even larger role in the next financial crisis. And the fatal flaw in Dodd Frank legislation? Well, as usual our elected leaders in the congress passed the buck. Not only did they fail to give specifics on how the banks and these instruments were to be reined in (in fact they exempted the lion's share of these derivative instruments from the rules themselves), but Congress abdicated their responsibility and punted to the regulators. The very same regulators, who failed to reign in Wall Street's worst excesses the last go around, that are prone to capture, and can change in the blink of the eye, with a change in administrations. That's right. Even the best and most well intentioned ministrations of Obama regulatory appointees can be reversed with the pull of a voting booth lever, and a Republican president entering the White House. Let us pray, not.

In short, Dodd- Frank is the bomb, and I'm not talking about a 50 yard aerial strike- pass play launched from the twenty yard line.

Perhaps Mr. Downey's line would be less comedic, and certainly more accurate, had he stated: Banking is a crypto fascist metaphor for nuclear warfare. Indeed, Mr. Blankfein's rule making appears, ultimately, to be to the detriment of society, business, the world, and ultimately to his reputation. Unfortunately, the joke is on us.

And while we're tilting at windmills this week, what about that other raging Leviathan, Exxon Mobil Corporation? Here again, the rules of capitalism, and society, have been so distorted, so as to cause many Americans, particularly Republicans, to think that Exxon is a capitalist enterprise. No, we hardly pay it a mind when they report out another record profits quarter. Now when demand is down or flat, supply is up, and OPEC says they have plenty of capacity to fix prices (um, provide a stable environment for world energy consumption), how exactly does Exxon make record profits? Well, that would be because they are, virtually, a government sanctioned monopoly, controlling significant amounts of market share. And as this blog has written monopolies and oligopolies are authorized by the government and can be controlled by the government, that is when there is the political will to do so; and this blog has also argued that monopolies, as creations of the state, are nothing short of socialism by private proxy. That's right, you - dear consumer - are the beneficiary of an energy industry that is not dedicated to evolutionary energy policies away from the burning of fossil fuels; but rather, an energy industry dedicated to the global addiction of a product produced by Middle-East tyrants and dictators, and maximizing profit at your expense.

No taxation (i.e. monopolistic profits) without Representation! Here is yet another industry that writes its own rules in Congress, and not only captures the regulators, but drugs and has sex with them. Witness B.P.' gulf disaster last spring, and their pet poster-boy, Representative Joe Barton (Republican-Dallas); and prior to that, the capture, drugging and sexcapades of the Minerals Management Service, supposed watch –dog for America. Given that monopolies are creations of government, and socialism by private proxy, windfall profits, like those made by Exxon, constitute a tax on society. But unlike the taxes levied by the government, where at the voting booth Americans have some say in the tax rate and distribution of government revenue, the American voter has absolutely no say in the price per gallon of gasoline, or the interest rate and terms of a bank loan they may receive. And the problem the American consumer is faced with? We now have several monopolies engaged in predatory pricing campaigns against the public so that America's ever shrinking middle class has little or no discretionary spending for goods and services, beyond the basics: food, gas, and interest payments to the bank! And we wonder why the alleged nascent recovery stalls whenever government stops spending stimulus money. Unemployment remains untenable.

Supply side theory/ Reaganomics, and the Laffer curve, an oft touted economic theory of the Republican Party, posit that tax revenue to the state actually diminishes at some progressive tax level. So that by cutting marginal tax rates, economic activity is actually spurred by animal spirits, entrepreneurial initiative is charged, and as a result, a rising tide of business activity causes the economy to advance ten yards up the field, and government receipts to actually increase. Democrats call this theory "trickle down." For the sake of the argument I'm about to make, I'm willing to give the theory some credit. The problem with supply side economics is that both political parties are good at cutting taxes to drive the economy up the field, but neither party has the will or discipline to increase taxes once the economy has run across the goal line; hence our colossal national debt. Witness the saga of the Bush tax cuts, over the last decade. By the way, it has been argued that President Kennedy was the first supply-sider.

That said, if Republicans believe that supply side theory actually works, why not apply the practice to monopolistic profits, or taxation by private proxy? If the government was to truly reign in the likes of big oil and the banking industry by taxing unseemly profits at the pump or by taxing the usurious interest banks charge (both are forms of taxation without representation), think about how much more discretionary spending the middle class would have to spend on other goods and services? If we believe Mr. Laffer and the Austrian school, the economy would certainly soar. And let's not forget rising fuel prices precipitated the financial collapse in 2008.

But if you believe the Republican Party is going to apply their economic golden-rule to the likes of Wall Street Banks or Big Oil than think again. Public be damned, the institutions of Wall Street and Big Oil, flush with monopolistic taxation, fill election campaigns with money, and their mercenary lobbyist roam the halls of congress, frequently and often.

If big oil and banks expect the government, and the public, to bail them out for their own disasters, whether it is gulf oil spills or financial crisis, might "the people" reasonably expect that their own government would protect them from monopolies worst pricing/taxation excesses? After all, democratically elected government allowed for these monstrous combinations. Unfortunately rule making, and the rule of law, has been hijacked by the plutocracy.... to the public's, business community', and nation's utter detriment.

History tells us that Coach Lombardi, a favorite of the business community, was both a Democrat and a friend to the Kennedy clan. One wonders if Mr. Lombardi would have supported a windfall profits tax.

GO GREEN BAY!

Blowback

*"Freedom is the right to tell people what they do not want to hear." —
George Orwell*

By J.M. Hamilton (2-20-11)

It's been awhile, but the arguments still hang in the air. One of the resolutions for my collegiate debate team went something like this: Resolved, the U.S. should not trade arms to non-democratic regimes. The affirmative argued that the U.S. should not provide arms to dictatorships, which are by their very nature oppressive; the negative argued that by providing arms to military dictatorships and authoritarian regimes, the U.S. was able to influence these regimes and had a greater opportunity to bring about democratic reform. The resolution came up in the eighties, as President Reagan turned the screws on the Soviets with amped up defense spending, and the cold war was rapidly coming to an unexpected conclusion. At the time the world to this young and naïve Republican appeared bi-polar, comprised either of democratic governments, or right wing dictatorship headed toward democracy, versus communist and/or socialist/totalitarian regimes. The ends appeared to justify the means, as, nearly, any regime that was a foe of godless communists bent on global domination, appeared to this debater worthy of U.S. military support.

The balance of the debate team, all of them liberals, thought I was mad, and that my case for supporting right wing dictatorships (the case for the negative) was "repugnant."

Nearly a quarter of century later, and with hindsight being twenty-twenty, I couldn't agree with my teammates more, that is to say, supporting military dictatorships and authoritarian regimes is, indeed, repugnant. A practice that unfortunately, the U.S. did not abandon at the conclusion of the cold war… when America road tall, was the only superpower left standing, and for a couple of decades anyway, truly had an opportunity to push these regimes towards democracy, reform, and may have helped to shape democratic institutions and parties within these countries.

We can see the results of U.S. foreign policy in the current wave of democracy sweeping the member states of the Arab League. For the last several decades the U.S., and Western Europe, have propped up dictatorships throughout the middle-east in the name of commercial "stability," by providing billions in economic and military assistance and a steady stream of petrol dollars into the region.   In the case of Egypt, we know that the U.S. gave between 1.3 and 1.5 billion in military aid, annually. Of course, there is nothing as unstable as authoritarian or totalitarian regime, if we believe Presidents Kennedy and Reagan, who both said that communism (i.e. authoritarian and totalitarian rule) was not the wave of the future, freedom is.

And it's really that simple, man craves freedom.   As important to man's inner core as air and water, political and economic freedom, for all educated citizens of the world, is an imperative. Freedom is instinctual.   In the present day, for U.S. leadership not to have seen the uprising in the middle-east coming makes one wonder what other blind spots exist? And now, instead being able to help shape events, the U.S. and the world must depend upon a military dictatorship, on the heels of Mubarak's departure, to bring about the necessary reform.

Omar Suleiman, Mr. Mubarak's vice-presidential appointee (aka Mr. Torture!), now runs the show, and the Egyptian economy, which is also said to be dominated by military run monopolies (sounds a lot like Iran's Revolutionairy Guard). Per the N.Y. Times: "…Mr. Suleiman has outraged members of the anti-government protest movement by saying that he does not think it is time to lift the 30-year-old emergency law that has been used to suppress and imprison opposition leaders and that he does not think his country is yet ready for democracy." So this story and democratic revolution is still very much playing out.

Of course, if the U.S. really wants both economic and political stability in the region, it should support democracy and democratic movements. *Realpolitik* would suggest backing dictatorships, but given demographics, the rising levels of education, and informational and social networks provided by the internet… true long term stability, economic and political, will come from democracy, not from authoritarian or even theocratic regimes.

The counter argument against democracy for the region offers up the same old bogey man, that of Muslim religious extremist, such as the Muslim Brotherhood.   This argument is specious at best, and at worst may only come to fruition, if democracy is not allowed to flower and take hold. The fact that some of the arguments made in this piece are even remotely novel, or even contrarian to U.S. foreign policy, shows the extent to which the short term thinking of commercial interests dictate both U.S. foreign policy and political trajectory within the region.   Observe German President, Horst Koehler, who was forced to resign in 2010 over remarks he made demonstrating that German foreign policy and military support in Afghanistan was not backed by idealism for democratic reform (the line we are often fed in this country), but rather, commercial, trade and economic self-interest. Shocking! Truth spoken here, so fire the poor man.

Fortunately, in this instance, doing the right thing, supporting democracy in the region, is actually in the United States foreign policy, commercial and geo-political self- interest. Military dictatorship is so *passé*. Democracy is *de rigueur*.

And the man of the hour for the middle-east… the catalyst, the spark, the dynamo who started the whole process? Well that would be Chairmen of the Fed, Ben Bernanke, whose policy of QE2/devaluing the dollar, has lead to rising headline inflation, and a speculative bubble in commodities. The Arab Leagues reluctant and nascent move towards democracy is fueled by hungry bellies. Many years from now, history may state that Mr. Bernanke, directly and indirectly, contributed to the birth of Pan-Arab democracy. Chinese and Iranian political leadership would do well to take note.

All of this and nothing

By J.M. Hamilton (3-12-11)

The first panacea for a mismanaged nation is inflation of the currency; the second is war. Both bring a temporary prosperity; both bring a permanent ruin. But both are the refuge of political and economic opportunists.

- Ernest Hemingway

In the song *All of This and Nothing*, Richard Butler's lyrics take us on a journey describing a shattered romantic relationship and the wreckage left in its wake. The song contains one of the most haunting saxophone intros known to rock and roll. Per Mr. Butler of the Psychedelic Furs, the abandoned flat that hosted the relationship doesn't contain much of anything, but assorted debris, painful memories, and "a picture of the queen." Inflation is a lot like a problematic relationship... perhaps a love story that comes to nearly the same ending throughout history, a very bad one.

Inflation often serves to provide temporary economic relief, and provides a smokescreen to a nation's real problems, which often require long term and economically painful solutions. Politicians and central bankers often deploy inflation, as a means to an end: namely, achieving victory during the next election cycle. The short term beneficiaries of inflation are the financial and political elite, who know better, but ride the wave – enriching themselves – while the general population, ultimately, suffers with the aftermath: unemployment, a stagnant economy, soaring costs for commodities and services, and a stumbling currency. The economic sugar rush that is inflation can have the look and feel of a normal economic recovery – initially, while hiding festering problems that desperately need to be addressed, like global banking, run away government debt, and the lack of a national energy policy driven by predatory oil monopolies.

Of course, inflation eventually catches up with everyone – even the elite: politicians fall, governments are overturned or change parties, corporations fail, and fortunes are eroded and spent.   Take a look at the following chart showing the S&P 500 results through the seventies, pretty stagnant stuff:

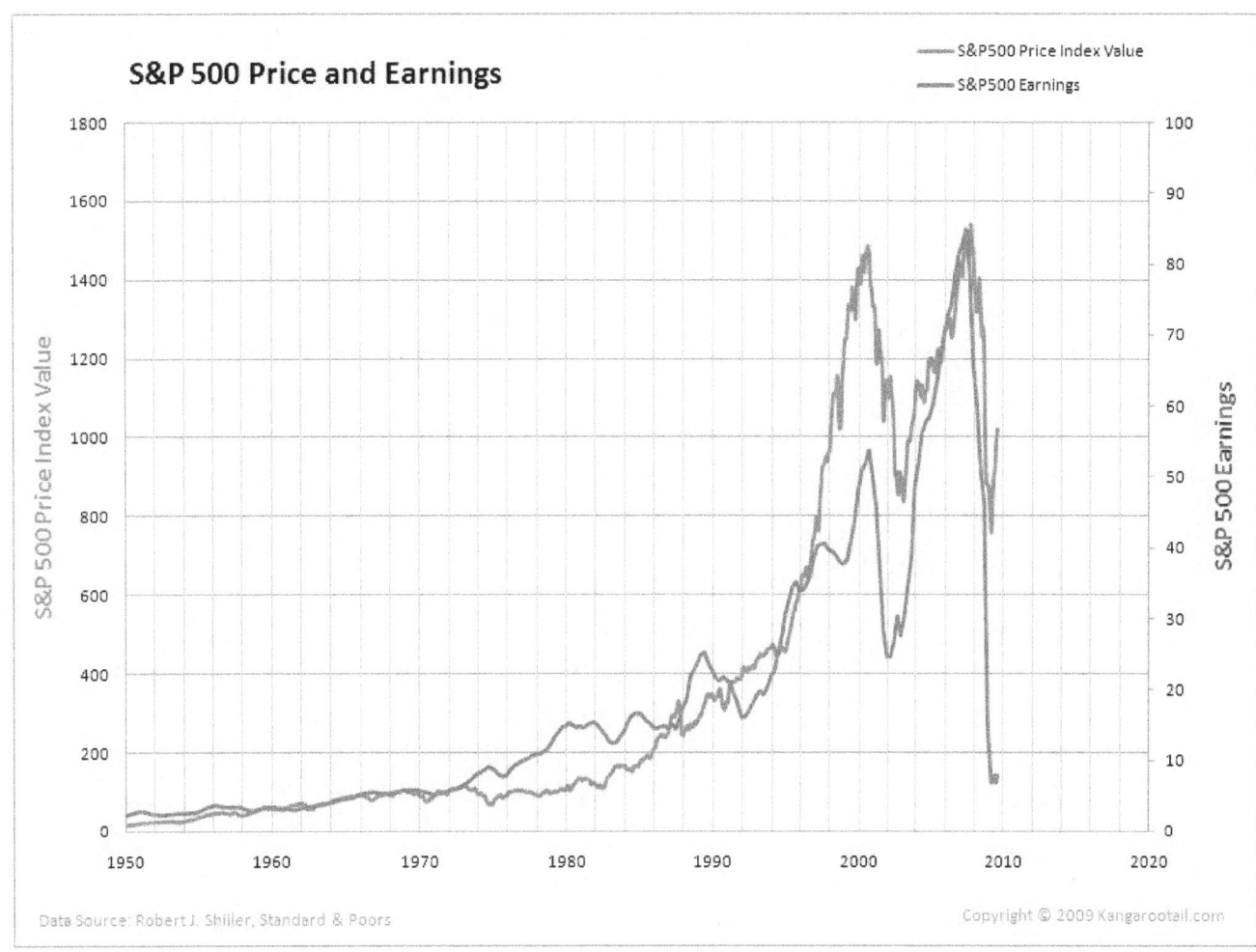

According to the CIA fact book, the median age in this country is thirty-six. This means nearly half of the U.S. population wasn't around in the seventies and early eighties, or was getting ready to enter kindergarten.   The hypnotic – sleeper effect quality of QE2, present monetary policy, lulls the nation into a false calm, a sense that something is being done about the public's problems, which gives our elected leaders an opportunity not to address the politically undesirable problems that lay before them: like cutting social security, Medicare, Medicaid, or reining in corporate welfare and tax breaks, and defense spending.

And the Chamber of Commerce was afraid of the "uncertainty" allegedly created by the Democratic Party's feeble, half-hearted, and weak attempts to overturn three decades of financial deregulation, culminating Dodd-Frank (banking legislation that is so pathetically weak that Republicans aren't threatening to overturn it). Brothers, sisters, and business community... you haven't seen anything until you have lived with double digit inflation. Inflation is the father of economic uncertainty, as we are all about to discover or rediscover. And it's already here.

Fear and unemployment will drive the 2012 election. No surprise. And this creates a problem/ opportunity, which is Washington feels the need to do something, like enrich themselves and their friends, the oligarchs. But with two wars going, record budget deficits/federal stimulus, and the Fed printing money like there's no tomorrow, if the power elite are still struggling to get this relationship/economy off the ground or put a dent in unemployment – then we as a nation are in very big trouble. Usually a war kick starts the economy. Trillions in deficit spending... the "relationship" heats up and goes into overdrive. Fed hits the switch on the printing presses and the economic honey moon begins.

The problem created by Washington's solution this time, as this blog has argued, is that all the government's efforts are directed at propping up Wall Street banks, the Wall Street produced fallout in the housing sector, or ameliorating the effects of same, VERY LITTLE OF WHICH IS TRICKLING DOWN TO MAIN STREET – UNLESS YOU CATER TO THE RICH. U.S. Republican and Democratic leadership replaces one bubble with another, via war-booms, deficit spending, or asset bubbles in housing, stocks or commodities – created out of thin air by the Fed. And with the herd stumbling back into the stock market in record numbers, how long before the elite banks, and the government, takes their profits out of the stock market and run?

Our "capitalist society" is hooked on a very bad relationship with big government, with 40 percent or greater of GDP coming from government spending. It is unsustainable, and as Mr. Herbert Stein, Richard Nixon's Counsel of Economic Advisors chairmen, so eloquently stated: "If something cannot go on forever, it will stop." Can a global restructuring of debt be around the corner? Watch the PIIGS in Europe closely, for the answer to that question.

Inflation stands for the ultimate debasement of the dollar, and the defilement of the American dream! And the unintended consequences of QE2 are stacking up like so many couples headed for divorce court. While the

Fed maybe trying to kick start the economy with a boom in manufacturing, to replace the boom it had previously helped create in housing, with easy money policies designed to make dollar denominated U.S. manufacturing goods more affordable overseas, this love interest may be short lived; this is because emerging and foreign markets are already raising interest rates to stave off QE2 induced capital inflows and inflation. Interest rate hikes in developing nations will have a contractionary effect upon their economies, and slow down demand for U.S. manufactured goods. So America manufacturing will be faced with less global demand at a time when demand here at home is very limited, because we are still suffering the ravages of the last crisis created by the Fed and Wall Street banks. Meanwhile, the inflationary effects of QE2 may very well be felt in this country for years to come (And can we see QE3 around the corner to bail out state, county and municipal government? Yes we can.).

One positive unintended consequence from QE2 is the democratic revolution throughout the Arab world. It appears that these folks have been under the boot heel of European and U.S. sponsored thugs for decades and they are not going to take it anymore. Rather than rejoice at the possible freedom of the enslaved and impoverished, the big fear here at home is that rising oil prices may stall a nascent economic recovery, and U.S. political aspirations for re-election. What our elected leaders and business community may fail to realize is that monarchies and military dictatorships are both highly unstable, and that Arab democracies will be just as hungry to sell BRICS, Europe and the U.S oil, if not more so, as the cutthroats who presently run the Arab world. And if, per chance, during this time of governmental transition throughout the Persian Gulf, oil prices should spike, than the U.S. should look upon it as an opportunity to, finally, reduce our dependence upon foreign energy, and start hooking up U.S. transportation and power facilities to natural gas and alternative energy. But I digress.

In 1979 my father, a smart man on many financial matters, explained certificates of deposit to me, and said that he could tie my meager amount of savings into a C.D. that would earn roughly 14%. I was young and distracted by other things, like skirts and hotties, but even with my short attention span fourteen percent seemed like a good deal. The problem was that by late 1979, early 1980, my "real rate of return," that is my return adjusted for inflation, at an interest rate of 14%, was probably negative or minus five to six percent. And that's inflation. No matter how fast your earnings and wages may climb the cost of goods and services, once those inflationary expectations are set, often rise faster. It is very destabilizing.

That is until a Gandhi – like figure comes along at the Fed, an economic marriage counselor if you will, and says enough is enough, we are going to strangle inflation, even if the short term economic pain or cure is almost as great as the inflationary illness, itself. Unfortunately, there are not many Paul Volckers in the world, and we have certainly not seen his like at the Fed, since his departure. Had Paul Volcker not saved us from inflation, the U.S. might have continued to plod along with stagflation, indefinitely, or worse, really gone off course, "Weimar style."

At the end of the day: When you weaken a country, as both our political parties have done for years, with excessive and unsupported government spending, weak business regulation, unfunded foreign adventures, and loose monetary policies, you set a country up for problems and possible failure.   Those in the know, the elite and the politicians, can sometime plan ahead and via currency arbitrage, protect their interests and assets (all at the expense of the nation). Shucks, politicians and the elite may even profit from the demise of a countries currency and economy, through the purchase of credit default swaps (C.D.S.) and derivative contracts; that is as long as the counterparty to that financial instrument has the assets to pay off, in the event of collapse or default.

You see, one really is gambling when Americans purchase C.D.S. betting against the dollar and the U.S., because if such a bet comes to fruition, in all probability there would be no U.S. government in any semblance of financial shape to bailout the counterparties.

As happened in Iceland, it has been written that many of the government officials who were responsible for the collapse of that nation's banking system, currency and economy, took out hedging positions against their own country.   So there's a flag right there. But with derivatives contracts not open to public purview on open exchanges, how is the U.S. public to know that we won't be left, like a jilted lover, with anything other than "a picture of the queen?"

P.S.
There are some who may still argue that there is no inflation, but if we study the history of the consumer price index (CPI), we know that the government took out unimportant items, such as food, commodities, and fuel a long time ago. Apparently, price spikes that affect the vox populi are inconvenient economic and political truths. As for interest rate inflation, as Mr.

William Gross so well noted on the PIMCO web-site this month, the Fed dominates, that is to say, purchases 70% of Treasury debt issuance; effectively crowding out the bond vigilantes, who would, undoubtedly, demand higher yields and insist upon Federal budgetary and monetary policy reform.

In response to the Fed's monetization of the national debt, both Messrs. Hemingway's and Stein's comments immediately come to mind.

http://blog.jmhamiltonpublishing.com/2010/07/05/thinking-the-unthinkable.aspx

Sorry, Wrong Number!

By J.M. Hamilton (3-26-11)

"How many yachts can you water-ski behind? How much is enough…"

- Charlie Sheen (aka Bud Fox), from the movie, *Wall Street*

History repeats. In 1974, the U.S. department of justice saw fit to break up the AT&T monopoly (aka Ma Bell), via an anti-trust law suit, into seven regional holding companies. The break up did not last. This week AT&T announced it would buy T-Mobile for a tidy $39 billion, which will essentially create a duopoly in U.S. wireless communications with its sister Bell Company, Verizon. There will be the usual regulatory scrutiny, perhaps a spin off or two to protect the consumer, and the usual arguments will be made in favor of the merger, like achieving "economies of scale" and "synergy" (read: pink slips).   There will be some chest thumping and grand standing in congress, a little noise, and then in all probability the merger will go through.

The consumer will not be protected, however, and the costs of the merger will be passed along to the cellular customers in the form of higher monthly fees, poorer service, and less innovation and possible cut backs in R&D. Management and congressmen, exempted from insider trading laws, will grow richer, and the employees at the combination – those lucky enough to retain their jobs – well, they'll just have to work a little harder.

Meanwhile, our government regulatory authorities (Justice, the SEC, and the FTC, Et Al.) will be kept on a very short leash, indeed, starved for funding by their handlers, the plutocracy. Can one envision a time when this script won't play out?   Not anytime soon.

Witness the pending play, rehearsed so many times before, as big oil, in all probability, gets called to take the stand for the umpteenth time before congress to explain why gas prices are soaring. If called upon, Big Oil, of course, will blame OPEC and trouble in the middle-east, but assure congress that the industry is competitive and properly functioning.   Not to hear Mr. Stephen Schork tell it, on a recent **Bloomberg Surveillance broadcast with Messrs. Prewitt and Keene.** Mr. Schork, an expert on energy matters, and an investor and speculator, informs us than 19 of 20 barrels of sweet crude sitting in Cushing are owned by speculators; moreover, thanks to the oil rich shale of Canada, the oil sitting in reserve in Cushing could be replaced six times over. Per Mr. Schork, the NYMEX futures market is "corrupted." As Mr. Keene notes, speculators are moving the price of oil; and therefore, the price at the pump. It sure wouldn't be market forces, but what market forces truly exist in an industry dominated by monopoly and cartels? Meanwhile the consumer will get soaked (not with inexpensive oil, however), and the newly minted nascent recovery, financed and sponsored by the Fed and QE2, will take it on the chin.

So when will the consumer prevail, and corporations fight the urge to merge? Possibly, maybe someday soon, when the monopolies themselves realize that they are literally financially disemboweling the consumer, world markets, and cutting into one another's profits, the monopolies will fully appreciate the instability myopic and unmitigated greed creates.

When gas prices spike, it eliminates consumer discretionary spending that could go into other businesses, or monopolies, goods and services; that is to say, when Exxon Mobil has a record quarter, the AT&T's of the world suffer because the consumer has less money to spend on cellular services (not to mention the overall drag on the economy, which may compound into recession). The extent to which a business (say AT&T) is harmed by the gouging another monopoly (say Exxon Mobil) executes upon the American consumer, depends upon where AT&T's goods and services fall within the consumer's, or market place's, hierarchy of needs. Sooner or later business and monopolies, of all shapes and stripes, are not going to appreciate the Wall Street banking cartel and the oil oligarchy taking out the U.S. economy and cutting into their profits. Of course, many businesses and monopolies, apparently, did not get overly upset that Big Oil price increases set the U.S. economy up for failure, and the Wall Street banking disaster finished the job in 2008, because there's always world markets to exploit and sell to.

But a very unfunny thing happened to the "globalization paradigm" in the last thirty days: namely, a quake, a tsunami, and a presently unfolding nuclear disaster, just north of Tokyo – Japan.

This blog, from time to time, has taken a crack at Apple, who many of us love and adore, because of their cool products, and their cultivated anti-establishment – snarky- image. Apple is perceived to be the anti-Microsoft. The reality, however, as this blog has documented, is that Apple **utilizes** Chinese "labor," and Japanese manufacturing to mitigate product cost and maximize profit. In short, Apple is about as establishment as it gets. Last we read, Apple had north of fifty billion in cash sitting on their balance sheet, courtesy – to some degree – of the fine purveyors of Chinese labor, Foxconn (see this blog for details). **I bring up Apple, because in many respects Apple symbolizes globalization.** Apple designs and engineers products here in the states, but outsources the manufacturing of product components and product assembly to the Pacific Rim. And the mark-up on Apple products is extraordinary because of the slave labor involved. The reality is Apple could manufacture and assemble in the U.S. and still make exceptional profit and returns, albeit less than they are making now.

But now, and this scenario is by no means limited to Apple, we hear there are going to be disruptions in the supply chain for the I-pad, because some components are manufactured in Japan, and the Japanese manufacturing facilities have either been washed away or are uninhabitable due to radiation.   Therefore, Apple cannot meet demand, which might turn off consumers, impatiently, awaiting product, and harm Apple's bottom line and image.   If and when Apple gets production up to speed, consumers may want to run a Geiger counter over the I-pad to insure its safety, but that would go for all Japanese products, post-crisis.

The bottom line and the lesson on Japan: Apple and other multi-nationals can no longer take for granted any given market, or country, to produce a revenue stream or a supply of products; and more importantly, it can ill afford to allow other multi-nationals or monopolies to trash a major world economy, like the U.S., as it may need that market again, either as a manufacturing, service, or revenue source. Good corporate governance and risk management dictates peripheral vision into economic and political areas beyond a corporation's next quarterly financial statement.

Does the Japanese disaster spell the end of globalization, or put another way, the end of labor, regulatory, and tax arbitrage? Not hardly, but it may make monopolies and multi-nationals reconsider their recent disdain for U.S. labor, and more greatly value the relative stability of the U.S. economy (still plugging along at roughly 25% of world GDP). If nothing else, multi-nationals and monopolies will be forced to hedge, that is Japan illustrates that they can no longer count on the stability of all developed or emerging markets and economies running in tandem all the time, neither as a source of revenue or supply. Instead, they will have to reconsider America (indeed, all markets), and this means they can no longer allow their brother monopolies, Banking and Big Oil, to prey upon the American consumer to the detriment of their financial statements, management bonuses and earnings, and their stockholders (not necessarily in that order).

In the near future, we may see a whole new side to the Apple's of the world. Instead of passively allowing Wall Street banks and Big Oil to trash the U.S. or world economy, upon which they depend, Apple, or like companies, may actually be on the forefront of advocating real and true bank regulatory reform (the antithesis of Dodd-Frank), and perhaps insist upon the break-up of the Big Oil monopolies, or be a leading advocate for alternative energy development. All the better to insure plenty of discretionary income and employment for their consumers, and healthy markets for their own products and services.

An enlightened and wiser Mr. Gecko may have responded to Bud Fox with, "Greed is good," particularly when greed is channeled for the betterment of society, the American consumer/labor, and corporate bottom lines (they are mutually inclusive). Mr. Gecko also advised Bud to read Sun Tzu: "Every battle is won, before it is fought."

Final thoughts this week: Hats off to President Obama for obtaining quick UN and European support for taking out Colonel Khadafy. Too bad, the Arab League is above the fray. American interests are being well represented by President Obama. Even more kudos and accolades will, undoubtedly, be heaped upon Mr. Obama with a quick and early American exit, after the Colonel takes a dirt nap. President Obama, and his Secretary of State, may very well be showing Americans the benchmark in how foreign policy and the use of force should be conducted. Too bad his predecessor, President Bush, didn't conduct our foreign affairs in a similar fashion in Afghanistan and Iraq.

Full Faith and Credit, Too…

By J.M. Hamilton (4-30-11)

Americans, per a recent NY Times/CBS poll, indicate that the country is headed in the wrong direction, and apparently S&P feels that the dollar is headed in the wrong direction, too. But fear not, Secretary of the Treasury, Mr. Tim Geithner, assures us all that there is "no risk" of a U.S. down grade, from its gilt edged AAA rating. This assessment by the Treasury Secretary would either make him omnipotent or extremely knowledgeable about the rating agencies' inner workings and politics. My guess is it is the latter.

Mr. Geither's assurances remind me of CFO's I have run into over the years, particularly those who have run financially troubled organizations. Now this particular brand of CFO must be ebullient with his creditors and suppliers, assuring them all is well and the company on the mend, and please keep the supply lines and credit flowing…. Lest said creditors and suppliers bolt, and send the whole enterprise into bankruptcy.

Or perhaps Secretary Geithner is merely planning, like any good CFO, to pull any number of accounting maneuvers, that the Wall Street Banks regularly perform, upon the U.S. budgets, her deficits and debt. Mr. Geithner might execute a Repo 105 and send debt to another country, when the CBO or the President's accountants get ready to perform their fiduciary responsibility. But that could get expensive, maybe Mr. Geither creates a special multi purpose vehicle and dumps the debt off the balance sheet, but off balance sheet accounting is already in play. Mr. Geither could enlist his friends at Goldman to obscure debt with CDS and derivative products, a la the products Goldman Sachs sold Greece to gain E.U. admittance. Mr. Geither could consult with the front runner for the European Central Bank's top post, Mario Draghi, a former Goldman Alum, on how exactly the process might work. Or perhaps the U.S. could like, Bank of America, create a bad bank, or "bad U.S.A.," and dump all the problems in a company that basically is a shell for failure? Why not a finite or reinsurance transaction to make accounting problems disappear, like those deployed by AIG and General Reinsurance?

Thanks to FASB and lax regulation the options are limitless.

And with the Fed purchasing U.S. debt nearly as fast as the Treasury issues debt, via quantitative easing, who needs to worry about militant bond vigilantes who might demand reform and higher interest payments?

Certainly not Mr. Geithner who recently offered his commitment to a strong dollar, when he said: "We will never embrace a strategy of trying to weaken our currency to try and gain economic advantage."

Amazing. And so, it is.

That is of course, until countries begin to lose faith in the dollar. For what is the dollar and what gives that piece of paper value? The dollar's value stems from a belief and faith that its value today and ability to purchase goods and services will be of like or similar value tomorrow. When that faith erodes, usually during highly inflationary times, when printing presses roll non-stop, the dollar's value plummets.

It gives you some idea of how bad things are with the dollar, when a shell shocked euro – complete with its own sovereign debt problems and all the incumbent potential for default – is in its ascendancy against the dollar.

But what do the Wall Street banks care if inflation heats up? They basically enjoy the equivalent to an endless flow of monopoly money coming from the Fed funds window at just a little over zero percent interest. And as more than one economist has observed, as well as this blog, Fed policy seems focused and centered upon keeping the Wall Street and European Banking cartels happy and above water. The Fed is not only the U.S. bank of last resort, but it is also would appear to be the E.U.'s, but that just comes with running the world's fiat currency.

The relationship between the mega-banks and government is both symbiotic and well established. The Wall Street Banks played a significant role in the creation of the last financial crisis, and both Republican and Democratic administrations bailed them out, and effectively transferred many of Wall Street's liabilities and toxic assets from the private sector to the public sector, via QE1, and a whole raft of programs (TARP, TALF, Et Al.) and special breaks. Despite all of the aid and assistance, many of the banks, even though reporting profits, still have not turned the corner (weighted down by unrecoginzed problem assets, such as sovereign debt and/or real estate). Meanwhile the general public is feeling the results of quantities easing with rapidly increasing inflation, at a time when their home value, if they still own a home, is in free fall.

And what does the government get out of propping up the banks? Well, they get compliant banks facilitating the financing of national debt, and an endless stream of campaign and political contributions, as long as a pol falls within the correct side of the political divide.

So what could cause Americans, indeed the world, to lose faith in the almighty dollar? Well, not that this blog is wishing for it, because the effects of a toasted dollar would probably feel a lot like, well, Armageddon. That is to say, economic activity would plummet, there would be capital flight, hoarding and rising unemployment, international trade would be rocked, endless negotiations and threats of war - as creditor nations demanded to be made whole, and a prolonged period of economic shock, dislocation, and stagnation, as a new currency is installed or an existing currency takes over the dollar's role. And unlike the rest of the world, who can depend upon the U.S. and the IMF for support during troubled times, who would the U.S. lean on in the event of fiscal and monetary crisis?

What could cause such an event? Any number of factors or a combination of factors, not limited to: China creating a middle class, a self sustaining economy, and no longer dependent upon dollar driven exports; the refusal of the Middle East to accept payment in dollars for the oil trade; a sovereign debt crisis compounded (read the E.U. and/or U.S. state and local governments), replete with another round of bank bailouts; systematic risk or a chain reaction triggering payment of any sizable percentage of the under secured and under collateralized CDS and derivatives market; rising global unemployment, and resulting anarchy and possible revolution. Global war. Soaring food prices and famine. Gee, come to think of it, many of these processes are in play presently.

And what would replace the dollar? Some economist argue a new global currency would replace the dollar, and others have argued that before the dollar was too far gone, it would form a monetary triumvirate with the Euro and the Renminbi. The question is how would sovereigns, like the U.S., surrender both the power to print money, and fiscal power and authority, that is to say, the ability tax and spend?

Don't laugh. There is a great fiscal and monetary science experiment underway presently in the E.U. that could be the template for future global monetary union. How the euro survives, and how the Fed and the E.C.B. manage the competing interests of many disparate nations, very well could signal how quickly the dollar falls from grace or joins up with the Euro and the Renminbi to form a new international monetary order. Businesses, too, may eventually support a universal currency, or basket of currencies, so as to protect profits from hyper inflation, and in order to save money on global currency arbitrage and profit repatriation. The ramifications of such a specie union or creation would be vast, but one thing is for sure, the international banking community would work to manage, capture, and infiltrate such an enterprise from the beginning.

So while an international central bank might be just what the world needs to rein in and control multi-national banking and too big to fail banking institutions, more than likely such an entity would be co-opted from its genesis.

In the interim, try not to lose faith... the Treasury Secretary offers great assurances.

P.S. Not only does Wall Street have an axe to grind with the Democrats and Dodd-Frank, but Big Oil and speculators maybe doing all they can do to unseat President Obama in 2012, via the power of the pump. Stay tuned.

Sherman, Scorched Earth and Goldman Sachs

Cost Benefit Analysis

By J.M. Hamilton (6-18-11)

"The trouble ain't that there is too many fools, but that lightening ain't distributed right." – Mark Twain

Mr. Twain was a very sharp man, and in addition to the above quip, he also offered up that "truth is stranger than fiction, because fiction is obliged to stick to possibilities." A better thought could never sum up the recent event of Jamie Dimon, a very sharp man in his own right, and the CEO of JP Morgan Chase, sidling up to Chairmen Bernanke, and asking if the Fed had done the cost benefit analysis on all the new financial regulation that was harming the banks and the economy.

The chairmen, possibly at a loss of words, admitted that no such analysis had been done. "'It's too complicated,' Bernanke said, adding that he said he thinks there's a way to safely regulate banks while preserving their ability to deliver 'basic financial services.'" Also per Bloomberg, Mr. Dimon is quoted as follows: "I have a great fear someone's going to try to write a book in 20 years and the book is going to talk about all the things that we did in the middle of the crisis to actually slow down recovery."

Many of us have a fear too, but it is quite the opposite of that which Mr. Dimon has expressed, and may be unfolding before our eyes in Europe, presently.

Now just too back up for a moment, the key focus right now among government regulators, politicians and the bank oligarchs, such as Mr. Dimon, is the regulation of credit default swaps, derivatives, and hybrid derivative products. These products when utilized correctly can have the impact of providing insurance to the direct counterparties of a business or contractual agreement; however, when these products fall outside regulatory purview (as has been allowed to happen by successive Democratic and Republican administrations), they have been allowed to turn Wall Street into, perhaps, the Universe's largest gambling casino. How so? Roughly 90% of all derivative products sold don't involve the counterparties to the contract itself, such as the sale of government bonds, but rather, are being sold to speculators who are betting for financial gain. Moreover, these products, worth hundreds of trillions in notional value, are inadequately secured or collateralized. So that when a calamity does occur, not unlike that presently unfolding in Europe, or that which occurred back in 2008 when Goldman, Wall Street banks, shadow banking, and AIG burned down the Western economies, it is not the too big to fail banking institutions who pay (like Mr. Dimon's bank), but rather, the governments who pay. That is to say, the tax payer, and we pay and continue to pay in so many ways for the last crisis.

Which brings us to the present day, Mr. Dimon, and the Wall Street cartel that, via its mercenary battalions of attorneys and lobbyist, have thwarted financial and derivatives regulation at every turn, actually played a large role in writing Dodd-Frank, and have engaged in regulatory and government capture, since time immemorial.

So how might have Chairmen Bernanke responded to Mr. Dimon? Well, if Mr. Bernanke channeled his inner Volker, we can imagine the following written response.

Dear Mr. Dimon,

Yes, the Fed has studied the costs of failing to regulate the derivatives market, please allow me to recap key costs for you; perhaps you may have observed them personally outside the window of your office, perhaps not. The source of our findings is the post financial crisis economy. The costs of the U.S. failure to regulate the derivatives/credit default swaps market are as follows:

$$$ Rising and sustained unemployment in the U.S., officially, set- as of this day- at greater than 9%; but per shadow government statistics the unemployed/under employed may be more accurately set at 20% or greater. That's a whole lot of pain and suffering, so that Wall Street can enrich itself from an unregulated product, and a financial product that Wall Street banks are ill-equipped to pay for in the event of a catastrophe.

$$$ Spiraling national debt to bailout the Wall Street banks, and the after math of our failure to regulate the derivatives market (with maxed out social spending, and cuts to educations, et al.), so that we are now staring at an eye-popping national debt in excess of $14 trillion. America, perhaps, is looking more like Greece by the day, Mr. Dimon, but for the grace of God, and holding the world's fiat currency.

$$$ A housing market, the sector leader in economic recovery, toasted and in ruins. Seems as though the foreclosure mill is gummed up with erroneous bank paper work, problematic debt securitization (CDO's- hybrid derivative products), robo-signers…. all Wall Street products and by product of the last liquidity bubble.

$$$ A probable double dip recession that maybe more acute than the original catastrophe, and a Federal government that can ill afford another round of bank bailouts, or continue to support those in need as a result of Wall Street's worst excesses.

$$$ Nascent inflation on the rise, and rabid speculation in commodities and oil, as a result of the Fed printing trillions in dollars to bailout the Wall Street and European banks. A greatly devalued and diminished U.S. currency, so that the talk is no longer when will the U.S. dollar stop becoming the world's fiat currency, but rather, what will replace it.

$$$ The Euro in crisis, brought to you by Greece (and assorted PIIGS), which purchased credit default swaps from Goldman Sach, Et Al., so as to obscure its national debt to gain E.U. admittance, not unlike a computer virus or Trojan Horse I might add.

Yes, Mr. Dimon, we have done the cost benefit analysis, and while you and Wall Street have enjoyed a prosperous trip back from the brink, courtesy of QE1, QE2, and a whole raft of government programs and subsidies, the balance of the U.S. economy stumbles on or fails. The U.S. consumer, as they like to say in Boston and greater confines, is "scrod." "Stagflation" and "Japanese Economy" are the watch words of the day, due to our failure to regulate your esteemed product. Please understand we would like to avoid another economic Hiroshima, and whatever hit your bank profits might receive as a result of the "regulation lite" that is Dodd-Frank, well, that's a cost we are willing to suffer.

Yours truly…. Ben.

The bitter irony is perhaps the person most capable of offering up grand insight and design into derivatives regulation is Mr. Dimon, himself; but that would require Mr. Dimon to abdicate responsibility to JP Morgan Chase, and realign his allegiance to ordinary Americans or roughly 99% of us. Let's hope that the lightening, that is financial deregulation in the 80's, 90's and 00's, doesn't strike the U.S. economy twice. My guess is a second bolt is descending upon Europe, as I write this editorial.

If parents don't allow children to play with guns and knives, and the Allied Powers did not allow post World War Germany to re-arm for a period of time, than why would the world allow Wall Street tycoons to play with unregulated derivative products?

P.S. It appears that the world will have to suffer at least another financial meltdown before we receive global financial regulation containing the utilization of derivative products. Hang on to your sports bras and jock straps gals and guys because this ride may turn turbulent. God bless us all.

A Golden Curtain has descended across the West...?

By J.M. Hamilton   (7-4-2011)

"I'd rather entrust the government of the United States to the first 400 people listed in the Boston telephone directory than to the faculty of Harvard University." – *William F. Buckley*

Per the NY Times obituary on Mr. Buckley, we the get the following: "All great biblical stories begin with Genesis," George Will wrote in National Review in 1980. "And before there was Ronald Reagan, there was Barry Goldwater, and before there was Barry Goldwater there was National Review, and before there was National Review there was Bill Buckley with a spark in his mind, and the spark in 1980 has become a conflagration."

To which this blog responds, what hath Mr. Buckley wrought?

As the political architect of the Reagan Revolution, the father of the paleo-Tea Bag movement (i.e. political conservatism), and after more than a quarter century of free market ideology and deregulation, Mr. Buckley, presumably, might have some misgivings about the way things have turned out.   One thing is for sure, there were some positives about the man, and his political knowledge and debating skills were something to be feared. In reading the above quote, one wonders if Mr. Buckley was more upbeat about the prospect of the first 400 people within the Boston phone directory running the affairs of the nation, or was he merely slamming the Harvard faculty?   My guess is a little of the both, because say what you will about the man, Mr. Buckley generally argued from a position of Christian altruism, the likes of which are rarely, if ever, heard in present Republican Party leadership. I would like to believe Mr. Buckley, a well known Libertarian, was also a populist at heart, who genuinely believed that his brand of free market ideology would be a boon to all.

History has yet to write Mr. Buckley's final epitaph; the political and economic wave he helped to unleash, more like a tsunami, is still very much with us – its troubled waters have yet to fully recede. Still one can't help but admire the man; and at the end the day, he was not a doctrinaire adherent to the political and economic ideology he helped mold and shape.   After all, any Republican who was not in favor of the Iraq war and who was not a fan of President Bush (W.) certainly deserves our acknowledgement, if not our respect; and any man who would sail into international waters to smoke a joint, so as to avoid breaking U.S. law certainly is, if nothing else, interesting.

Damn, I miss *Firing Line*.

But we move on, and deal with the wreckage of our present economy, and what a week it was. *Bloomberg* released a story highlighting that the revolving door between the most nefarious bank known to mankind, Goldman Sachs, and Western Governments continues unabated. Goldman not content to rule the known financial universe must also control the highest chambers of government and central banks. Proving that we do, indeed, live under a bankocracy. Mr. Forsyth of *Barron's Magazine* wrote, if I may have license to paraphrase, that the banks of the E.U., particularly those in France and Germany, are being propped up on the shoulders of the poor of Greece and what remains of their middle class, come to think of it not unlike what has transpired in the U.S. since 2008. Austerity, a shrinking economy, and low employment prospects are what await Greece and the West, that is as long as our political elite remain slavishly devoted to propping up the banks.

And it doesn't look like it's going to get better any time soon. Christian Lagarde will head up the IMF. And while it is wonderful that a woman will finally run the IMF, she most certainly will continue the policies that have indentured 99% of us to the banks, many of which are insolvent. And Tim Geithner, it appears, will stay on at the Treasury for the "foreseeable future," perhaps the worst news we received all week.

Charles Munger, the Vice Chairmen of Berkshire Hathaway (the bastion of all things Ayn Rand) had an epiphany of Tourettes, when he offered up the following gems, as reported in *Bloomberg*:

"The bubble in America was caused by some combination of megalomania, insanity and evil in, I would say, investment banking, mortgage banking."

"Alan Greenspan is a smart man," Munger said. "He just totally overdosed on Ayn Rand at a young age."

"I would guess that Dick Fuld has not a single ounce of contrition wherever he sits today."

Mr. Munger, the story goes on to report, is a fan of Elizabeth Warren.

My guess is the "Morning with Charlie" show will be permanently cancelled. Mr. Munger is a reported Republican, and the Republican Leadership must be foaming at the mouth over these "revelations."

Might have Mr. Buckley have also thought along the lines of Mr. Munger had he lived through our present financial crisis? Quite possibly so.

But are the Democrats really any better? This week we learn in the NY Times that Democrats and the Obama administration were about to sell out the American worker once again, with proposed passage of several Bush era free trade agreements; that is as long as Republicans were going to aid and abet this catastrophe by expanding the welfare state for all the displaced American workers, who would lose their jobs as a result of the wage, tax, and regulatory arbitrage that is "free trade." Of course, as this blog has written there is absolutely nothing free about "free trade." A friendly note to the Democratic Party: America needs jobs, not an expansion of the deficit and more welfare programs, so that your party can appease the chamber of commerce, multi-national manufacturing and banking interests.

Do you ever get the feeling that we live in a one party state? With both parties pandering to Wall Street, both parties propping up the banks, at the expense of us all…. If you think about it, we really aren't that dissimilar to the Greeks who felt betrayed by their own elected officials this week, or the upset German populace, who will now have to bailout E.U. periphery nations, not to mention their own banks, again and again and again….

Of course the banks, always several steps ahead, are international in scope, hire the best and brightest, make them rich, and turn them out to run our "democracies," perhaps to circle back again for more tax payer funded loot. Meanwhile the G20 and the IMF (and I might add Basel), as written about by Barry Eichengreen in *voxeu.org*, just can't seem to get it together long enough to thwart the interests of the Wall Street cartel, always dissolving into petty recriminations, disputes, and bickering, not unlike a bad marriage counseling session, as Mr. Eichengreen observes

On March 5th 1946, Winston Churchill gave a famous speech in Fulton, Missouri. At the time the speech was dismissed as more war mongering from the often bellicose and belligerent Mr. Churchill; but Mr. Churchill turned out to be quite right because an *Iron Curtain* was indeed descending across the continent of Europe, and much of the world, that would form the basis of the cold war for the next forty years or more. Behind the curtain was the unfathomable, but we now know, as Mr. Buckley may have observed, it was one vast gulag archipelago, complete with slave labor, backward and underperforming economies, and absolutely miserable human right conditions. Most importantly, personal, economic, religious and political freedom were crushed under the boot heals of communist masters. It took the likes of Messrs. Churchill, Reagan, Buckley and Truman, with a whole lot of help and sacrifice from the West, to bring down the Soviet empire (in of all places a small country at the cross roads of the world, Afghanistan).

Today, if Mr. Churchill were alive might he warn of a *Golden Curtain* descending across the Western democracies? This curtain is made of gold for our elected officials, and the insiders and banking interests protected from within. Outside the curtain, the middle class is crumbling, unemployment and inflation are rising, and U.S. and European economies are in shambles. And the liberty we take for granted is under threat from within. In Greece, and coming soon to a country near you, order and peace are at a premium, as are jobs. Crony capitalism, like some defunct Soviet era economy, is often how business gets done; likewise Monopolies, or put another way socialism by private proxy, prey upon the population with taxation without representation. And seemingly no elected official or appointee has the political will to, consistently, say or do what is right. Where is FDR, a traitor to his class, when you need him? Where is Teddy Roosevelt the trust buster? Where is Harry Truman?

Political economist will tell you that black markets are dangerous things because they offer unregulated and unsafe products, and make obscene profits, which can in turn be used to subvert democratic governments, institutions, and elected officials. But Mexican drug cartels cannot hold a candle to the banking interests who traffic in the ultimate narcotic, money! It is banking and shadow banking, armed with a *Citizens United* supreme court decision and the unlimited flow of money, that has woven the golden curtain that separates us from the our elected leaders, and perverts our democratic institutions.

P.S.

On this Fourth of July weekend, a few lines from Mr. Jefferson, who had quite a disdain for monarchs, like the Kings who rule us all on Wall Street:

"He has plundered our seas, ravaged our Coasts, burnt our towns, and destroyed the lives of our people."- Declaration of Independence

"A Prince whose character is thus marked by every act which may define a Tyrant, is unfit to be the ruler of a free people." – Declaration of Independence

"He has combined with others to subject us to a jurisdiction foreign to our constitution, and unacknowledged by our laws; giving his Assent to their Acts of pretended Legislation: For imposing Taxes on us without our Consent (In the modern day this would be monopolistic profits and usurious interest rates)." - Declaration of Independence

"And I sincerely believe, with you, that banking establishments are more dangerous than standing armies; and that the principle of spending money to be paid by posterity, under the name of funding, is but swindling futurity on a large scale." - Jefferson's letter to the political philosopher, John Taylor.

Stealth Coup

"The chamber and other business groups have pressed with increasing urgency for Congress to raise the maximum amount that the government can borrow. " — NY TIMES, 7-26-11

By J.M. Hamilton (7-31-11)

The country continues it's seemingly inexorable tilt to the right and mayhem, despite Americans living with the lessons, daily, that markets do not self-regulate and that the vast majority of us are but a pink slip away from humility. It's like the financial disaster in 2007-2008 never happened; and both parties, Republicans and Democrats, and apparently even the President, are attempting exceed one another in learning just how far they can shift the political center and discourse further right. It seems to have been that way since Reagan came to power.   And while the man of the eighties talked a great "conservative game," the fact that he raised taxes eleven times during his presidency, and perhaps was one of the greatest Keynesians ever to enter the White House (perhaps second only to George Bush – W), seems to have been lost altogether on the Tea Party movement, and recalcitrant freshmen congressmen (who appear to be doing their best to level the national and world economies). It is as I have long suspected, namely, that certain elements of the Republican Party would like to destroy the Federal Government.   What else is one to conclude from the comments of Dick – Deficits Don't Matter –Cheney, and recent happenings?

The Koch brother's stealth coup seems to have taken hold … all the better to let the law of the jungle take over and monolithic commercial interests call the shots, without the gadfly of the federal government nipping at their heels. Of course when you're a member of the plutocracy who really needs government anyway?

As for the poor, "Are there no workhouses?"

And just so you don't think this blog has finally and completely gone off the rails… a couple of observations to back my premise:

$$$ Roughly 50% of discretionary Federal outlays goes to military spending, but despite having finally brought down the arch nemesis of the free world, the U.S. is still neck deep in Afghanistan with 100,000 or more boots on the ground to tackle what? As the New York Times reports, 100 to 200 Qaeda,

and yet, nary a word from our elected leaders about reigning in the biggest barrel of pork known to mankind, the military industrial complex. The fact that this nation spends more on defense than the G-20 combined seems lost on fiscal conservatives and budget hawks, within both parties. Perhaps the Department of Homeland Security should dust off the recently retired multi-colored terror alert chart, so that we can all be properly afraid again? All the better to justify the insanity that is the defense budget. Apparently cutting back on government welfare only applies to benefits allocated to the weak and infirm.

$$$ Closing revenue loopholes on personages and entities, so that instead of paying no taxes, the same actually pays taxes, apparently constitutes tax increases to the radicals who are calling the shots in the House, and holding the nation's economy hostage. Demagoguery at its worst, and yet where are the Democrats to expose this fallacious reasoning? And when did paying ones fair share of taxes become a source of derision or scorn? To hear the tax and accounting department at General Electric tell it, or as one is to discern by their actions, apparently anybody who pays taxes is a sucker, and all one needs to do, to right the wrong of paying taxes, is to hire former Treasury officials to chart the loopholes, and game domestic earnings and the tax code. The fact that Reagan actually closed loopholes, when he learned that his former employer, General Electric, was paying few if any taxes in the eighties, showed just how selective the collective memory of the *res publica* can be.

$$$ Allowing the Fed to devalue the dollar and therefore, allowing the Fed to make weak and only slightly effective attempts at addressing fiscal, trade, domestic and foreign policy, so that the legislative branch doesn't have to — is a cop out. The Fed, and Mr. Bernanke, is effectively carrying our elected leaders on its back so that they do not have to address the issues of the day, and can abdicate responsibility. The Fed should stop providing aid and comfort to the Charlatans, and begin to raise interest rates, which would force our elected officials to govern. With an interest rate rise the harmful effects of QE1 and QE2 might soon vanish as well: inflation might wane; the saving class would enjoy more income to spend in the economy and have a greater incentive to save; some of the banks that should have failed three years ago might finally go under – helping to clear markets; and it would provide a signal to many in the stock market that it might be time to move on, before the inevitable tumble occurs. Most importantly, rising interest payments on the national debt may create the – up until now – missing sense of urgency for elected leaders to deal with budget deficits and national debt.

Funny, one hasn't heard about either party complaining about the Fed recently. Apparently, trashing the world's fiat currency is perfectly acceptable when it provides cover for political failure to perform!

$$$ Even the Chamber of Commerce is starting to sweat bullets. Having helped the Koch brother ensconce the freshmen class, they have been rather reluctant to push the ideologues. Mr. Axelrod, a chief political advisor to the President, had the following to say in the *Times* last week: "I just think that there was, at least on the part of the chamber, a reluctance to tangle with, or pressure, the same group in the House that they're depending on to gut financial reform and undo environmental regulation and so on. But I think the gravity of the situation is now clear." Yeah, it's all good when your pit bull is mauling the opposition, but when your monster starts to glare at you, hungrily, look out.

Running the world's fiat currency translates into great responsibility. If the U.S. defaults because of political theatre, there will be a lot of oligarchs, who are going to quite possibly find the business environment and the economy less conducive to making money, perhaps globally. Of equal or greater importance, expect a new outcry from world leaders for a new global currency to replace the dollar, especially if the rating agencies down grade the U.S.

The right thing would be for the Congress to pass the debt ceiling, and then enter into good faith negotiations with the Democrats that embraces both spending cuts, and tax reform; but doing the right thing and the "political thing" are as often as not diametrically opposed. There's always the next election cycle around the road, scheming and contrivance trumps prudent action, and the public always seems at the mercy of the politicians and the elite who pull their strings. Of course, if this novice class of politicians trash the world economy, and do reparable or irreparable damage to the dollar and the U.S. credit rating, they will quite possibly have the shortest political careers, as a group, in the nation's history. And the Koch brothers and the chamber may lose this round in their venture into politics. There's a happy thought.

Let us weep for the Koch Brothers and the Chamber of Commerce, and let's remember, who they put in office, come November 2012. This might be a very short lived coup. The question is will the Democrats learn from their 2008 mistakes, and govern more effectively and efficiently? And will President Obama be given a second chance?

P.S. One wonders how many of the freshmen class, including their staff and wealthy supporters, took out CDS and derivative bets against the dollar in advance of the spectacle that lies before us. By having a transparent derivatives market, on open exchanges, we could quickly learn if some of the faux patriots in Washington, and their money men, have a vested financial interest in political stalemate, a U.S default, and in shorting the dollar, at the expense of us all. Another argument for free and open derivatives exchanges? Perhaps.

http://blog.jmhamiltonpublishing.com/2010/10/16/otis-rawl-chief-executive-officer-of-the-south-carolina-chamber-of-commerce—we-wanted-to-bring-the-debate-away-from-the-tea-party-and-back-to-the-middle.aspx

http://blog.jmhamiltonpublishing.com/2010/08/29/if-you-believe-the-tea-party-is-a-grass-roots-movement—think-again.aspx

QE3... With Teeth? A Modest Proposal

By J.M. Hamilton (8-7-11)

Mr. Bernanke, can you hear it in the distance? They are beckoning you...that's the whine of Helicopter rotors.

By now we all pretty much know how America got here: a democratic government that would rather campaign than govern, fiscal incompetence, two wars, government failure to regulate, regulatory capture, bankers run amok, underwriting prudence tossed out the window, hyper-leverage, debt securitization, funky accounting, unlimited campaign contributions (thank you Supreme Court) ....bank bailout after bailout, and a total lack of monetary temperance. And, there it is, the inevitable ratings down grade.

Yup, ma, we are just like everybody else now: in hock and broke!

It's almost enough to make you weep for our children's and the nation's future. And of course, its one thing to blog about it, write and complain about it, but how about a solution? J.M. Hamilton was not a fan of QE1 or even QE2, but we understand why Mr. Bernanke engaged in it, primarily because of the extreme dysfunction of the congress, and their near complete inability to govern. After all, someone has to conduct domestic, foreign, and trade policy. That said, monetary policy is a crude instrument with which to conduct the affairs of state.   In a perfect world and with the Congress willing to govern, responsibly, it would be much better if Mr. Bernanke set the interest rate, presumably above zero, and went to bed for the next four or five years. But that ain't gonna happen.

The pressure will build as never before for the Fed to engage in another round of quantitative easing, or debt monetization, after all election season is upon us. Many scribes have said it is unlikely, but both the Street and the economy appear to be crying out for it, so addicted has the nation and business become to the largesse of Rome, and currency mechanization. This economy is not healed by a long shot.   And the primary reason for the struggling economy is that the engine of economic prosperity, the American consumer, is still financially under water or unemployed.   Up until now, QE1 and QE2 were focused on the supply side of the credit market. The Fed got out its bazooka, and flooded Wall Street with cash, which it promptly leveraged and invested in T-Bills, the stock market, commodities, or sent offshore to much more favorable financial climes. Ah, our patriotic banker friends…. You gotta love 'em. We bail 'em out, and they sell America short or invest elsewhere.

My point is… up until now Mr. Bernanke has been dumping the cash from his helicopter on the wrong side of the demand and supply curves. What America needs is not another back door Wall Street bailout, but rather, what America needs is some consumer relief from its 14 trillion in mortgage and personal debt. In other words, if the Fed is going to turn the spigot one more time, that is if we are going to roll the dice… the money should be directly allocated to pairing down consumer debt (all the better to free up Americans to begin buying, purchasing and consuming again). If Americans are buying and consuming again, demand increases, which should set off a round of hiring as business seeks to keep up with demand. The rising economy increases the tax base and receipts at the IRS, helping to alleviate our national debt, or giving both political parties an excuse to spend more. Things - uh, maybe, get better.

As for our friends the bankers, well perhaps they can be put to good use after all.

F.D. R. was alleged to have said, "It Takes a thief to catch a thief," which was in reference to placing Joseph P. Kennedy as the first head of the Securities and Exchange Commission. And perhaps it takes our Wall Street banker friends, and some creative thinking, to get America out of the jam the bankers helped put us in?

What if QE3 was launched by the Fed with strings attached, or caveats and conditions governing its use? QE3 could be leveraged, turned into 30 year debt, and sold to investors, with the idea that at least half of the proceeds would go exclusively to paying off U.S. consumer debts and obligations (which would show up as a reduction in the consumer's monthly mortgage payment). The debt and servicing of the same could be set up in LLC's or SPV's, away from the bank's balance sheets. It would then fall upon Wall Street to utilize their wizardry and the other half of the proceeds from the QE3 debt sale to pay down both the principle and interest of the combined QE3 debt, over a thirty year run. It would be patriotic to buy such an offering; and even more patriotic for a banker to serve such an organization, and quite possibly lucrative. Just as the banks transferred their debts and obligations to the government and the public sector, perhaps a percentage of the mountain of personal or consumer debt, the banks helped to create, could in like manner be transferred back to Wall Street?

Think about it, if we added up all the bailout programs launched since this crisis began (TARP, TLGP, TALF, Fiscal Stimulus, QE1 and QE2, etc. etc.), and if it had been allocated to the writing down some amount of the $14 trillion in private sector debt, this economy may have already returned to normalcy. The housing market might have become liquid again.

There might be some outcry about socialism from some, perhaps even the banks; but those arguments went out the window, when we bailed out Wall Street. Of course, CEO's in manufacturing and the service sector would have to do their part, that is to say, utilize the increase in demand to employ Americans.

What's in it for Wall Street banks? In addition to getting to write down a percentage of debt from their balance sheets without taking a hit, the Fed and the government could play this any number of ways. In exchange for the bank's assistance and cooperation with the QE3 plan, it could help the banks out with a tax holiday or perhaps they get a break on some of the foreclosure problems they have been having; or if that wasn't working for the Street, maybe the government could audit our friends, institute mark to market accounting, and nationalize the bastards, as should have be done in 2008 and 2009! After all, GM was nationalized, re-orged and turned loose again to the private sector, and just reported an 89% increase in profits in the latest quarter. Why not our buddies on Wall Street?

Some people speculated that perhaps Mr. Milken's (of Drexel/ junk bond fame) talents could have been put to better use, when he was convicted/jailed in the late 80's for some creative financial engineering... like using his financial acumen to help reduce the national debt.

Maybe America should consider putting Wall Street to work for Americans? What a wonderful way for the Banks to redeem themselves, the Street could deploy it's greed for the betterment of mankind and a reinvigorated world economy. Shoot, if the banks can't hack it, private equity might step in.

Desperate times call for desperate measures. Cue up the Flight of the Valkyries!

Heart of Darkness

By J.M. Hamilton (9-5-11)

"Mistah Kurtz — he dead."

For thrills and chills, I have never been much into fiction. The cold hard realities of this world provide all the excitement, drama, and surreal energy I'll ever need. Why just open up your New York Times, and be prepared for shock and awe. However, on occasion I have come across a piece of fiction that hits home. The story puts the hook into me because of the core truth it exposes about the human condition. Such a work is **Heart of Darkness** by Joseph Conrad, which I believe is the greatest story ever told. This story has everything: empire, anthropolatry, mass murder, and capitalist excess. Oh, did I mention cannibals?

And of course, ultimately, it's a love story!

Heart of Darkness is a study in what Carl Jung would refer to as the "duality of man," unchecked power, and the megalomania that often follows. Having studied power for decades, the story rings true on many levels. A *wunderkind* goes into the jungle to seek his fortune so that he can marry above his caste. Driven by this love and his passions, Mr. Kurtz loses himself, and with his tribe of warriors in deepest dark Africa begins cutting off heads, so as to gather more ivory. As more ivory accumulates and is sent back to Mr. Kurtz's corporate masters, his fame and reputation grows, often to his business colleague's dismay. The more Mr. Kurtz enriches others the greater the license he is given. Sound familiar?

Heart of Darkness was published in 1899, and the story is set in the colonialism of the period, but examples of Mr. Kurtz and his behavior can be seen everywhere at the genesis of the twenty-first century. The troubled times we find ourselves in amplify and magnify these figures as they stride across the business and political landscape, indeed across the globe. Many of these figures exhibit myopia that excludes nearly all social conscience, an all consuming goal, great economic or political power, and in some instances enjoy a cult following. Often some or all ethical and moral restraint is abandoned so as to achieve "the dream," even at the expense of the destruction of others, and ultimately, themselves. That pretty much defines what I like to call Heart of Darkness syndrome or HDS. Please read on, as the blog offers up examples of HDS here in 2011.

$$$ Mr. Lloyd – Doing God's Work – Blankfein exhibits many of the characteristics of HDS. His problems are legendary, but to sum up include selling short the American Dream and the American economy, and of course, client double-dealing. His singleness of purpose is manifest to all; his ethical bypass complete, as he continues to fight and lobby for the very rules and regulations (or the lack thereof) that brought this nation's economy to its knees. Not content to having enriched his company, Goldman Sachs, and his management team many times over, he has insured his and Goldman's success by purchasing all the politicians Goldman's money can buy, and placing his employees in the highest chambers of global government. And he probably believes he is doing "God's work," after all Mr. Blankfein does his best to operate within the confines of the rules Goldman's attorneys lobbied for, created, and helped to legislate. Mr. Blankfein and his cadres seem oblivious to the human toll and suffering he and his banking peers on Wall Street have created. And my favorite thought from Goldman, recently released, was the assurance that the hiring of Reid Winegarten, criminal defense attorney, was "routine."

$$$ Secretary of the Treasury, Tim Geithner - Mr. Geithner, as the former head of the New York Fed, we are often told helped save this nation from ruin and another great depression, with a little help from his friends Messrs. Henry Paulson, Fed Chairmen Bernanke, and Larry Summers. But three years into the economic quagmire many Americans and businesses find themselves in, Mr. Geithner and his colleagues appear not to have saved the American economy so much, as have bailed out the banks, repeatedly. And the trickle down from these banks just hasn't happened, just ask Shadow Government Statistic, who show true unemployment and underemployment creeping north of 22%. By not restructuring the Wall Street banks and not writing down home loans, when America had a chance, Mr. Geithner and his colleagues have consigned the U.S. housing market, and indeed the Western economies, to years and years of economic turmoil and malaise. Trust me, the fun is just beginning. However, the ultimate cost will not even be borne by this generation, but rather, it will fall upon our children and future generations. It is they, and ourselves, who will have to deal with a devalued currency and debt piling ever higher, as good money is thrown after bad – all for the enrichment and aggrandizement of a few, and at the expense of virtually all.

If President Obama loses his bid for re-election in 2012, he will have to thank Tim Geithner for the outcome. By the way, the transparent assurances of Mr. Buffet aside, it's never too late to nationalize and restructure the banks, starting with Bank of America. Why look at GM, who was nationalized and restructured, and just reported record sales figures, up eighteen percent!

$$$ The Republican Party and the Politics of the Heart of Darkness – The Republican party's disdain and visceral objection to the President taps right into the Heart of Darkness. What does it say when the Senate Republican Leader's primary goal is not the betterment of his home state of Tennessee or the country, the job for which he was presumably elected, but rather unseating the President of the United States. This party of which I was once a proud member, has completely run off the rails, and now is run by megalomaniacal billionaires, the intolerant, and those who politically exploit the evangelicals and Christian community. Ironically, the party of Christ, as the Republican Party would have you believe, worships money and is the lap dog of corporate interests, often at the expense of all other considerations. If the GOP was really adhering to the teachings of Christ they would be providing aid and assistance to the poor and the elderly, not shutting down government assistance or attempting to privatize same. Governor Rick Perry's connections to the plutocracy and fund raising capabilities are legendary, and yet, he wants to kill social security.

There's just one problem, the Republican Party and the Chamber of Commerce are rapidly finding themselves turned inside out, by the alleged extremes within the party tent, many of whom are anti- multinational, anti-Wall Street, and anti-Fed. Seems that some of the elements within the party can appreciate, greatly, American business and capitalism, but don't share a similar fondness for cartels and monopolies who exploit government largess, tax loopholes, and the legislative process. This party claims the mantle of fiscal responsibility while often presiding, from the White House, over the greatest Keynesian raid heretofore known to man, from Reagan through Bush (W). Hypocrisy defined.

$$$ Steve Jobs and Apple Computer. Talk about singular focus, look no further than Mr. Jobs. The man truly is great, and has changed America and the world in so many different ways, often for our betterment. But could Mr. Jobs be greater? By hiring U.S. labor, instead of exploiting labor on foreign shores, one economist estimates Apple's profit margin on the iPhone would drop from 60% to 50%. Not a terrible price to pay for helping out your home country, right? Or by insisting that Apple's vendors in China pay a fair living wage, with a normalized work week, Mr. Job's would set a standard for multi-nationals, and bring the differences between U.S. labor and China's labor market one more step closer to parity or equilibrium. Mr. Jobs could also insist that vendors in the Pacific Rim not hire child labor, or pollute. Mr. Jobs will go down in history as a tremendous talent and inventor, but might he have been greater? Instead of employing more American's we have a company that exploits U.S. tax law and is sitting on more cash than the U.S. Treasury presently has on hand.

With great power comes great responsibility; U.S. corporations want to be treated like royalty, but often eschew a great deal of the social responsibility that comes with that privilege. That is to say, corporations often enjoy greater privilege and deference under the law, than any single citizen would ever be accorded; and yet, often get away with crimes that no citizen could ever escape, individually. If corporations want to be accorded great privilege should they not be held to a commensurate standard?

The annual drive for the United Way is great, but could Corporate America do more? Apple computer, and the cult of personality that follows Mr. Jobs, could change the corporate/social responsibility dynamic if they so choose, and with a minimal hit to their bottom line. In fact, this blog argues that any short term reduction in income – as a result of a renewed commitment to the United States and its citizens – could be made up for, in terms of profits, many times over in the intermediate and longer term.

Speaking of great works of fiction, probably the greatest lie told over the last three years has been that the Obama administration is anti-business. Take a look at the productivity gains of the American corporation, the increases in net income, and the mountains of cash many of these entities lay upon, and convince me that this administration is anti- business. Meanwhile, American labor has not seen a real increase in income over the last two decades.

$$$ Exxon Mobil: This story is priceless, but first a little history. On August 23, 1939, Adolph Hitler signed a deal with the devil, Joseph Stalin. Also known as the *Molotov – Ribbentrop Pact*, the deal basically carved up Poland and Northern and Eastern Europe between the two ambitious men. The "deal with the devil" eventually disintegrated with Hitler's Operation Barbarossa, and the Russian winter. (Hitler apparently learned nothing from another person exhibiting HDS, Napoleon Bonaparte, who made the same mistake in attacking Russia too late in the summer, and was also fighting wars on too many fronts. We can all be thankful that Hitler was apparently not a student of history.)

Fast forward to this week, when Rex Tillerson's Exxon Mobil signed, perhaps, another deal with the devil, Ex- KGB and now Russian Prime Minister, Vladimir Putin. For a look into what Exxon stockholders can come to expect from a deal with Vlad, examine the tough love dished out to a present Russian partner, British Petroleum, from this week's N.Y. Times:

MOSCOW — Police officers armed with assault rifles Wednesday raided the Moscow offices of the British oil giant BP, carrying out a type of ritual armed search of white-collar premises that is common enough here to have a nickname, "masky show."

The timing of the raid, however, highlighted this peculiar type of Russian risk for another company — ExxonMobil, which just a day earlier agreed to take over the very Arctic exploration deal that fell through for BP.

BP is still involved in a dispute with its Russian partners over that oil-exploration deal; the police search was related to a lawsuit pending in a Siberian court.

Russia is as important for BP's oil production as the United States, so even though the company has had such problems here for years, its share price often nudges up or down in response to police raids or the arrests of employees.

The police raids on Moscow's glassy high-rises where foreign banks and oil companies have offices unnerve employees and disrupt business. They are called "masky shows" for the balaclavas often worn by the black-clad police.

What makes Tillerson's deal so unique is not that he is getting into bed with a reformed commie, after all President —" I can do business with this man" — Bush was snookered by Mr. Putin, too; but Exxon must know that the prospects for any longevity to this partnership cannot be good. Many multinationals have sought to do business in the former Soviet Republic, only to find themselves shaken down by corruption, subjected to police state tactics, and with little recourse in a country where the rule of law often does not exist.

Of course, the allure of drilling in the Arctic Sea has to be a huge draw for Exxon, what with the U.S. still concerned about the Alaskan coast and its environment, why not do an "end around" U.S. energy policy and hook up with the Ruskies? Selah! If there's a catastrophe, who's likely to know if a few million barrels of the sticky black stuff dumps into the Arctic Ocean during a period of endless polar nights? (Polar bear au chocolat? Exxon appears down with that.) Since this deal will have to be ratified by the congress and involves giving Mr. Putin's Russia a share of Exxon's U.S. assets, how much of this "dance" by Exxon is sincere, and how much of it is a way to put pressure on the U.S. government to open up the Alaskan coast to Exxon?

Only time will tell, however, one thing is clear: If you thought the banking crisis threw a wrench in the global economy take a look at the economic and foreign policy ramifications of the largest U.S. corporation, and a key energy provider, doing business with the Russian Prime Minister. Does the U.S. really want a Russian Premier (who often exhibits HDS) holding U.S. policy hostage via his arrangement with Exxon? Mr. Putin, said of the deal: "The scale of the investment is very large. It's scary to utter such huge figures." Scary, indeed.

The Heart of Darkness syndrome is everywhere these days, and you don't even have turn on the news to see it first hand, why look right next door. One might see HDS exhibited in local judges, politicians, school superintendants, and even teachers, anywhere where near absolute power has the potential to corrupt, absolutely. Men and women will often make mistakes, and become entranced by a goal, mission or dream. And it's this passion that can also, if channeled correctly, drive men and women to achieve great things. The question is can the person with HDS pull up before it's too late, or like Kurtz will the situation end in personal destruction and substantial collateral damage?

Mr. Kurtz died before reaching his goal of being reunited with his lover, his "intended."

She never came to know his final words, which were: *"The horror! The horror!"*

At the end, Mr. Kurtz came to rest where all the indispensable men and women of the world ultimately come to lay, in a dark grave, and possibly answering to a much higher power.

P.S. I know the economy sucks, but is President Obama kicking some serious tail or what? I mean if these were normal times, this guy would be coasting to victory in 2012. Let's look at his foreign policy score card, shall we?

Osama bin Laden: Check.

Colonel Gaddafi, check.

Wind up Mission in Iraq, check.

Start and conclude a war in Libya with multinational political, economic, and military support to prevent genocide by a ruthless dictator, setting a new benchmark for U.S. foreign policy: Check again.

Ushering in a new — hopefully less costly — age in the U.S. military, that of covert operations, drones, cyber-ops, and less dependence on standing armies: CHECK!

Pulling the hell out of Afghanistan... Under Review/Pending.

Foreign Policy grade for the Commander in Chief, and showing the Republican Party how to actually hunt down scum bags and win: A

Note: If Obama was a Republican, the GOP would be singing his praises right now.

Note, if the U.S. can exit Afghanistan, possibly as the election nears, we predict that the President's poll numbers will enjoy a boost. Then America can say, definitively, "mission accomplished." Coming soon, the Presidents score card on U.S. domestic policy. This blog has seen some promise from this administration on domestic matters, like having the Justice Department take on the AT&T monopoly, and combination with Sprint. The government's law suit against the banks, initiated this week, over the fraud associated with mortgage debacle is another great start. Potential here is limitless, as an agent of real change. Obviously, jobs is priority one!

Finally, see the film adaptation of Heart of Darkness with Mr. Francis Coppola's Apocalypse Now. I highly recommend it.

Power is never dearer as when it is fleeting or under threat…

"The Department of Justice law suit against the AT&T/T-Mobile combination, hopefully, sends a message to the nation's monopolies and oligopolies that it is no longer open season on the American consumer, the economic engine that drives demand and top line growth."

By J.M. Hamilton (9-11-11)

It is the political season, which means for some of us the synapses will be burning red hot, and the serotonin, the lubricant for the brain, will be evaporating off the cranial engine. It's not easy being a political junkie, but as far as blood sports go nothing else quite compares. That said, why the political season must start just a couple of months after the last election is beyond reason. Don't these guys and gals ever work? Apparently not. As noted by **Arthur Levitt** (former SEC Chair and Policy Advisor to Goldman Sachs) on a recent *Bloomberg podcast hosted by Tom Keene and Ken Prewitt*, Congress has passed only 28 pieces of legislation this year, much of which was not germane to our economic nightmare.

Nice. The country is staring into the abyss, and the 112th Congress takes a two year holiday to campaign. Of course, the only thing more unpopular than President Obama is the Republican lead congress, with their approval ratings at half the Presidents.

It seems that the Republican lead congress is more interested in scoring points with its political base than in helping this President tackle the really tough issues; the thought being, come November 2012,the nastier the economy is the greater the chances of an Obama defeat. However, with Obama willing to meet the Republicans half way on most issues (and in some instances actually co-opting the GOP), the public, and maybe even the Chamber of Commerce, may end up supporting the President in 2012, as the sane and rational choice. Stranger things have happened. Comparatively, Obama is looking good, as opposed to radicals on the right who sent the nascent economic recovery careening into the ditch, over the debt ceiling increase.

As noted in last week's editorial, *Heart of Darkness*, the President on the foreign policy is batting near a thousand, showing great moxie and courage. So much so that even the most ardent Neo-Con should be applauding: President

Reagan wanted Kaddafi, and President Bush wanted OBL.... President Obama took them both out.

On domestic policy however, it has been a different story, and the shame of it is the President didn't hit the ground running harder on the banking crisis, or the jobs situation, at the very beginning of his term. But perhaps the President, under the advice and direction of Messrs. Geithner and Summers, wasn't told just how bad things were or how bad they were going to get. What is clear is the tremendous focus and political capital spent on "Healthcare Reform" appears to have been wasted energy and time, given our pressing economic state. President Obama probably felt that if so much money was going to Wall Street, how come a pet Democratic project, like universal healthcare, could not be addressed. After all, President Bush (W) expanded big government with Medicare, Part D (or as we like to call it, the Big Pharma entitlement act).

All Presidents, however, deserve time to learn on the job, and Obama inherited a complete economic nightmare scenario from former President Bush (W); the inverse of what President Bush inherited from President Clinton. In fact, J.M. Hamilton would argue that the President was set up and robbed of his "F.D.R. moment" by Messrs. Henry Paulson, Fed Chair Bernanke, and Tim Geithner, who bailed out the banks rather than letting them collapse into bankruptcy and reorganization (hence setting up this administration for the drawn out economic catastrophe the U.S. and Europe finds itself in). Of course with this President picking Mr. Geithner as his Treasury Secretary, and Larry Summers on the President's Council of Economic Advisers, the continuation of the Bush Presidency – Wall Street bailout policies was all but guaranteed.

What we now know, based upon the G.M. example, is that the country most likely would have been much better off had we let the banks collapse into an expedited re-org, nationalized, haircuts delivered to bond holders, mortgages and commercial loans written down (providing immediate relief to American business and the consumer), and when the smoke cleared release the financial institutions back into the wilds of the private sector, albeit broken up – so as to prevent future moral hazard – and under the scrutiny of a much deeper regulatory regime.

If this had been done, the country would already be on the mend, Europe would have had a road map, and Japan might have had some regret, instead of looking upon the American economic scene knowingly.

Instead we crawl along, Japanese style, in global economic malaise.

The great thing, however, about the predicament the U.S. finds itself in is the President and the Congress have a tremendous opportunity; that is to say, the nation's economic situation is so dire that they have a golden moment to address real problems, rather than use the Fed and monetary policy as a crutch, or throwing more money at a problem, which is the standard fiscal audible in Washington. The Fed has used up all its monetary policy ammunition, and is gambling with intermediate and long term health of the dollar with each new round of quantitative easing (not to mention severe inflation). Moreover, this blog argues that as long as the Fed continues to throw money at the banks, instead putting caveats and conditions on QE3 and its use, expect more of the same: in short the Fed is just enabling the banks. The Federal budget is in shambles, so that each new round of fiscal stimulus actually creates greater debt or taxation (both of which are, ultimately, contractionary). In short, the fiscal policy shell game we have been privy to for the last couple of decades is played out.

This means that the President and the Congress must address real problems head on, if they are to pull the nation out of this mess. And since we all agree jobs is priority one, this means the government must address impediments to job creation. Some of the largest hindrances to job creation are: the insipid taxation monopolies impose upon the American public, a house marketing that is illiquid and still in decline, and banks that do not function in their traditional role, that of lending money to the private sector (but rather, gamble with bailout money in the stock market, commodities, or in offshore investments, a la BRIC nations).

And we are already seeing signs that the President is making an effort to confront some of these issues: namely, by taking on the AT&T/T-Mobile combination, and in filing suit, via Freddie and Fannie, against the Wall Street Cartel that defrauded and took down this nation's economy.

This blog has made the argument over many editorials that the nation's monopolies, like Big Oil, Big Pharma, and the Wall Street banking cartel, create a huge drag on the U.S. and global economy and in fact, are a detriment to the many U.S. businesses that operate, legitimately, in competitive environments.

Why? Because when you're a monopoly, if demand is inelastic enough, you can charge pretty much whatever you damn well please, and the resulting tax on society (read: usurious profits) kills discretionary spending, kills jobs, and saps economic opportunity.

It's the Republican supply side argument applied to private sector monopolistic taxation; it's the mirror of the Laffer curve held up to opprobrious monopolistic profits.

The Department of Justice law suit against the AT&T/T-Mobile combination, hopefully, sends a message to the nation's monopolies and oligopolies that it is no longer open season on the American consumer, the economic engine that drives demand and top line growth. If the DOJ was properly funded not only could it take a harder line on future M & A activity, where appropriate; but it might begin to revisit some of the past combinations that occurred over the last couple of decades, and take on industries that prey upon Americans, such as big oil.

Besides with stock prices trending down, the breakup value of some of these too big to fail institutions is greater than their present market cap. In shorthand, stockholders, too, would benefit from knocking some of these Goliaths down to size.

The Federal Housing Finance Agency law suit against the Wall Street cartel is, possibly, another effort by this administration to tackle a becalmed U.S. economy. An effort that could potentially force Wall Street banks into reorg. And what is the problem? Many bailouts later, many uber banks are still financial basket cases, loaded up with impaired assets, illiquid assets, and much of it erroneously valued on their balance sheets. Tack on billions of liabilities in prospective litigation costs and outcomes, over underwriting fraud, securities fraud, and robo-signing from the 2008 debacle, and if these firms were audited under legitimate "mark to market" accounting guidelines, many banks would have to be restructured, immediately (which means write downs, and relief for the American consumer that could turn this economic ship around).

As it stands however, the banks are in denial, management teams are intransigent with siege mentality, and bank investment is focused not upon American business, but upon on playing the stock market, as noted recently by **Alan Abelson in** *Barron's Magazine*: "… banks have gone whole hog into high frequency trading, which accounts for seventy percent of the turnover on the exchanges."

And we wonder why American small business is shut down, crippled and can't find a banker to lend them a dime....it's because the banks are gambling on Wall Street with U.S. bailout money, or choking on sovereign debt.

If this administration finally forces Wall Street to restructure, directly or indirectly, through any number of means (litigation or regulatory), it could unlock the key to economic recovery by unfreezing credit markets, and clearing out residential and commercial real estate markets; in short the President appears to be rolling up his sleeves and tackling some of the key road blocks to economic recovery (albeit not as aggressively as we would like): bank restructuring, consumer debt restructuring, and reining in job killing monopolies, like the Wall Street cartel.

The administration appears to be on the right path, the question is can and will Obama seize the moment, or is it too late to have a real impact on the economy and the 2012 Election results? With his presidency under threat by unemployment and underemployment, President Obama maybe pressed into taking bold action.

Power is never dearer as when it is fleeting or under threat.

Undoubtedly, taking on banks could take awhile, with opaque accounting rules being what they are, the banks can hide their insolvency for years, and the DOJ, SEC, FTC, CFTC, Et Al., are all being held back, budgetarily, by the Republican lead congress. As such the Republican Party, who proudly withholds money from these regulatory bodies, would appear to be in favor of job killing monopolies, and the credit and housing market's worst nightmare, the Wall Street cartel.

P.S.

And the other shoe that must drop if the jobs issue is to be addressed is globalization and unfair trade practices; that is to say, the fallacy of "free trade" must be tackled. Ronald Reagan, as reported by the Cato Institute, was one of the greatest protectionist Presidents of the 20th Century, despite his rhetoric. And after decades of Republican and Democratic administrations exporting U.S. jobs offshore, it's time for both parties to emulate Reagan and start negotiating fair trade agreements that benefit U.S. labor and the U.S. tax base. But that is for another editorial and another day.

Coming Soon to the Street…. A Nixon Moment?

"How strange is the illusion by which men sustain themselves!" – Doctor Henry Kissinger

By J.M. Hamilton (10-9-11)

"He stopped at the door of the Lincoln bedroom. And he suggested that he and I pray there together. There was no good way to end that evening or to put a period to such a tempestuous career. And I am not sure that this was not as meaningful as any other and more appropriate than most. Nixon's recollection is that he invited me to kneel with him, and that I did so. My own recollection is less clear on whether I actually knelt. It is a trivial distinction. In whatever posture, I was filled with a deep sense of awe which seemed its own meaning so that I did not know exactly what to pray for. A passage of Aeschylus kept running through my mind – the verse that, as it happened, was a favorite of one of Nixon's obsessions, Robert Kennedy:

Pain that cannot forget

Falls drop by drop

Upon the heart

Until in our despair

There comes wisdom

Though the awful

Grace of God

Shortly after midnight — after about a half hour in the Lincoln Bedroom — I returned to my White House office. Within a few moments Nixon called. I must not remember our encounter that evening as a sign of weakness, he said. He hoped that I would keep in mind the times when he had been strong. How strange is the illusion by which men sustain themselves! There were many occasions that Nixon identified with strength that made me uncomfortable. This evening when he barred his soul I saw a man of tenacity and resilience.   And so I told the stricken President that if I ever spoke of that evening, it would be with respect. He had honored me by permitting me to share with him his last free night in the White House where so many memories had united us."

August 7, 1974 – Henry Kissinger, Secretary of State – from the book, *Years of Upheaval*

Hardcore! And if you saw the speech two days later, Nixon's farewell address to his staff, you knew it was an iconic event in American politics, if not the key political event in the last hundred years: where a man of humble origins had climbed to the pinnacle of success, culminating in his 1972 landslide victory, only to see it all come crashing down.   Nixon said it best: "It's not the crime that kills you, it's the cover up."   The creator of the EPA, the author of wage and price controls, and the underwriter of double digit inflation (as America left the gold standard and monetary supply was goosed to aid Nixon's '72 re-election bid), would appear to be some whacked out liberal freak by today's Republican Party standards. But he was one of the brightest individuals to ever enter the White House, and on foreign policy he was a genius, witness the ultimate cold warrior's embrace of Red China, all the better to drive a wedge between Soviet – Sino relations. At the end of the day, Nixon was hoisted upon his own petard, and America sat paralyzed for over a year, glued to the televised Watergate hearings. The resulting "Nixon Moment," so well described by Doctor Kissinger, is forever branded upon the American psyche.   And indeed that is what ultimately makes this country great.

No one is above the law, at least not in the long run.

Could a similar moment of truth be coming to Wall Street? All the signs point to yes. After three years of economic decay and misery, a continuation of the financial crisis from 2008 to this present day, and watered down financial regulation and rules…. The Nixon Moment may soon be visited upon the Street. Fate appears to demand it. After all, Wall Street and European banks, and our elected officials governing same, appear to have learned little from the events that transpired in the fall of 2008, events that appear to be overtaking us all, here and now in real time.

$$$ Many economist and insiders agree that the primary reason the U.S. economy has not regained its footing is a stagnant housing market. And the root cause of this stagnation is the banks. Not only can they not foreclose upon a property, but for the very same reasons, I suspect these same banks are reluctant to refinance and write down mortgages. To back up for a second, allowing consumers to refinance at record low interest rates would give consumers (aka ordinary Americans) more dollars in their pockets, that is to say discretionary income, the spark that could drive this economy forward, and transform an illiquid housing market back into recovery. Writing down these same loans to market value would send the U.S. economy into overdrive: recession over!

The banks, and the governments, unwillingness to allow refinancing all goes back to debt securitization and the MERS system or the electronic registry of mortgages. As we know and have widely read, mortgage foreclosure has fallen apart because of shoddy paper work, an inability to find out what bank or institutions actually possesses the mortgage, and an apparent failure of the MERS system, etc. Plus banks also benefit, to some degree, from a seized up mortgage foreclosure process, since they no longer have to write down impaired assets on their balance sheets. These very same reasons may also account for why banks are reluctant to refinance mortgages, which has been painfully slow. The short answer? During the housing boom, banks securitized mortgages and sold them to wealthy individuals and large institutional investors (Freddie and Fannie, et al.), who have come to expect a certain rate of return; however, if these same mortgages were suddenly refinanced at lower rates than the financial returns to the owners of CDOs would suddenly drop below expectations. And there's already an entire industry built upon litigating against the banks, which created collateralized debt obligations (CDOs), with billions in prospective legal fees and settlements on the line. With the banks already under attack for securities fraud, lousy mortgage underwriting, and client double-dealing, the last headache they need is to lower the returns on CDO products, or to write down assets through debt forgiveness.

How big is this problem? The New York Times reports that half the mortgages holders in the state of Arizona are underwater. And nationwide one in five mortgage holders are a couple of fathoms below the surface, carrying debt above the value of their homes at approximately 700 to 800 billion dollars. That's almost a trillion dollars that could be funneled back into the economy, not to mention interest on same, instead of into the hands of banks, wealthy institutional and sovereign investors. This same article goes on to report that even the Federal Housing Finance Authority is against debt refinancing, in direct contrast to the Obama administration's stated refinancing goals. And the oft given reason the tax payer supported banks, and the tax payer owned Freddie and Fannie won't forgive debt or refinance…. Well, these fine upstanding tax payer funded organizations are all very concerned about… wait for it….. here's the punch line…. consumer "moral hazard."

$$$ Meanwhile, the sovereign debt crisis threatens to implode in Europe, quite possibly pushing a troubled world economy over the brink.   Despite assurances from Treasury Secretary Geithner, in last week's congressional testimony, that the fiscal and monetary crisis in Europe doesn't threaten the U.S. directly, J.M. Hamilton, and many of our readers, understand the opposite to be true.

"Our direct financial exposure to those governments and their financial institutions is quite small, but Europe is so large and so closely integrated with the U.S. and world economies that a severe crisis in Europe could cause significant damage by undermining confidence and weakening demand." – Treasury Secretary Geithner.

The "closely integrated" that the Treasury Secretary is referring to would be the systematic risk posed by the six hundred trillion dollar derivative/swaps market, underwritten by Wall Street banks. Derivatives/Swaps, legitimately, provide insurance against bank and sovereign default; derivatives/swaps, illegitimately, fuel gambling, speculation, and unprecedented economic risk to the citizens of the world. Of course it is derivatives, hybrids, and swaps that nearly brought down the world economy in 2008, a la AIG. Wall Street has and continues to lobby for an unfettered and unregulated derivative/swaps market place (i.e. a continuation of the financial Wild West show, which is ultimately financed by the U.S. taxpayer).   The banks get the profits from this unregulated – black -market, and the tax payer enjoys the privilege of cleaning up the mess. There's just one problem.   Nobody on the planet, individually or collectively, has several trillion, or even tens of trillions, to put up if European defaults trigger these swaps. Simultaneously, the U.S. Commodity Futures Trading Commission keeps putting off rule making on these financial weapons of mass destruction; and likewise in Europe, the regulation of these products continues to be delayed and watered down.

No wonder Mr. Geithner likes to travel across the pond, and tell his European brothers to continue to bailout insolvent governments and insolvent banks.   Default, after all, just might trigger financial Armageddon.

$$$ Election season, and the Republican Party is trotting out the same old failed fables, only the message has grown more radical and shrill. Ayn Rand has become the Party's goddess, and the problem with our economy, per the leading candidates, is excessive government regulation; such irony when Wall Street proves, again and again, that the economic problems staring the nation down are the lack of government rules and regulation. Meanwhile the only viable candidate, Mitt Romney, visits Jamie Dimon on Wall Street and makes pledges to boost military spending beyond the obscene amounts already spent (all the better to take the nation to war in the future, so as to distract our citizens from the economic Hiroshima that three decades of free market ideology have visited upon us all). So much for fiscal sanity. Meanwhile the only rational GOP candidate, John Huntsmen, isn't even in consideration or a serious contender for nomination. Mr. Huntsmen is too establishment, too Herbert Walker Bush, too, well, uh... sane, cultivated and erudite, when all the Molotov throwers within the Tea-Party movement want is to do the plutocracy's bidding and dismantle government once and for all. The smartest GOP candidate would appear to be New Jersey Governor, Chris Christie, who decided not to run. Brilliant!

And the ultimate bellwether of the times we live in…. my mother recently came to me and asked if she should pull her retirement money out of stock and bond mutual funds, and place said funds into FDIC insured accounts?

"Yes, mom, and while you are at it, buy some gold on the next dip. It's all about capital preservation now, thanks to the Fed."

They say there are no atheist in fox holes, and that on the weekend after 9-11 normally empty churches and synagogues were filled to the rafters. My guess is that a Nixon Moment is not too far around the bend for our elected officials and the Wall Street plutocracy. I pray not, but the writing appears to be on the Street. Could the next boom market be in Bible, Torah, and journals of faith publishing?

And, possibly, coming to the Street soon, the sound of rampaging bulls, albeit not the kind of "bulls" we normally associate with the Street – signifying a rallying market. No the bulls I have in mind maybe covered in Kevlar and armed with mace, rubber tipped bullets, and riot shields, all the better to protect the denizens on the corner of Wall and Broad from angry U.S. citizens.

P.S. "Alas, how terrible is wisdom, when it brings no profit to the wise."
– Sophocles

Fear and Loathing – Globally

By J.M. Hamilton (10-16-11)

"Politics is the art of controlling your environment." – **Hunter S. Thompson**

"Strange memories on this nervous night in Las Vegas. Five years later? Six? It seems like a lifetime, or at least a Main Era—the kind of peak that never comes again. San Francisco in the middle sixties was a very special time and place to be a part of. Maybe it meant something. Maybe not, in the long run . . . but no explanation, no mix of words or music or memories can touch that sense of knowing that you were there and alive in that corner of time and the world. Whatever it meant. . . .

History is hard to know, because of all the hired bullshit, but even without being sure of "history" it seems entirely reasonable to think that every now and then the energy of a whole generation comes to a head in a long fine flash, for reasons that nobody really understands at the time—and which never explain, in retrospect, what actually happened.

There was madness in any direction, at any hour. If not across the Bay, then up the Golden Gate or down 101 to Los Altos or La Honda. . . . You could strike sparks anywhere. There was a fantastic universal sense that whatever we were doing was right, that we were winning. . . .

And that, I think, was the handle—that sense of inevitable victory over the forces of Old and Evil. Not in any mean or military sense; we didn't need that. Our energy would simply prevail. There was no point in fighting—on our side or theirs. We had all the momentum; we were riding the crest of a high and beautiful wave. . . .

So now, less than five years later, you can go up on a steep hill in Las Vegas and look West, and with the right kind of eyes you can almost see the high-water mark—that place where the wave finally broke and rolled back."

- *Hunter S. Thompson, Fear and Loathing in Las Vegas, Circa 1971*

Could a tide of sixties idealism, a tide- also – of pure economic and political survival, be rolling back in? As I explained to my Texas friend, Bubba, this week, while the caricature of the sixties is one of free love, drugs, and tie dye, the reality is the sixties were a time of political rebellion against the establishment and the economic-political elite.   The military industrial complex and the politicians, who fed same, LBJ/Nixon, put the fear of god into all classes of society with the Draft and Vietnam War.   Americans felt excluded from the decision making process that significantly impacted their lives, with their son's and daughter's – of all classes of society – drafted into a badly managed war that no one appreciated or wanted, except for the power elite, the corporations, and stockholders, who profit from war.

Separately, the social fabric was torn further when Post WWII black servicemen and GIs, treated as equals in Europe, returned to America's Jim Crow, and decided they had enough. These black men and women, who had risked their lives for America to help defeat Nazism, and would later help stop the tide of Communism, were not going to allow themselves any longer to be marginalized and excluded from the American dream.   And a mass movement was born.

The resulting rebellion, the sixties, was born out of desperation and a feeling that the political elite, and the corporations who rule same, had ignored, or worse, abandoned them.   In short, this was a rebellion born of fear, a struggle over life and death, and the realignment of economic and political responsibilities and sensitivities. Once the goals were realized (the end of the Vietnam War, and much later the end of the Draft, and the birth of civil rights), the better part of sixties rebellion was eventually co-opted into the mainstream, while the excesses of the movement were used by the establishment to tar and vilify it, as run by *dilettantes* and undesirables. Might history repeat itself once again?

Today's budding struggles in both Europe and the U.S., indeed globally, are also driven by fear and instincts for survival, and the feeling of societal abandonment by the plutocracy, who are catering to banks and major corporations, at the expense of the politically disenfranchised. People may laugh at the naiveté and the innocence of the Occupy Wall Street crowd, but they are possibly the vanguard of economic and political rebellion that will be with the U.S. and Europe for as long as the financial crisis continues; and as the liabilities and excesses of Wall Street, and European banks, are transferred from the private sector onto the backs of those who can afford it the least, the poor and the middle class, this crisis is likely to be with us for awhile. With Japan pointing the way to America's and Europe's foreseeable future, one of endless bank bailouts, wealth destruction, and an economic fugue of recession and depression, Occupy Wall Street is a possible prelude to much darker forces that could, eventually, rip the lid off social stability. This nascent movement will likely metastasize into what remains of the middle class, as the real unemployment and underemployment rate continues to rise, economic opportunity and the safety net is rent and shredded by cries for fiscal austerity, and reactionary forces continue to advocate for and insist upon living with the fantasy/delusion of a free market economic system (when the reality is we are all living under quasi- free market/socialist regimes, globally).

If we examine how America and Europe got here, it appears that the worst excesses of both capitalism and socialism have collided, and reanimated into crony capitalism and crony democracy, the worst of all worlds. Let's then examine some of the recent political and economic events and trends for a snap shot in how we got here and what might be done.

As Mr. Thompson said, "Politics is the art of controlling your environment," and the plutocracy manages the 99% of us, politically, like a virtuoso violinist plays a Stradivarius. The plutocracy actually fears democracy and the law of large numbers, because it is something that they cannot control; but where there is a will there is often a way, for what the the one percent lack for in votes, they more than make up for it in money, and money is how the one percent control "democracy," their political environment, and 99% of us. With the Roberts Court's *Citizen's United* decision, the plutocracy can control the public through a flood of unlimited political campaign contributions, and hence control party nominees, the political parties themselves, and who gets elected in the vast majority of instances. Money then is the river that feeds the political sea, and controls and reigns in populist impulses, at the expense of the majority. Money controls the politicians, the political message, and the issues that are debated and discussed (e.g. during the recent Republican presidential debates, the issue of unemployment, bank bailouts, and possible solutions for the housing market are rarely if ever mentioned or discussed in any kind of detail). These same power brokers to a very large degree also control the media and its output, and hence the questions posed to candidates. Those politicians, who are elected, are so beholden to monied interests that they might as well be remote controlled robots, operated via remote feed; these politicians, in turn, vote for and maintain the lower tax rates that allow for the massive accumulation of wealth into the hands of a few, who in turn use this font to perpetuate their power (i.e. through the subversion of democracy).

If you think I'm just some crank with too much time on his hands, let's hear what the King-Daddy of all plutocrats has to say on the matter, Mr. Warren Buffett (the living embodiment of F.D.R.):

"There has been class warfare going on," Buffett, 81, said in a Sept. 30 interview with Charlie Rose on PBS. "It's just that my class is winning. And my class isn't just winning, I mean we're killing them."

The global power elite also use their money to subvert populist uprisings, internationally. Witness the Royal House of Saud' deft and expert management of the *Arab Spring* (recently written about in **Foreign Affairs**), with the removal of the Egyptian Dictator, which was replaced by the far more oppressive Egyptian military and intelligence apparatus. The Egyptian military, of course, dominates the Egyptian economy and politics. The prosecution of Egyptian President Mubarak is nothing more than a side show, a distraction, red meat for the masses, while the popular uprising is subverted and controlled from within, by the money and power of the oil rich Saudis and the rise of the Saudi supported Muslim Brotherhood. This example reminds us of how another popular uprising in America, the Tea Party movement, was co-opted and harnessed by the billionaire Koch Brothers, ultimately to serve their own ends (i.e. the continuation of their privileged tax status, and to insure the rules and regulations that govern their industries remain pro-Koch – all under the guise of perpetuating free market principles).

Of course the plutocracy is all for the "free market," as long as it serves their ends, but the free market also has a nasty downside, which is bankruptcy and putting corporate management teams on the street when they fail. Hence, the plutocracy is not in favor of the free market when it threatens their own interests, and this is when they go running to the government tit for bailout monies (e.g. Wall Street during the 2008 financial crisis, up to the present day). Hence, the plutocracy also favors socialism, when it favors them, although you'll never hear them endorse it.

What this all adds up to is crony capitalism and crony democracy. As predicted by J.M. Hamilton, the masses it seems, the 99%, are beginning to wake up, and they don't like what they see: the instability the massive concentration of wealth creates, and the subversion of democratic institutions that results from same.

The ninety-nine percent are controlled politically and economically, like a puppet on a string. Economically, globalism, free market ideology, and free trade dogma also insure that the masses and the message are controlled, via the number of jobs that are made available, and the opportunity that is created, when, where, and in what country, by the oligarchs and interlocking boards.

"Free trade" is nothing more than regulatory, tax and labor arbitrage by any other name. Large multi-national manufacturers scour the globe, looking for the most advantageous trade laws, regulatory regimes, labor costs, and tax laws and rates. Factor in the logistical costs of transporting foreign manufactured goods and services to their ultimate destination/market, and you have "free trade." There's just one problem, practiced in the extreme, arbitrage leaves advanced economies, and its citizens and labor, in a state of economic and political paralysis, as production, jobs, and tax revenue are shifted to emerging markets. And while advanced economies and consumers maybe the beneficiaries of cheaper imported goods, from arbitrage and emerging markets (i.e. BRIC nations), those inexpensive goods and services don't do the consumer a damn bit of good, if said consumer is unemployed. At the end of the day, one can't dine on iPad.

To combat "free trade" dogma, and encourage emerging markets to develop their own self –sustaining middle class and economies, America needs to embrace the actions of President Reagan and focus on **fair trade agreements** that benefit American labor and the U.S. tax base. The best way to do that is via trade policy reciprocity, that is to say, with the imposition of taxes and tariffs upon imported products that neutralizes to the manufacturer the benefits that accrue from arbitrage. Until there is global parity in tax laws, labor markets, and rules and regulation governing industry and business, there is no other way than import taxes, tariffs and trade barriers, unless Americans are satisfied with high unemployment, declining economic opportunity, deficit spending, a shrinking tax base, and the resulting social upheaval. In short, if you like one in five Americans being on the government dole (and a 25% childhood poverty rate), with those numbers likely to rise, then continue to embrace free trade. This is why the Obama administrations support and passage of three Bush-era free trade agreements last week was so disappointing to many Democrats and labor.

Reciprocity should also be the U.S. tax policy in regards corporate profit repatriation.

By managing the economy, the plutocracy also manages our elected officials and their prospects for re-election. By inflating prices at the pump, or inflating the price of basic consumer goods and services (or by decreasing the number of jobs, as a result of same), through financial speculation, or simply by controlling supply, and the deployment of capital, the monied interests can also expand and contract the economy, and the political fortunes of our elected officials. President Obama and some of the "manufactured economic conditions" he has had to contend with, some possibly of his own making, immediately come to mind.

What can be done then to prevent the resulting societal unrest? These proposals are neither novel nor new; they are basically, just common sense.

Push for higher tax rates on the rich, who are better organized and smarter than we are, or certainly have the resources to accentuate their god given talents, in the furtherance of their goal of global economic domination. By raising the tax rates upon the rich, we effectively de-fang them and preserve democracy. It also pushes the plutocracy to focus and work harder on sustaining and preserving their own wealth and status – this means they have less time to "screw over" the 99%. Republicans like to wax nostalgic about the 50's and the Eisenhower Presidency, when the upper income tax rate was 90%... why not return there?

Advocate and push elected officials for caps on campaign contributions, the amounts of money that can be spent on campaigns, and push for limits on the amount of time our politicians can campaign. The year around campaign cycle, with unlimited flow of money, has lead to an abdication of responsibility, and a vacuum that the elite exploit. The Supreme Court might not like it, and view such restrictions as a violation of free speech, but in its present incarnation, the Roberts Court is just another plutocratic tool. Besides, our system of checks and balances allows our legislative body to create new laws to counteract the worst tendencies/rulings of this judicial body, and vice versa. The judicial smoke screen about money and free speech aside, what makes a democracy, ultimately, is the citizenry's ability to vote (not the amount of money spent on a campaign, or the duration of the election cycle).

Encourage your elected officials to adopt fair trade agreements that protect America, American labor, and the U.S. tax base. America has been exploited long enough by multi-national manufacturing interests to maximize their profit margin, and developing nations, as a dumping ground for their social problems (i.e. poverty and unemployment). It's time for emerging markets to create their own advanced economies and their own middle class, all the better to create greater opportunity for all, globally, and as a countervailing force against the downward economic spiral advanced economies present to the world today. At the end of the day is the world better off with more advanced economies or fewer?

Advocate against excessive corporate combinations, oligopoly and monopoly. We have seen time and time again, where these combinations are risk management nightmares, lead to greater inefficiency, and ultimately failure (e.g. UBS just lost a couple billion and saw their CEO dismissed). The failure of these institutions often leads to great economic stress, and bailouts at the public's expense (take for instance, the Wall Street cartel). What these excessive combinations do achieve, however, is the greater enrichment of the elite at the expense of their clients, consumers, and the general public.

Communism doesn't work, which is the ultimate combination of the means of production under a single entity…. Why would the free market's equivalent to communism, monopolies and oligopolies, work any better?

It's time for an honest conversation with the American public, and the citizens of the world, about the right mix of free market principles and socialism, as a matter of economic policy. I call it the big girl/big boy conversation. The free market demagoguery that reactionary forces have foisted upon us all for so long has lead to some of the greatest economic and political abuses in the 20th and early 21st centuries, often with the 99% paying the price. Socialism, and free markets in there purest forms, presently, do not exist, and would lead to the worst of all worlds: it's time that the public was educated accordingly. Therefore, what should be open to debate and discussion, among the electorate and candidates for office, is the appropriate capitalistic and socialistic mix within the economy and society?

The plutocracy is at a cross roads… ultimately, they can rein themselves in via reform, or allow events to continue to spin out of control, and watch in dismay at the rising tide of economic instability and social unrest. The current picture is none too bright for anybody: the 99% or 1%. Ultimately, the political wave that broke in the sixties and receded, so well described by Mr. Thompson, did so because the plutocracy yielded to public demands for a more politically just and civil society. However, this victory did not come easily or quickly, and was paid for at tremendous cost.

Now the question, some forty to fifty years later, is will the plutocracy yield and allow for a more economically just society? There's only one way to contain the fear and loathing unleashed, globally, and that is to contain the worst excesses of the ruling class. Flexibility is key.

P.S. *On this date in history, the NY Times reports: "October 16, 1793-Marie Antoinette was beheaded during the French Revolution," seems that the Parisian 99% were not content with their cake.*

The Good, The Bad and The Ugly

By J.M. Hamilton (10-23-11)

"Such ingratitude after all the times I have saved your life." – **Clint Eastwood (aka The Good)**

Perhaps I'm dating myself, but I still think **The Good, The Bad and The Ugly (GBU)** is one of the greatest movies ever filmed. Shot by Mr. Sergio Leone, GBU is the final act of the Dollars Trilogy, starring Clint Eastwood (as Blondie, the Good), Lee Van Cleef (as Angel Eyes or the Bad), and Eli Wallach (as Tuco, the Ugly). Together these three seek their fortune in a Civil War landscape, with all the mayhem and moral ambiguity that often surrounds war. For even "the Good" in this movie doesn't exactly have a heart of gold. Mr. Eastwood was no Gene Autry, or even Gary Cooper, and the story would be disfigured if he was. The menace coming out of Mr. Eastwood's eyes is only matched by pure evil pouring forth from Mr. Cleef's fearsome visage; and Tuco, Mr. Wallach, looks throughout the movie like a rat that has been cornered and can't decide to fight or flee but either way, you know better than to turn your back. Tuco is always trying to figure out his next three moves.

This story of course is a love story, although the love interest is gold.

Without giving away the ending, the movie concludes at the center of Sad Hill Cemetery in what is referred to by some as a **Mexican Standoff**; that is a three-way gunfighter face off, in which almost assuredly someone is going down. Only one of the three knows in which grave a cache of gold is buried and a ticket to a much easier life.

Today's global financial crisis is not dissimilar to a Mexican Standoff, with the three principle actors in our play being the public, the banks, and the politicians. Politicians are being held accountable by the public, who are beginning to reassert themselves after a long period of bank bailouts, and wealth transfer from governments/public to the banks (whether it be through the inter-generational wealth larceny that is the Fed's quantitative easing, or via an alphabet soup of government programs designed to give the banks billions at every turn, or through a stream of favorable court ruling that are pro-bank). The American and European public has never really had say in any of these government programs, Fed policy or judicial rulings, and has not been the beneficiary of trillions in government largess. No that degree of love and financial assistance appears only destined for the one percent, the banks. And now, *res publica,* the 99%, is beginning to reassert itself with violence in the streets, protests, and the power of the ballot box (its weapons in our story).

Of course, the banks too, perhaps presently best personified by Deutsche Bank's Mr. Ackerman, play their part, literally holding a financial and economic gun to the heads of the politicians and the public as well. And the bank's preferred financial weapon of choice is a global web of credit default swaps and derivatives contracts with hundreds of trillions in notional value. That and the banks, if they are made unhappy, just might go on a capital strike, the equivalent to a nuclear first strike upon the global economy that governments and the public depend upon. The politicians caught in the middle realize the solutions to the sovereign debt crisis, which have been peddled to date, are no longer working: monetary easing, fiscal stimulus, and sovereign debt piled upon more sovereign debt. In short the political game of Russian Roulette many *pols* have been playing has nearly run its course.

The politicians have increasingly found themselves cornered, faced with choices and solutions that may cost them their careers, outright public revolt at election time, or cut off from future bank contributions to their re-election campaigns. Clearly Greece and many sovereign nations need debt restructuring, and the banks – prolific holders of sovereign debt – don't want to take the hit (i.e. "haircuts" and write downs). Nor does bank management want their stock holdings and options watered down with public money and yet another government capital infusion (such a buzz-kill to any bank CEO's stock portfolio).

The public, and in particular within Europe, the German community , are tired of carrying the freight for the excesses of others.

The "excesses" being: nations and politicians, who have lived beyond their means, and who refuse to hold the banks accountable; and of course, banks, who thrive upon the incompetence and moral depravity of some elected officials, and insist upon (and obtain through regulatory and government capture) the continuance of an unregulated and an opaque CDS/Swaps market …. all the better to hold the public, world governments, and economies hostage, guarantee future bank bailouts, and insist upon fiscal austerity – born by the middle and lower classes – as the solution to the debt crisis.

Politicians and banks are staring back at the public, who has learned too to vote themselves largess, via social spending. Ah the pitfalls of democracy.

I don't' have to tell you who the Good, the Bad or the Ugly is in our current picture… you can figure it out, but let's just say that no one actor is entirely pure, but some of the players in this drama, clearly, are less evil.

Either way, this movie too, will have a denouement, and just like in **The Good, The Bad and The Ugly**, there will be winners and losers, and someone will ride away with the gold.

Mexican standoffs are never pretty.

P.S. For those who didn't like last week's editorial, *Fear and Loathing – Globally,* **and its central message against free trade/arbitrage…. Please take a look at China with all its barriers to trade, and its tremendous economic success, and tell me once again why free trade is beneficial to America?**

Democracy in Flames and Sovereignty under Fire!

By J.M. Hamilton (11-11-11)

"Thus was parliamentary democracy finally interred in Germany. Parliament had turned over its constitutional authority to Hitler and thereby committed suicide…" - **William L. Shirer, The Rise and Fall of the Third Reich**

It doesn't take much to overturn a democracy or democratic institutions: economic chaos, unchecked fear, a couple of gallons of gasoline, and a few matches.   That's all it took in Germany in the 1930's, when the Nazis burned down the Reichstag (Germany's emblem of democracy and the equivalent to the U.S. Congress). Communist were of course blamed and used as scapegoats. In the resulting fear and turmoil, civil rights were suspended by Germany's President Hindenburg, allowing Hitler to round up and exterminate any and all political opposition without due process. A short time later the aptly named "Enabling Act" was passed and a dictatorship was born – *all perfectly legal and sanctioned by the state*. Hitler said the suspension of both German civil liberties and democracy itself, was all for the German peoples protection. It was through fear and uncertainty that Hitler seized that which the Nazis could not obtain democratically, hegemonic and absolute power over the German state.

Today in Europe and America we see the erosion of democratic institutions at every turn.   And what global banking oligarchs cannot accomplish by a flood of money into the political process, or by the purchase of politicians, is won through the coercive power of the state, as former bank executives cruise through the revolving door and operate key government positions – *again, all perfectly legal and sanctioned by the state*. (e.g. Witness the recent coronation of Goldman Sachs alum, Mario Draghi, as head of the E.U.' central bank, who is said to have wrote the book on hiding government debt via the use of swaps and derivative products; or check out another Goldman alum who runs the Commodities Futures Trading Commission (CFTC), Mr. Gensler… and some people wonder why the CFTC has delayed implementation of new derivative/swaps rules and regulations?)

Per the New York Times' Thomas Friedman, there's a reason why 61 house members sit on the congressional Financial Services Committee.

In the cradle of democracy last week, Greek Prime Minister, George Papandreou, dared defy the established order of things, that of *banking uber alles*, and actually sought a referendum by the people on the proposed E.U. Greek bailout package. Now this bailout package promises a write down on Greek debt of 50%, when the market values the haircut to bond holders at no less than 80% (what a deal for the bank or institution who picks up this debt at the fireside sale price, because if the bailout holds, they will more than double their money, all at the expense and suffering of the taxpayer – both U.S. and European); moreover, the proposed bailout would in all probability consign Greece to austerity and economic decline for at least a decade or more. Not that the alternative, default, hyper-inflation, capital flight magnified, and a return to the drachma, would have been much better. But the resulting outcry from the European and U.S. political elites was so stunning and sharp in response to the referendum, it merely proves the point that the J.M. Hamilton blog made in an editorial a couple of weeks ago (entitled, **Fear and Loathing – Globally**), namely, that the elites fear democracy. Mr. Papandreou retreated and cancelled democracy/the referendum, which would have finally given Greek citizens an opportunity to weigh in on their nation's financial crisis.

Meanwhile, in Italy, a media mogul and a septuagenarian playboy, also known at the Italian Prime Minister, has "voluntarily" submitted his government and its budget to International Monetary Fund (IMF) oversight and scrutiny. Now, submitting your government budget for IMF review is very much like the indignity, and an infringement upon sovereignty, that the Greeks have already endured and continue to suffer, that of sovereign budgetary oversight by interested third parties.

Moreover, it is an indignity and threat to sovereignty that the United States Congress would never tolerate, at least not yet. You've got to hand it to the bankers, however, they would never tarnish and soil their bespoke suits with gasoline and matches. That's entirely unnecessary, especially when the banks can burn down democracy with threats of a "Lehman event," a capital strike, dumping sovereign debt, or by making financial bets against the very nations that have repeatedly bailed them out. (**Note:** In yet another assault on pesky democracy, both the democratically elected Italian and Greek prime ministers, Berlusconi and Papandreaou, are being replaced by "technocrats," which is a fancy word for saying that Messrs. Monti and Papademos are more than likely BBF or Banker Buddies Forever. Messrs Monti and Papademos have not been popularly elected, but will most likely run both Italy and Greece, presumably, for Wall Street's and E.U. Bank benefit.)

Three years after the last financial crisis, politicians are desperate to avoid another "Lehman event," which is code for the global systematic risk posed by international banking, derivatives, and credit default swaps. Aside from the economic damage such an event would cause the global economy, already strained state budgets, and the havoc it would reek upon global currencies, the political elite are worried that the European and U.S. electorate might begin asking very pointed questions. Namely, what have these same politicians done over the last three years to prevent the banking crisis that is unfolding before our eyes, here and now in real time?

And that's a question no politician, who wants to be elected or re-elected, appears to want to answer. Why? Because in the U.S. both political parties share blame for catering to Wall Street, and the lack of rules, regulation, and oversight since the 2008 financial crisis.

At the end of the day, international banking is the tail that has been wagging world governments, democracy, and the global economy with ever more frequent and deleterious effects. Multi-national corporations wised up to the games these Wall Street sharks play a while ago, and have hoarded colossal amounts of cash, in essence becoming their own banks, so as to avoid dealings with same.

But the public isn't quite as fortunate.

Ultimately, the only thing that will rein the banks in, and the threat to global security and stability they represent, is to allow them to fail and subsequently nationalize them. If the global banking model the world is headed towards, willingly or unwillingly, is that of utility banking (i.e. elementary/pedestrian lending without the proprietary trading), then why not nationalize the cartel, install new management, and preserve as many banking jobs as possible, when these institutions inevitably fail again? As it stands, the banks often prey upon anybody or any institution, private or public, they come into contact with; and as often as not operate to the detriment of legitimate business, the world economy, and world governments. World governments are tapped out after bailing out international banking, repeatedly, and now the banks are demanding fiscal austerity, so that governments have the means to bailout the banks, yet again.

And to insure that the global political system continues to favor banks, these same institutions now appear to be installing their own heads of state. Democracy be damned.

Outlawing and unwinding existing *naked shorts* (e.g. speculative derivatives instruments) is also a must, if we are avoid repeating the same mistakes *ad nauseum.* In the last bubble, the speculative instrument of choice was mortgages, and in the coming crisis, as predicted by J.M. Hamilton, it is sovereign debt. In both instances, the banks have suspended all business prudence in exchange for the fast buck, with the full knowledge that governments will bail them out again, since they are too big to fail. Isn't it time to stop this cycle? The failed banking institutions can always be returned to the private sector, post re-org.

As this blog has alluded to before, global democracies, as a general rule, don't allow megalomaniacs to hold and operate standing armies or to possess nuclear weapons (or they do a great deal to suppress, contain, and avoid the reoccurrence of such individuals as Herr Hitler).

Containing these rogues is a matter of global security for world markets and the consumers within those markets.

If that's the case, then why would business leaders and global governments allow something possibly more insidious than nukes, say international banking in its present incarnation, to be left in the hands of private sector dictatorships?

PS: For those who think that our banks, shadow banking, and exchanges are over-regulated... please explain it to the fine investors of MF Global, who relied upon CME -the self- regulating futures trading exchange — to protect their interests. A lot of farmers and investors are missing millions of dollars, because of this unregulated market and exchange, and some could face financial ruin.

A Pending U.S. Workout?

By J.M. Hamilton (11-24-11)

"I know who exactly who I'm talking to, Mr. Croker." Croker's voice was low and strong, but Harry's high grinding whine cut through it. "I'm talking to an individual who owes this bank half a billion dollars and six other banks and two insurance companies two-hundred and eighty-five million more, that's who I am talking to. And you know, there's an old saying here in Atlanta, too, and that saying is 'Money talks, and bullshit walks,' and the time has come to talk with money, Mr. Croker. All I'm telling you is what's already obvious. All I'm telling you are some home truths in the privacy of this room. You wanna throw this thing open to all seven banks and the two insurance companies and have a real workout session? We can do that! Happens all the time. It'll have to be in an auditorium. Nine different lenders? We're talking about more than a hundred people sitting in an auditorium with an audio system and microphones, and it'll be incumbent upon every one of those lenders to pick up a microphone and tell you something over the wall speakers that I'm gonna tell you right now, very quietly, in the this little room, across the table, on behalf of only one lender, PlannersBanc, and it's this Mr. Croker.... " Seeing that Croker was suitably stunned by his belligerence, the Artiste paused for maximum effect and then said in a menacingly calm voice, "This is one of the worse cases of corporate mismanagement... one of the grosses violations of fiduciary obligations.... I've ever seen... And in my job I look down the gullet of mismanagement and malfeasance every day. You and your corporation have taken five hundred million dollars from the bank, Mr. Croker...."

From the book *A Man in Full,* by Tom Wolfe (Writer of *the Right Stuff* and *the Bonfire of the Vanities)*

Can you see it on the horizon? I can.

The workout that is taking place in Greece and in Italy, where popular democracy has been suspended and new heads of state have been installed by the banks, could eventually arrive in the U.S.

Granted European parliamentary democracy makes the pretense of keeping up democratic appearances so much easier.

Mr. Papademos, Greece's new Prime Minister, was formerly employed by the E.U. central bank, and Mr. Monti, Italy's new Prime Minister, does have strong ties to Goldman Sachs (neither were popularly elected); and both bankers/technocrats/prime ministers received the blessing of the E.U.' central banker, former Goldman alum, Mario Draghi.

So how did Europe get here and what does it bode for the U.S.? Greece and Italy are mired in debt, and in both countries the "bond vigilantes" (read: banks, hedge funds, private equity, mutual funds and wealthy individual investors) have driven swaps spreads and state bond yields to the breaking point. The "breaking point" is where interest on the national debt takes up such a large portion of the government budget that states must engage in either fiscal austerity or default. Fiscal austerity is paid for by the 99%. And default threatens the 1%. Default also triggers credit default swaps, and the equivalent to economic Hiroshima or Nagasaki in Athens or Rome. The contagion then spreads to Northern Europe/Deutsche Bank, and across the pond to the corner of Wall and Broad.

To buy more time, and to postpone economic Armageddon, the banks and Germany are presently engaged in something called a workout in Greece and Italy. Now for the uninitiated, a "workout" is a "come to Jesus/Yahweh/Muhammad moment," where bank(s) and creditor meet and all kinds of nastiness ensues. In the private sector, assets might be sold off to repay bank loans, labor cut, new management installed, and the bank may install "friends" on the board of directors. Debt might even be "voluntarily" restructured. That's if things go nicely. An alternative to the aforementioned is bankruptcy, Chapters Seven or Eleven. And although the popular press hasn't picked up on it yet, a workout is exactly what is happening in Greece and Italy right now…. The banks have effectively installed their own men in the key positions in government to workout on state finances.

And as with the private sector, the workout solutions in government are not dissimilar: raise taxes (preferably upon the middle class), cut spending and social services, sell off state assets to the connected bidder (privatize), and stack government with bankers or banker friendly politicians.

So as to avoid a write down or a default, the banks want to squeeze every last drop out of fiscal policy. Think of private equity/shadow banking buying out a company on Friday, popping champagne corks on Saturday night, and handing out pink slips to employees on Monday morning. Choose your analogy.

At the end of the day, the debt must be serviced.

And the banks will do everything in their power to insure that they win, and that the creditor, in this case the public sector – the government/democracy/taxpayer – takes the hit before they do. It's the banker's code! After all, the creditor borrowed the money, and no matter how many financial artifices of war were deployed against said creditor/government/taxpayer, or no matter how usurious the terms, the creditor must pay.

The fact that many of these troubled governments presently under fire for their profligate ways, the U.S. included, bailed out the banks and continue to do so, repeatedly, is an entirely separate matter, as far as the banks are concerned.

In the eyes of the bank, whether it be John Q. Public maxing out his credit card, a major corporation who borrowed one too many hundreds of millions in the face of an economic downturn, or the Sovereign Government of Greece, who hid its fiscal intemperance via advisors from Goldman Sachs and the use of CDS and swaps… they are viewed all the same. They are all freaking dead beats!

Again, how does the public and private sector get here? The parallels are not dissimilar for the private and public sector. It is usually financial mismanagement, combined with rotten timing. The quote from Mr. Wolfe's banker -the man with the Death's Head suspenders – the workout artiste – says it best: *"This is one of the worse cases of corporate mismanagement… one of the grosses violations of fiduciary obligations…. I've ever seen… And in my job I look down the gullet of mismanagement and malfeasance every day."*

For the public sector this means, simply: Politicians have over promised on public services and social programs (or failed to reign in the costs of those programs by conducting fair and honorable negotiations with the vendors for government programs, say Big-Pharma), underfunded their liabilities, low balled taxes to appease the rich (or in the case of Greece haven't even bothered to collect taxes), and presto… you have massive amounts of government debt, that the bankers assume is bullet proof and/or are all too happy to fund. Besides, aside from interest payments, the bankers clean up on the issuance of government debt with fees and commissions, arbitrage generates more fees, and so does CDS, swaps and hedges, which insures government debt or allows gambling against same. The bankers also assume, when it's convenient, that world governments will not default, and can always raise revenue or print additional monies. Always.

Yes, having a little debt or venture capital is all good, when the economy is rocking, the birds are singing, and demographic trends favor your government. But when the advanced economies budgets are shredded by bank bailouts and the resulting chaos, central banks who pushed the pedal to the metal on printing presses, the birds are dying, and demographic trends are sucking the state dry…. Well, it's no time to be beholden to the banker, because bankers don't do sob stories.

If you are a winter enthusiast, don't worry about climate change and it's impact upon ice and snow… why just stop by any Wall Street bank branch, and look into that banker's heart and soul and find a veritable winter wonderland. 'Tis the Season!

But I digress, because as flinty and as cold as a banker might be as an enabler, there's always the enabled. And in the case of the United States of America, the Republican Party "pimped" the nation out to Wall Street, through mismanagement of state finances for the last thirty years. The GOP, or certainly their laissez faire ideology, did it to us. Starting with Reagan, the Republicans gave us the credit card economy, they took the governors off the economic engine of capitalism (by stripping away bank regulation), they floored the printing presses at the Fed (courtesy of the Maestro), and they removed all fiscal sanity with monolithic tax cuts for those who could most afford to pay, the rich. A neo-gilded age was born, complete with excesses that F. Scott Fitzgerald never dreamed of. Western governments were overrun with newly minted plutocrats, bankers, and plutocratic wannabes, complete with Bunga-Bunga parties. Of course, the bankers were there all along, right by the side of the GOP – dispensing campaign contributions and whispering sweet nothings, like 'the economy will roll forever, the good times will last forever, the U.S. is strong – it can always pay down its debt at some future date.' Shortly after the 2008 crash…the mother of all fiscal hangovers kicked in, and now the mirror that reflects the state of the union is fractured… not that many heads of state from that era want to look into the mirror.

When's the last time this country heard profound wisdom from former President Bush (W)? Surely, Mr. Bush has ideas on how to cure the nation's ills. No? Or how about the former VP, the man without a pulse, who said deficits don't matter?

Democracies perish when special interests learn they can vote themselves public largess, and many advanced economies/democracies have often become nations of special interests. This is why strong democratic government with strong government leadership is so important, and the word "NO" is the most powerful word in the English language. Ultimately, to rein this fiscal mess in and remove the bankers from the seats of government, there needs to be real reform on taxation, but just as importantly, on the supply side of the government equation. That is to say, if America wants to get its fiscal house in order, we need leadership who is willing to offend very wealthy and powerful special interests, who provide government services: that would be doctors, hospitals, big pharma, defense contractors, and bankers, just for starters.

Failure to do so may just mean that we see a President Blankfein in our lifetimes. Ah, his hair is not right, make it Prime Minister Dimon.

As this blog has stated previously, J.M.H. will take a tax and spend Liberal, over a borrow and spend Republican any day. Both parties favor big government… the difference between the two parties lies in whom the respective parties believe should be the beneficiary of government largess: the Democrats favor the people, the Republicans favor the Three Bs: banks, big oil, and billionaires. At least with the Democrats, you get fiscal responsibility and you pay as you go. With Republicans you get massive debt and the Wall Street cartel's frosty embrace. I call it a death grip.

Finally, there are some who say that the solution is to turn on the printing presses. But we have already seen this movie. Piling debt on top of more debt, w/out real fiscal reform just buys a little more time and a lot more agony. Ultimately, this global train wreck we are all witnessing has a date with destiny.

And Destiny, she's been stood up and she's pissed!

P.S. We would all do well to remember the last thirty years the next time Republicans and Wall Street propose to privatize Medicare and Social Security.

We'd also do well to remember where Presidential Candidate Romney made his money, with Wall Street's co-evil twin, shadow banking' Private Equity.

And speaking of workouts, how about the workout purchasers of derivatives and swaps are receiving over Greek sovereign debt, presently. The International Swaps and Derivatives Association (ISDA), run by you guessed it, the Wall Street Cartel, appears to be putting pressure on the holders of credit default swaps to "voluntarily" accept a haircut on Greek debt of up to 50%, w/out seeking the insurance protection afforded by same. Seems that the banks, many of whom probably reside on the other side of the transaction, or put another way may in fact be the swaps counterparty, surprise, don't want to pay out. Hence, investors who haven't figured it out already are learning the obvious once again: the banks, who control governments and politicians, write their own rules. Contracts and the rule of law be damned!

What does this bode for the future of the swaps and derivatives market? The impact could be immeasurable. If purchasers of these swaps and derivatives feel that the game is rigged and banks, or counterparties, don't intend to pay out on these insurance products in the event of default – governments, business and individuals will stop purchasing them, and so follows the purchase of debt and other obligations derivatives and swaps are designed to insure.

Happy Thanksgiving!

A Tsunami of Cover-ups and Lies

By J.M. Hamilton (12-4-11)

"As Ferdinand Pecora, the Depression-era prosecutor, is supposed to have said of the events leading to the Wall Street crash of 1929: Pitch darkness was among the bankers' stoutest allies." **- Gretchen Morgenson – NY TIMES**

In a land where back room dealing, and double dealing, in government, banking, and many other facets of our lives, has become the norm, Judge Rakoff's position on the Citigroup/SEC deal was a breath of fresh air.

The Judge's position, unfortunately, would appear to be – by current standards – anachronistic. Mr. Rakoff's appears to be standing against the tide of history, more akin to a tsunami of cover ups and lies, and yelling "Stop – a little honesty and integrity, please!"

Please recall Judge Rakoff, a Federal Judge, was supposed to rubber-stamp a deal between the Securities and Exchange Commission and Citigroup, a bank that has been bailed out by the U.S. taxpayer, *ad nausem*.   In fact last I checked the U.S. government still holds a substantive stake in Citigroup, as a result of the bank's failure in 2008. The "deal" was Citigroup would cough up just north of a quarter billion dollars, and its role in selling, possibly, fraudulent security products, like derivatives and CDO's during the height of the financial crisis, would vanish w/out any admission of responsibility or wrong doing.

How convenient.   And yet this is the norm in our two tiered justice system, where the public deals with one set of courts, and banks get fast track justice with no trial, relatively light fines, and where the fines, themselves, are considered a cost of doing business.   Americans, of course, have become numb to Wall Street's recidivist activities. And so for Judge Rakoff to say "no more," was truly exceptional.

And we can see why the Judge's behavior was novel, almost rebellious: the Wall Street cartel has co-opted our government, regulators, our judicial system, rating agencies, and our laws and law making. Our opaque accounting system is laughable, when we consider how derivatives and swap are not accounted for in financial statements (often only receiving a footnote); and Repos – an accounting maneuver/derivative product that helped bring down MF Global (not to mention Lehman), and with it possibly a billion plus in client money disappearing – are an all too common practice.

Granted Judge Rakoff's decision could possibly mean more trials and the SEC spending more time proving its case against the major banks – at a time when, as recently noted by **Arthur Levitt on Bloomberg Radio (Hosted by Tom Keene and Ken Prewitt)**, Republican's are starving the organization of money and funds. Mr. Levitt is the SEC's former chairmen. The Republicans, lap dog of Wall Street, and advocate and stander bearer for the one percent, quite possibly may believe they are doing "god's work," by supporting a monopolistic cartel and restraining government agencies, like the SEC. However, the SEC is the first, and often only, line of defense against the predatory Wall Street oligopoly, in the protection of ordinary Americans, investors, business – both big and small, and of course, the government, itself.

But can you hardly blame the Republicans? With all that money coming their way from Wall Street, and presidential candidate Romney meeting with Jamie Dimon, (Mr. Romney, himself making his bones on Wall Street with private equity's Bain Capital), why not perpetuate crony capitalism and crony democracy? After all, and gee-whiz, Wall Street paid back its TARP loans with interest….isn't it time to get off the cartel's back?

And therein lies the problem, because as much as Republicans would like to wish away the financial crisis of 2008, and assure us that the banks' have paid back the U.S. taxpayer in full, quite the opposite has in fact happened. The Banks, who have received 7.0 plus trillion in handouts and government benefits, as reported by Bloomberg last week (that's half of U.S. GDP), have not paid for the damage they have caused to the real estate market (the cornerstone of life savings and equity for many Americans), the economy, nor for their share of the fiscal mess our government and economy is in.

Not by a fraction.

Republicans are often portrayed as being unfeeling, uncaring, and against the welfare state… that paradigm does not hold up, however, when the welfare is gifted to the Republican Party's core constituency, the one percent.

So for Judge Rakoff to shine a bright light of truth on an unacceptable practice, tantamount to a banking whitewash and cover-up, was both brave and the kind of iconoclastic practice Americans need to see more of, in both business and government.

Some might call Judge Rakoff a bully. I call the Judge a hero.

In the land where who you know and one's connections, as often as not trumps the truth, Judge Rakoff's act was a singularly courageous event.   Kudos and accolades to Judge Rakoff!

Dien Bien Phu & the Last Empire

by J.M. Hamilton (12-25-11)

"Colonial policy is the daughter of industrial policy." – French P.M. Jules Ferry

Lost in the fog of war and the mists of time is a long forgotten battle. A battle fought on the other side of the world, between the French and a proud and indigenous people, who wanted nothing more than their freedom from colonial rule. The U.S., at that time, pumped what would be considered an exceptional amount of money into the French military. Fought in the decade following WWII, and with the Korean War very much on the minds of U.S. policy makers, surely the French could defeat this revolutionary tribe. But it was not meant to be, the French decided to roll the dice within Indochina's isolated hill country, near the enemy's Laotian supply line. The French opposition knew the importance of this battle, as international negotiations were underway in Geneva over the regions future. The French, who had brought with them into battle mobile bordellos, were caught off guard when they found themselves surrounded by captured artillery pieces and anti-aircraft guns, strategically placed on higher ground. The subsequent battle of Dien Bien Phu ended French colonial rule in Southeast Asia, and became a rallying cry globally for nationalist movements seeking independence from occupying western powers. The country was subsequently divided in two at Geneva, and Ho Chi Minh was given a foothold in North Vietnam and international legitimacy, with which to launch a civil war that would eventually end in American defeat two decades later.

The New York Times reported on 5-9-54 the following: *"The fall of Dien Bien Phu marks the end of an era. The ultimate military, political and psychological reactions may either make or break the anti-Communist front in the Far East and France as a great power... A lost battle has tipped the scales of history in the past; Dien Bien Phu may prove, in future accountings, to be the balance point in contemporary history."* - **After Dien Bien Phu, What?**

Could the Iraq war be America's Dien Bien Phu?

Before answering that question, let's take a look at the similarities and differences between America's wars in Iraq and Indochina. And then let's examine the cost allocation of war.

History repeats. Both wars, Vietnam and Iraq, were started at a time when the American public was hyper vigilant about a perceived and real menace in the world: Communism and Radical Islam. In both wars, political authorization for U.S. involvement was obtained under dubious and questionable circumstances: In Vietnam it was the Gulf of Tonkin incident that provided a catalyst, and in Iraq it was concern over weapons of mass destruction. In both wars the political goals and objectives were nebulous over time, and finally denigrated into "nation building;" and in both wars, America was either forced to leave the battlefield or requested to leave… no longer wanted, and leaving under less than auspicious circumstances. Time would also show that the twin threats of Communism and Arab Radicalism would dissolve considerably with the collapse of the Soviet Union and the rise of the Arab Spring/pro-democracy movements.

And as Vietnam proved, and as pointed out by **Alan Abelson** in last weeks **Barron's**, Americans will not know the true cost of the Iraq war for many decades. The Iraq war will more than likely exceed a trillion is net cost, but that doesn't begin to account for the tremendous forgone opportunity costs incurred by the nation, when we consider that Iraq war debt could have been allocated to helping Americans achieve a higher education, or if said funds were allocated to paying down the national debt, or not expanding same. Even by today's standards, a trillion dollars is still real money. Nor does this begin to factor in the additional economic burden placed upon ordinary Americans, and returning soldiers, post war, when monetary policy inevitably swings towards war debt monetization – resulting in inflation and lower living standards.

That the real political achievement of the Iraq war was the permanent removal of Saddam Hussein calls into question the efficacy of Executive Order 12333, which supposedly forbids the assassination of foreign heads of state. The reality is there are plenty of exemptions to Executive Order 12333, and so if we compare the cost of the Iraq war to say, the cost of the mission to eliminate Osama bin Laden, well there really is no comparison. What's the nominal cost of a bullet or a drone, versus the extraordinary cost of Iraq War…. all to remove one man? To push the point a step further, compare the cost, in blood and treasure, to remove Col. Gaddafi versus Saddam Hussein?

Separately, "nation building" (code for we no longer know what the freak we are doing here, so we have turned this mission into a philanthropic enterprise) was a failure in Vietnam, and only time will tell if it will prove successful in Iraq. Recent actions by the Iraqi prime minister, like issuing an arrest warrant for the Iraqi Vice President and further consolidating his hold on power, already call into question whether or not a nascent Iraqi democracy will flower and grow. What nation building really has come to symbolize is a run up of conflict costs and expenditures, and a financial "pig-out" by private contractors and commercial interests within a war zone, all at U.S. tax payer expense.

Despite many similarities, a key difference between both wars was the utilization of conscription by U.S. forces fighting in Vietnam, versus an all volunteer military fighting force in the Iraq War, and the resulting passive objection to the Iraq war by U.S. society, versus the near public rebellion over the Vietnam war. Some how it makes it more acceptable to some Americans if the poor and the down trodden are voluntarily sacrificed upon the altar of war, instead of the sons and daughters of the wealthy and the middle class, via the draft. And the military industrial complex (MIC) knows this. Former Defense Secretary Robert Gates warned of a separation in society between an elite warrior class and ordinary Americans.

Also of critical importance, we can see a tremendous disconnect in the way the costs of war are passed onto society as whole, in lieu of armed conflict's true beneficiaries. J.M.H. argues that because of this, wars have a tendency to drag on indefinitely. In other words if the true costs of the war were allocated correctly, than wars would become more efficient, cost effective, produce swifter results with less loss of human life, and pull out and withdrawal would become more rapid. More thought might also be given to entering into war in the first place.

So who or what truly benefited then from the removal of Saddam Hussein, aside from the Shia majority inside Iraq? Well as clearly alluded to by French Prime Minister Jules Ferry, commercial interests clearly benefit from war without end, colonization, and/or nation building. Big Oil was clearly chomping at the bit to return to Iraq. And of course the U.S. military industrial complex expanded and grew, significantly, over the last decade, more than doubling in budgetary outlays. Not surprisingly banks benefit with the issuance of martial debt and financing. The fact that the U.S. government spends more on defense than the G-20 combined says it all.

As with all wars, there are often unintended consequences. An unintended beneficiary of Mr. Hussein's removal was Iran; and Iran has been working to obtain a foothold inside Iraq, with success, ever since the U.S. lead invasion.

America has to figure out a way to be less subservient to what President Eisenhower referred to in his farewell address to the nation as the military industrial complex; failure to do so may mean that Iraq could become America's Dien Bien Phu. How then might America control the costs of war, and prevent taxpayer money, sometimes with good intentions, from being wasted on nation building? If the cost of Iraq war was amortized over the costs of the products and services produced by the MIC, and passed onto foreign consumers (America being the largest arms dealer on the planet), the price of a prolonged and protracted war would become too great for the MIC to endure and would make MIC products and services considerably less competitive. Likewise, if the price of the Iraq war were presented as a cost of doing business to Big Oil or mining interests, they would balk at the cost; and maybe the Iraq war truly would have ended when Mr. George Bush landed on the deck of the aircraft carrier, USS Abraham Lincoln, with the now infamous sign, "Mission Accomplished." Thanks to the manner in which American wars are presently billed, there is no financial incentive to rein in the cost, since the U.S. has been living on a credit card economy for decades, and the MIC, via its all volunteer military, has all but eliminated serious protest.

Ultimately, if America is unsuccessful in reining in MIC costs, it could result in a threat to national security, the loss of international prestige, as well as, possibly cause unmitigated hardship here at home, as defense spending takes away government services from the 99% and ultimately leads to an increase in taxation upon all Americans, the 100%. (By way of example, take a look at the financial situation of the so-called PIIGS in Europe… and ask yourself, are these nations in any kind of financial condition to fight a war on terror or handle any other sovereign threat? The PIIG's fiscal policy, and deficit spending, is a threat to their very own national security.) Equally tragic, back in America, nation building exercises may leave the MIC winded and the public less likely to support the use of force in the future, when the U.S. may actually have very good reasons for going to war.

"Of all the enemies to public liberty war is, perhaps, the most to be dreaded because it comprises and develops the germ of every other. War is the parent of armies; from these proceed debts and taxes … known instruments for bringing the many under the domination of the few…. No nation could preserve its freedom in the midst of continual warfare."

There is some reason for optimism however. Not everyone who enters the White House is an opportunist or a poor war strategist. Look at George H.W. Bush and his management of the first Gulf War; this was a war that was fought with great precision, finite goals and objectives, and clearly big oil and the House of Saud were among the beneficiaries of that war, not to mention the Government of Kuwait. Arguably, the U.S. should have submitted a substantive portion of the bill for that war to the various governments in the Middle East and to commercial oil concerns operating in the region.

Better yet, observe President Obama and his deft and expert management of the overthrow of the Libyan dictator, Colonel Gaddafi. These are excellent examples of where the U.S. military was utilized for its intended use, as opposed to an unending nation building exercise that only served to enrich the private contractors of war, and the commercial interests that sweep in post-war – all at the expense of the American people and the men and women who serve. Are we naive enough to believe that these same commercial interests, in our present form of democracy, do not have a considerable say in how and when America goes to war? Do foreign governments and the MIC lobby the congress? Assuredly and big time!

To be sure, there are many reasons to go to war, and American leaders may in fact have the best of intentions and the highest of ideals (humanitarian, the spread of democracy, and otherwise), but our leaders nor the American people should never lose sight of the fact that there are tremendous profits to be made in war, as well as, many interested parties and unintended consequences and expense.

J.M.H. is a fan of President Obama's foreign policy, and the world owes him a debt for his substantial contribution towards the Libyan dictators removal; and America owes the President another debt for finally extricating our service men and women from the Iraq war.

That said, it appears that we plan on colonizing Afghanistan for years to come, in yet another nation building exercise. Witness last Wednesday's NY Times story, which quotes a U.S. general as stating that America may be in Afghanistan beyond 2014. How ironic that Afghanistan, under Americas watch, has been and remains the worlds foremost opium purveyor. Americans, fiscal conservatives, and liberals, who find endless war objectionable, or too damn corrupt and expensive, may find that Republican Presidential Candidate Ron

Paul provides sharp and welcome contrast to mainstream political pandering to the MIC. Perhaps Mr. Paul can help drag the mainstream towards his line of thinking?

J.M.H. is grateful for the men and women who serve their country. And Americans, as responsible participants in our democracy, owe it to our armed forces to make sure that when our elected officials send these men and women into harms way – it truly is for the advancement and protection of the national interest, and not just another nation building exercise. These men and women would also be better served if the true costs of U.S. involvement in armed conflict were allocated to commercial entities and foreign governments, with vested economic and political interests, when and where possible.

After all, blood and nation building are a huge expense.

P.S.

"The most powerful weapon on earth is the human soul on fire."

-Ferdinand Foch

Americans should not confuse a quick willingness to go to war with patriotism, or subservience to the MIC as a rational political agenda. Ronald Reagan, who never started a hot war in his two terms in office, is model for current political leadership to emmulate, in this regard.

A very happy holidays!

The Ultimate GOP Candidate has yet to Step Forward....

By J.M. Hamilton (1-8-12)

"Today we have a similar debate over this... anyone know what this is... class? Anyone, anyone, anyone seen this before?... the Laffer Curve. Anyone know what this says? It says at this point on the revenue curve you will get exactly the same amount of revenue as at this point. This is very controversial. Does anyone know what Vice President George Bush called this in 1980? Anyone, Anyone? Something D-O-O economics... voodoo economics."

- Ben Stein from the movie, Ferris Bueller's Day Off

Happy New Year!

I don't get it. The GOP candidates are running around destroying each other, trying to figure out who will lead them out of diaspora and back to the White House. Debate after Republican debate only shows which leper has the least spots (hopefully that's not politically incorrect?)

Have you ever seen such a fatally flawed crew?

The only one in the mix with real gravitas, who could pose a serious challenge to the incumbent, is the only one who hasn't bubbled up as the monthly Republican candidate *du jour,* that would be Mr. Huntsman.

Romney, who seems destined to get the nod, is going to become the "Bain" of private equity. Seriously, if you are an executive officer for TPG Capital, Blackstone Group, KKR, Carlyle, or any number of private equity firms, you've got to be pouring money into the campaign coffers of anybody other than Romney.

Why? Because with a Romney nomination will come intense and withering scrutiny of what private equity is and does: which is kill jobs; liquidate, flip and merge companies; and increase the concentration of political power and wealth in this country into fewer hands.

And the real irony of a Romney nomination (?)… Evangelicals, who make up a substantial percentage of the core Republican base, fear a new world order and one world power. Evangelicals believe a one world power cabal is a sign of the end times and the antichrist…. if I have that right. If that's the case imagine evangelical dismay when they learn that private equity is probably one of the largest single contributors to globalization and the concentration of power on the planet, aside from the Wall Street Cartel. Yep, the likely Republican nominee, Mr. Romney, is the poster boy for private equity and the concentration of economic, and hence, political power. President Reagan was not a huge fan of concentrated power, by the way.

Separately, just imagine the scrutiny Mr. Romney is going to bring to the "carried interest tax?" A tax benefit that is near and dear to every private equity exec's heart.

Moving right along… as much JMH finds the most interesting Republican candidate by far, to be Ron Paul, he unfortunately carries with him some baggage; baggage that afflicts many of his generation, and unfortunately successive generations, as well. That people, and even political candidates, can grow, evolve, and shed intolerance over time appears lost on many who rabidly oppose Mr. Paul. Nevertheless, racism of any kind is a very serious charge, rightfully so, and is likely to stick to his candidacy, even with earnest disavowals. The real irony is that the twisted brother of racism, he goes by the name of Religious Bigotry, would appear to be on full display with another Republican candidate, Mr. Santorum; and yet, Religious Bigotry appears more widely tolerated in Republican circles. J.M.H. is not the first to write it, but it bears repeating…. at least a President Ron Paul would not seek to legislate religious beliefs/morality from the White House (shucks, a President Paul just might close up shop and sell the White House), while a President Santorum would likely set up a theocracy, and a religious police force that would make the Taliban pale in comparison.

As this blog has suggested before Mr. Paul and his follower's single biggest contribution to this election cycle is to draw attention to just how similar both parties, Republican and Democrat actually are, and how both parties are addicted to big government. J.M.H. actually believes in the importance of the U.S. government, but also acknowledges, as Mr. Paul does so well, that our government often overextends its reach into our personal lives, through incursions upon our civil rights, and globally, in the form of taxpayer funded foreign adventures, aiding and abetting war profiteering, and nation building.

Mr. Paul, personal failings aside, has a contribution to make to these upcoming elections, that of providing competition to the duopoly that runs our country; let's hope he stays in the race, and starts a third party.

Which brings me finally to the *uber* Republican candidate… this man has out "republicaned" the Republican party, by stealing their foreign policy thunder. On foreign policy, he is second to none in protecting America from her enemies. He hunted down and killed Osama bin Laden, and made significant contributions to Dictator Gaddafi's immolation (both were Republican targets). He brought our troops home from that legacy catastrophe of a war in Iraq – handed down to him from the Bush administration; and this individual has plans to exit Afghanistan.

This gentlemen has shown international leadership and the path to how America can enlist allies, and not go it alone, in Libya, a preferred model for future martial efforts; and he has also shown us how 21st century military engagements can often be handled with technology, manless drones, and lightening quick raids. He has almost made Al Qaeda leadership extinct. And he is the process of stream lining the DOD to fit our national interest and budget. On foreign policy, President Obama makes the prior Republican administration look like amateur hour, and I would suggest to my readers that no current Republican candidate could step into his shoes and do as well.

And like prior Republican administrations, President Obama has kept strong ties to our ally in the middle-east, Israel. As quoted in the **Washington Post, Chicago Mayor Rahm Emanuel** had the following to say about the President's commitment: "As I listened to the president's speech on the Middle East, I heard him reaffirm his strong commitment to Israel's safety, security and prosperity."

On domestic policy, corporations have never been richer, profit margins are high, and balance sheets – in many instances – are rich with cash. Fed policy under the President's watch has been very generous to: the wealthy, Wall Street Banks, and multi-national corporations. As for the Wall Street bail-out, again, this was a legacy project – initiated – by the Bush administration and Mr. Henry Paulson. How this President handles the next, and inevitable, financial crisis remains to be seen; Mr. Obama's administration will own the next crisis.

And while jobs are scarce – how much of this present economic environment is created by the plutocracy, via capital strikes, globalization, and unfair trade agreements? These are issues that could be addressed, if the nation had a fully functioning Republican Congress that was interested in helping out the American economy, instead of holding same hostage for prospective political gain. Unlike a President Romney, whose economic policies call for "borrowing and spending" as reported by **Bloomberg** last week, President Obama is more fiscally conservative and would prefer to pay as we go through a combination of spending cuts and tax increases.

President Obama does not appear to believe in what former President H.W. Bush referred to as "voodoo economics." He's a pragmatic man and probably understands that politicians/congress doesn't have the self-discipline to increase taxes in good economic times, which is the Keynesian paradigm's shortcoming.

The argument I'm clumsily attempting to make is that, in essence, a moderate Republican already occupies the White House, and that by the standards of a H.W. Bush, or say, either an Eisenhower or Nixon, Obama should be the Republican nominee. It is because the zealots within the Republican Party have moved the political center of this nation so far right, as to be rendered unrecognizable to many establishment Republicans from yester-year, that we have such a conservative and pro-business Democratic administration.

What this says for the economic and political aspirations of Democrats and Liberals is another story. If I didn't know better, it's almost as if the plutocracy installed into the White House a Trojan Republican President, wrapped in the Democratic Party's mantle. It is because President Obama is the calmest, most rational, and most presidential choice, versus the Republican field of candidates, that J.M.H. supports him for a return to the White House. Besides, the nation hasn't had a foreign policy guru in the White House this gifted, since Nixon/Kissinger teamed up to conquer the world.

Bubba and the Socialist in South Carolina

By J.M. Hamilton (1-21-12)

"We are all socialist now." – King Edward VII

I rang up Bubba this week to get his take on the South Carolina primaries. I very much respect Bubba's opinion on political matters, after all – he called the 2010 midterms.

My readers may recall that Bubba is my red meat inhaling, beer guzzling, mescal snorting best friend from Tejas. Yes, Bubba has proven that you can snort mescal, but the worm does tend to get stuck in the straw. Bubba and I go back to younger days and simpler times, summers spent water skiing, drinking PBR, and chasing skirt (not necessarily in that order). I spent many a summer night looking up at the stars of Texas through bullet holes in Bubba's trailer ceiling…. Lying on his living room couch in the middle of the night (yes, we drank responsibly), and at the right kind of angle, you could sometimes see satellites pass by.

"The socialist dream is over. ObamaCare is dead. Just wait until the Roberts court rules," he yelled into the receiver. "You can't force people to buy insurance."

"But Bubba by that same logic," I responded, "shouldn't all entitlement spending be eliminated then? After all, what is social security? It's an insurance program we all pay into. Ditto Medicare. Why I don't think there's a single Republican candidate, save Mr. Perry, who favors elimination of social security. And look what happened to your governor! And didn't Bush (W) expand Medicare with Part D?"

"Look," Bubba rejoined, "Americans despise Euro-Socialism, period. Comprende?"

"Bubba, Americans should not fear Euro-Socialism, but rather, they should fear American-Socialism, which is far more expensive and dangerous to any country's health."

"What you talking about Willis?"

I'm talking about the most insidious kind of socialism, the kind that is rarely discussed and all but ignored in the South Carolina Republican debates:

Like the bailout of Wall Street and European Banks.

- **Bloomberg** recently put the Fed's bailout lending to the Wall Street Cartel at $7.7 trillion.

- A GAO report of 7-21-11 placed the Fed's lending to the banking cartel at $16.0 trillion. Conveniently, that lending is at near zero percent interest. Free money!

- TARP and Quantative Easing (QE1) transferred hundreds of billions in toxic assets (CDO's and MBS) from the Wall Street Cartel's balance sheets and onto the public's balance sheet, that would be the Fed's and GSE's – like Freddie and Fannie.

- And the Fed is rolling over and reinvesting its earning in yet more toxic assets, as reported by Mr. Randall Forsyth in **Barron's magazine (New Call for the Fed to Spur Housing, 10-21-11).** Just another form of bank bailout.

- Now this same practice, American-style Socialism, is all the rage Europe, after the Germans swore they would never go there, courtesy of Mr. Mario Draghi – Goldman Sachs alum and European Central Bank head.

- Mr. Draghi has lent out $640 billion dollars to bailout European banks, which suddenly have better bond ratings than many of the sovereign nations they operate in.

- As in America, the European bank bailout was designed to encourage lending to individuals and small and mid-sized businesses (primary drivers of the economy, employment, and top line growth); but instead, European banks either deposited the money with the central bank or re-invested the money in sovereign debt.

- Meanwhile the Cartel (presently lead by Mr. Josef Ackermann as head of the IIF) has fought all legislation, regulation, and planned transparency and collateralization, governing derivatives and swaps, which are the very same products that nearly brought the global economy down in 2008.

- After all, if America regulates derivates and swaps, Wall Street may lose business to insolvent European banks.

- **By way of comparison, social spending – or entitlement spending within the U.S. Federal budget – is running just north of two trillion dollars per annum, a fraction of what has been given to Cartel and IIF members over the last couple of years.**

- The Cartel all but refuses to refinance mortgages – which would spur the economy, as do the GSE's, because it would crimp CDO and MBS earnings.

- Banks are given trillions, in both America and Europe, and the public is told by Republican candidates to suck it up and get a job!

- Banks are given trillions, and the public will have to pay for those trillions through higher taxes and higher headline inflation. Inflation the Fed conveniently refuses to recognize within its CPI calculation.

Republican candidates have a keen dislike for social spending for the elderly, disenfranchised and the poor (what they have dubbed "Euro-Socialism"), but these same Republican candidates have little to say about America's biggest – and most recent – export to European shores… American Socialism (aka Crony Capitalism).

"I need a beer," said Bubba.

P.S.

And to see why American-style Socialism is alive and well let's surf over to Opensecrets.org, and review 2012 campaign financing by economic sector.

Sector Totals, 2011-2012

http://www.opensecrets.org/industries/index.php

http://www.opensecrets.org/industries/indus.php?Ind=F

http://blog.jmhamiltonpublishing.com/2010/08/15/bubba-called.aspx

London Calling

"The most effective way to destroy people is to deny and obliterate their own understanding of their history." **- George Orwell**

By J.M. Hamilton (2-3-11)

Let's face it. As much as central banks, and their bankers, like to say they're looking out for the public, their core constituency and the masters they serve are the Banking Cartel. The Feds mandate is stable prices and maximum employment; but a closer look at the Fed's policies and its results reveals the opposite has in fact happened, since the crisis in 2008, to the benefit of Wall Street (the 1%) and to the detriment of the public (the 99%).

And to show you what I mean, the Chancellor of the Exchequer, George Osborne, was making the rounds at Davos and lobbying on behalf of both his country's interests and the Banking Cartel's position: namely, the Volcker Rule must be abolished or significantly watered down. At issue the Volcker Rule requires that U.S. banks not gamble with public/taxpayer money, and the same rule also means that same should no longer hold foreign debt, at least not to gamble with. (Sovereign debt is no longer what it once was, bulletproof, and in more than an uncomfortable number of European instances as of late, it has become highly speculative.) Mr. Osborne, or perhaps it's Sir Osborne, hails from the U.K. and more precisely London.

London, of course, is where all that is "whack" (please excuse the slang) goes down in world financial affairs.

"But J.M.," you reply, "you're kidding…. Wall Street is the epicenter of all things financial, both catastrophic and magnificent."

Not any longer. And here's why.

As reported in Bloomberg this week in a piece entitled, **Goldman Sachs among Banks Lobbying to Exempt Half the Swaps from Dodd-Frank**, penned by Ms. Silla Brush, we learn that the majority of swaps are now transacted overseas, possibly in the hopes of skirting future swaps regulation under Dodd Frank. And where exactly is "overseas?" Per Ms. Brush, "New York-based Goldman Sachs's largest counterparty for credit derivatives on the eve of the credit crisis in June 2008 was Deutsche Bank AG (DB)'s London branch; its third-largest interest-rate derivatives counterparty was JPMorgan's

London branch; and its largest counterparty for currency products was Royal Bank of Scotland Plc's London branch, according to a 2010 report from the Financial Crisis Inquiry Commission, a U.S. panel that investigated the crisis."

So London appears to be the prime destination for the derivatives trade, which are rogue insurance products that the American taxpayer reinsures, and the Banking Cartel profits from; that is to say, the banks keep the premiums, and you, Dear Ninety-Nine, pay for the losses when things go bust.

To drive my point on "The City" a little further, please recall it was London that housed Mr. Joseph Cassano and the fabled AIG Financial Products Unit. This was the unit that was taken down by Goldman Sachs in 2008, and demonstrated to the world what systematic risk truly was… a lesson that we are still learning to this very day.

It has been rumored and speculated that some of the $1.2 billion in missing MF Global client money has vanished around London environs, quite possible pledged as collateral in Repo transactions.   **Repos** are the very same accounting transactions that are said to have fooled business partners, lenders, exchanges, and regulators, when both Lehman Brothers and MF Global went down. (Repos can be off balance sheet transactions.) Repos involve transferring risky assets, for some period of time, off one's financial statements and sending them quite often to London, where for a fee, the client is given cash or more warmly received/perceived assets.

Sort of a duplicitous accounting bait and switch…. if you will.

Depending upon the duration of the transaction, and the maturation date of the instrument, and with proper timing, a Repo may even be posted as sales revenue.

Repos are nasty enough, but what happens next to the collateral in London is altogether insane, because under British law, rules and regs, the collateral can be pledged and re-pledged, used and reused, in a process called Rehypothecation. Reusing collateral, again and again, is risky enough in good times, but throw into the mix some volatility, add a dash of uncertainty, with equal measures panic and default, and poof, collateral/client money all gone. Rehypothecation is, conveniently, an off balance sheet transaction.

Ultimately, where I'm going with this is…. U.S. bank regulation in today's global economy is only as strong as its weakest link. And the weakest link in the financial world today, the king daddy of systematic risk, and moral hazard, is London. There's a reason why so many banks set up shop there, and so many derivative/swaps counterparties operate in London. It's called regulatory capture and regulatory arbitrage, or London by any other name.

If U.S. lawmakers and policymakers want to avoid a repeat of the mother of all financial crises, then pressure must be brought to bear, and applied directly to London's financial district. Perhaps the tables should be turned and Mr. Geithner should be lobbying Mr. Osbourne for U.K. banking regulatory reform?

On a historical note, the nickname for London at one time was "Old Smoke," perhaps the new nickname should be "Old Smoke and Mirrors."

And going full circle back to the topic of central banks, Mr. Randall Forsyth, of **Barron's Magazine**, paraphrased Ms. Stephanie Pomboy this week as stating (he also detected a similar note from Mr. Bill Gross of PIMCO fame): "…the 'transmission' for monetary policy is broken. Easy Fed policy lifts prices but, owing to consumers' reluctance or inability to borrow, doesn't translate into spending increases."

Which is a nice way of saying Fed policy is great at servicing the Cartel, but the Cartel no longer serves the American public, no, in fact, the Cartel serves, you guessed it, only themselves. But what else would one expect from an oligopoly? Ms. Pomboy goes on to note: "That suggests the counterintuitive conclusion: expansionary monetary policy could be restraining the economy.

I believe what these three wise persons are driving at is that the paltry less than one percent interest the Fed pays out (the Fed can get away with this because the Euro is trashed, and the Fed is monetizing U.S. debt) is providing zero relief for consumers, savers, or the economy, because the banks are not lending the money out…. No Wall Street is either investing in commodities, the stock market, T-Bills, or the carry trade (or in the case of European banks, placing the money back into central banks or sovereign debt). Meanwhile retirees and savers are not earning a dime in interest income, and are being squeezed hard by fiscal austerity, higher headline inflation, and declining property values.

Nor are the Fed's policies exactly good for corporations or multi-nationals, who would like to see: wealthier consumers, an increase in consumer spending, a resulting rise in top line growth, and an increase in profits.

It seems that Wall Street banks don't want to soil themselves with untidy residential lending, and they have been off loading illiquid and impaired CDOs and MBS onto the Fed's and the nation's balance sheets ever since the 2008 crisis began. The Fed into the breach, once again, to bail out the Cartel, but Mr. and Mrs. John Q. Public will just have to cope. Of course the near zero percent interest rate the Fed charges banks, also enables the Leviathan to hold illiquid and damaged assets on their financial statements, such as CDOs and MBS. That is until, the Fed can take it off their hands.

After all with essentially free money, courtesy of the Fed, the banks have no incentive to mark residential mortgages to market, which would spur refinancing, begin the residential housing recovery in earnest, and ignite the economy.

Why oh why would the Cartel want to refinance mortgages and kick start a U.S. economic recovery? After all, Wall Street banks have a Democratic President they need to run out of office

But wait, it gets darker, because, as we learned this week, there may be yet another reason why the Fed is keeping interest rates at zero percent. Both **ProPublica and NPR** put out a joint piece this week, entitled **Freddie Mac Bets Against Homeowners**. (Shucks, it might as well have been titled: Taxpayer bailed out Institution $cr@ws Americans and the American Dream.) Per the article, it seems as if this GSE has taken out some sophisticated bets, which wager that much of the U.S. residential market will not be refinanced. Of course, with the GSEs essentially controlling the nation's residential market portfolio, it's sort of a guaranteed win. For Freddie that is.

And the wider the spread between the Fed's interest rate, and the rates U.S. homeowners pay, the more money Freddie makes off its bet: "The inverse floaters carry another risk. Freddie gets paid the difference between the high mortgages rates, such as the Silversteins are paying, and a key global interest rate that right now is very low. If that rate rises, Freddie's profits will fall."

Hmmm… sounds like the Fed has yet another reason to keep interest rates low, and that's so Freddie (and possibly other institutional investors?) can make a killing off inverse floaters, while Americans – the 99% – pray the stuttering nascent economic recovery, this time, is for real.

Isn't that special?

So just to get this straight, the U.S. economy is being held back – homes are not being refinanced – so that taxpayer funded/taxpayer bailed out/taxpayer owned institution, named Freddie, can make profit from CDOs and the MBS the banks off loaded on to the tax payer at list price; and this same publicly owned institution, Freddie, has wagered/doubled down – through highly leveraged and speculative instruments called reverse floaters – that homeowners and the economy won't heal, so that they can make a mint. Moreover, this is a bet that Freddie controls, as one of the largest suppliers and reinsurers of U.S. residential mortgages.

And who sold Freddie these exotic products? My educated guess is the Wall Street Cartel.

Meanwhile, the Fed pledged in late January to keep interests rates at their super low values for yet another year. Seems that the FMOC is worried, terribly worried, about the economy.

Thank you FHFA Director Edward DeMarco!   Thank you Chairman Bernanke!

Perhaps "Old Smoke and Mirrors" isn't so slippery after all.

Not aloof just disciplined...

"Santino, come here...Never tell anyone outside the Family what you are thinking again." – Marlon Brando (aka Don Corleone, from the Godfather)

By J.M. Hamilton (3-1-12)

This week we go where no man should go. I'm talking the third rail of polite discourse, politics and religion. But heh, blog site traffic should soar. So lets boldly step forth.

Being a political junkie, I have observed President Obama for some time, and have also watched with equal alacrity the Republican primaries unfold. Of conspicuous interest as well, I have read the economic, financial, and political pundits comments on same.

One of the common threads of accusation/complaint against our current White House inhabitant is that he is, perhaps, aloof, possibly arrogant, proud, and not fully engaged in the right causes. Some of this might, in fact, be true. It's also been argued that our President does not fight, speak up, or lead properly: if you're a Liberal, the President has fallen short on just about nearly every pet cause; if you are corporatist, Mr. Obama has failed to defend the Wall Street Cartel properly – per the Chamber of Commerce; and if you are a Tea Partier, perhaps you think the President is, well, aligned with... sinister and other worldly forces.

But having thought this through, and having watched the Republican primaries, I have concluded that our President is, in fact, extremely intelligent. And here's why, the longer the Republican candidates speak, the more the American public (Republican, Democrat and most importantly, Independents) comes to realize that this is not the grand ol' party of our fathers. Surely, this isn't Ike's party, nor is it Reagan's, and had Mr. Buckley been alive to witness this disaster unfold, he would have packed up National Review and fled the country (e.g. Switzerland or if desperate enough maybe France). The longer these gentlemen talk, the more many of us are coming to realize that silence is a virtue.

Okay, so President Obama doesn't rise to the bait, he doesn't pander, and judging from his foreign policy he doesn't react, he acts. But given the immolation of the Republican Party, and given the overwhelming challenges President Obama inherited, aren't we glad he's not monopolizing the media on a nightly basis?

Lao Tzu said: "Those who know don't speak; those who speak – don't' know."

And the Bible (James, Chapter Three) offers up the following: "So also the tongue is a small member, but boasts of great things. How great a forest is set ablaze by such a small fire. And a tongue is a fire, a world of unrighteousness. The tongue is set among our members, straining the whole body, setting on fire the whole course of life, and set on fire by hell... "

Proud, aloof, indifferent or otherwise (or maybe he's just very focused on doing his job), our President appears to know the limits of the tongue, and may have studied both the Bible and Zen Buddhism. Who knows maybe he even studied the Godfather? It's one of the reasons our President looks presidential and the Republican's look well, like they do.

In a world of 24/7 buzz (where infotainment trumps real news), celebrity worship, twitter and assorted social media, where nothing is too mundane to share with the planet and gossip rules... aren't we fortunate that we have a President who is disciplined enough not to share his every waking thought with us? The President, in this regard, appears to be leading by example; perhaps it's an example we can all learn from?

And speaking of Christians, particularly the Religious Right.... I remember discussing Mr. Romney's prospects, back in 2008, with a friend from Massachusetts. My friend was fairly upbeat about Mr. Romney's chances of obtaining the Republican nomination that year. And I assured my friend that Mr. Romney didn't have a chance in well... hell. "Why," my friend questioned.

Because quite simply, I responded, Mr. Romney is a Mormon, and as far as the Christian Right is concerned he might as well as be the devil incarnate. They just aren't going to nominate the man. Of course, I called that one, correctly. And my guess is Mr. Romney maybe out of luck, once again, here and now in 2012. Mr. Romney is of course, a victim to some degree of religious bigotry, some subtle – some not so subtle. And even if he gets the nomination, he may find Evangelical turnout to be a little lackluster on election-day.

The good news for Mr. Romney? After he fails to get the nod this go around, or win the prize, I know of a party that I – and other Republicans – recently migrated to, that is a little more tolerant, a little more open minded, and has a wide and broad enough tent that will accept a former private equity CEO (even if they're Mormon and once governed the State of Massachusetts). Imagine that!

The Democratic Party can use a few good men and women, Mr. Romney. Isn't it time you, and your clan, fled religious persecution?

Which brings me to the Religious Right itself, and a few more bible passages:

Mark 12:31 Thou shalt love the neighbor as thy self; there is none other commandment greater than this.

John 8:7 Let he is who is without sin among you cast the first stone.

Matthew 7:1 Judge not that you not be judged.

In examining these three passages Christians, myself included, would do well to remember that it is not our place to judge others. And as for the golden rule, a common theme in many of the world's core religions, I have never seen Mark 12:31 amended to state: Love your neighbor '…. as long as they are Catholic, Pentecostal or Baptist, look like you, and come from the right socio-economic background.'

At the end of the day, based upon the little we know, Christ was if, anything, tolerant and extremely patient. He wanted to give everybody an opportunity at salvation, again and again. The Lord even extended the gift of eternal life to the gentiles, so much for being judgmental. But today's Religious Right appears to have already judged everybody, and its leaders have for some time now sought to hijack the Republican Party to advance its goal of legislating morality. Or, as I have argued to friends and family members, conversely, these militant Christians have allowed themselves to be used by a Republican Party, who only cares about them when it's time to vote; but once in power, the GOP places Evangelicals – and the Catholic extreme – in the back seat.

"See ya in four years, fellas!"

Either way, one gets the feeling that this is not what Christ had in mind, who discussed of all things, the separation between church and state when he said render under to Caesar the things that our Caesars.

Assuming his sincerity, Mr. Santorum appears to be the current poster-child for this group, and he is full of righteous indignation for the alleged persecution of his Catholic values, and the Evangelical base. Mr. Santorum, seemingly, would gladly set up a religious police state to advance his values and views. How sad that these "ambassadors" of Christ may actually be doing more harm than good in turning people away from God and his values.

Yup, I just re-read the commandments and there's nothing in there about launching jihad against "godless" Democrats, Mormons and Ecumenism.

Some say there's not enough religion in the world to make people love one another, just enough religion to make people hate one another.

One of the core reasons I jumped the Republican ship about four years ago – and was more open to the Democratic party – was via an epiphany: perhaps – just maybe – the Democratic party with its focus on tolerance, a more just and civil society, and a desire to help those less fortunate and in need…. was a little more closely aligned with the teachings of Christ, than the party of the one percent.

But who's judging.

PS:

SOLA FIDE!

And speaking of faith and prayer, perhaps we should all send one up for the ISDA, who will make a determination today as to whether or not the derivatives and swaps that insure Greek bonds will be triggered. Quite a Faustian decision: It seems as though bankers and those who give bankers succor (i.e. politicians and regulators) have finally painted themselves into a very dark corner. Does the ISDA, and the Cartel that controls same, acknowledge Greek default and possibly set off financial Armageddon, or do they not acknowledge Greek default and make these highly profitable, and taxpayer subsidized, instruments useless and unsalable? Either way, CDS and the like are about to come under a great deal of scrutiny once again, and hopefully, a great deal more financial regulation.

Mr. Demagogue?

By J.M. Hamilton (3-17-12)

"The State Department is infested with communists. I have here in my hand a list of 205—a list of names that were made known to the Secretary of State as being members of the Communist Party and who nevertheless are still working and shaping policy in the State Department."

-Senator Joseph McCarthy – Wheeling, Virginia speech (2-9-50)

"Until this moment, Senator, I think I never really gauged your cruelty or your recklessness ... Let us not assassinate this lad further, Senator. You've done enough. Have you no sense of decency, sir, at long last? Have you left no sense of decency."

- U.S. Army's chief legal representative, Joseph Nye Welch – Army\McCarthy Hearings (June 9, 1954)

They seem to arrive during troubled times, be they economic or political. A leader arrives on the scene, and offers up a seemingly simplistic reason for a nation's problems, and often a simpler solution. They may be charismatic and, ultimately, enjoy a cult of personality following. Demagogues play upon the public's fear, and often their ignorance. The elementary, and often times extreme, positions they take offer solutions for a bewildered and frightened public, all too eager to put a bad situation behind it and looking for an earthly messiah. Above all, what a demagogue offers is a short cut to thinking. The fear and misery that propels these individuals into a nation's spot light can be so great that otherwise sane, rational and intelligent academic, business, political and spiritual leaders offer no rebuttal, for fear of being ostracized, castigated or worse.

It reminds me of Mr. Burke's famous quote: "All that is necessary for the triumph of evil is for good men to do nothing."

The spell is weaved, the die is cast, and the next thing one knows a nation has an even bigger problem on its hands; the fallacious and specious solution that was offered often delays the inevitable (the more arduous path to resolution), or serves only to aggravate and prolong the crisis. Examples of U.S.

demagogues in the 20th Century would include Huey P. Long of Louisiana. Visualize Governor Long calling the shots in the Louisiana legislature, from the dais with a bottle of whiskey in his hand. Or Wisconsin's Senator Joe McCarthy – who actually did more harm than good to the anti-communist movement. Across the pond and beyond, Adolph Hitler – another demagogue – offered up a final solution and in the process, nearly killed off a race of men, destroyed a nation, and obliterated a generation's collective soul. Mr. Stalin was indiscriminate in the genocide he perpetrated within the USSR, but according to Andre Solzhenitsyn, Stalin's body count made Hitler look like a piker (that is not to diminish Hitler's crimes against humanity in any way). Further east think of Pol Pot and the killing fields in Cambodia. These men often possessed by messianic and revolutionary vision, lead their nations to destruction.

Fortunately, this country's demagogues – at least in the last century – have been less harsh in terms of generating body count, but potentially were just as dangerous. Here and now in the 21st Century, we appear to have a demagogue presently in our midst; and like Senator Joe McCarthy before him, Mr. Norquist – who holds no elected office, and with no binding legal authority whatsoever – has a list. The list, however, doesn't name communist but rather, a list of Republican congressmen, who have pledged to Mr. Norquist not to raise taxes.

To which JMH responds: When did the Republican Party become Mr. Norquist's sock puppet, or this weeks buzz word – "muppet?" Ninety-five percent of all Republican congressman and, I believe all Republican Presidential candidates, have suspending rational thought, and have signed Mr. Norquist's pledge, maintaining that they will not increase taxes. (I remember another highly respected Republican President, who your humble blogger voted for twice, who lost his re-election bid in '92 over a similar commitment, in which he stated "read my lips;" his own political party turned on him when he rationally bailed upon his pledge not to raise taxes.)

Now nobody, including Democrats, likes paying taxes but as stated by Justice Oliver Wendell Holmes: "Taxes are what we pay to live in a civilized society." Besides, the only thing worse than taxes is government debt and deficit spending – and the U.S. has mountains of debt brought upon it by successive Republican administrations.

Just how fiscally conservative is the Republican Party, and Mr. Norquist then, when they offer no concrete or realistic recommendations to reduce government spending, but are all for tax cuts for the wealthy, when we are running trillion dollar deficits per annum?

The answer is: Not very! Analysis from major news organizations reveals that Mr. Romney's budget plans for the nation, if elected, would lead to an even greater accumulation of debt than the present administration. And lets not forget Republican Vice President Cheney's infamous quip that President Reagan proved deficits don't matter. One only has to look to the PIIGS in Europe to see where this fiscal insanity will eventually lead; and but by the grace of the printing press and possession of the world's fiat currency, the U.S. doesn't find itself among the PIIGS already.

Of course rarely mentioned, if ever, by Mr. Norquist, or his minions – the Republican Party, is that the wealthy, the rich, and any major corporation worth it's salt, often don't pay taxes, or pay taxes at exceptionally low rates versus the middle class. Now, if your middle class, say within the ninety-nine percentile, you likely cannot afford lobbyist, or pay to hire former U.S. Treasury personnel to run your tax department, or spend exceptional amounts of money electing politicians – who will vote for and protect your favorite tax loophole(s) or dodge. But for the elite, it's just another day in a tax paradise.

Mr. Norquist is correct in that marginal tax rates are too high in this country, for the individual and the corporation; but where many part company with Mr. Norquist is in the belief that closing catalogue upon catalogue of tax loopholes, exploited by the powerful economic and political interests, is tantamount to a tax increase, and must be fought at every turn.

The middle class and future generations are being robbed by U.S. tax policy, as it presently stands. The middle class, what remains of it, cannot escape paying taxes, and pay a higher rate to subsidize those entities, individuals and organizations, which often pay at half the tax rate we do, that is if they pay any taxes at all.

Here's what Mr. David Brooks of the NY Times had to say on the matter. Mr. Brooks isn't exactly known for his liberal views.

The Organization for Economic Cooperation and Development recently calculated how much each affluent country spends on social programs. When you include both direct spending and tax expenditures, the U.S. has one of the biggest welfare states in the world. We rank behind Sweden and ahead of Italy, Austria, the Netherlands, Denmark, Finland and Canada. Social spending in the U.S. is far above the organization's average.

You might say that a tax break isn't the same as a spending program. You would be wrong.

David Bradford, a Princeton economist, has the best illustration of how the system works. Suppose the Pentagon wanted to buy a new fighter plane. But instead of writing a $10 billion check to the manufacturer, the government just issued a $10 billion "weapons supply tax credit." The plane would still get made. The company would get its money through the tax credit. And politicians would get to brag that they had cut taxes and reduced the size of government!

And we are not talking about the usual list of suspects here when it comes to IRS avoidance, but rather, when we talk about those who make a sport of ducking payment into government's revenue stream (be it America's or Europe's), we are talking about a pantheon of venerable corporate entities and institutions, some of the finest America has to offer.

How do they do it?

We know that private equity likes to front load profits by soaking balance sheets in debt, and via the tax deductibility of interest payments on same. It's what makes private equity work. Moreover, private equity dividends paid for with debt are not taxed until the debt is retired. And a takeover target that is saddled with debt is likely to have diminished earnings, if any, to pay taxes on. In fact, it might carry forward financial loss (brought on by excessive debt) to offset future earnings for purposes of cutting taxes. Separately, payment of carried interest to the pirates of private equity is at the capital gains tax rate, presently set at 15%. So in many instances, not only is private equity doing harm to the U.S. labor force by stripping away CAPEX and human capital (which actually does pay taxes), in order to service an artificially high debt load; but private equity loads take over targets up with debt so as to pay themselves and in turn, coincidentally, lower the effective tax rate paid on debt encumbered earnings. In short, Americans get robbed both ways, when private equity runs a company, through the loss of jobs and the debt-ladened company's diminished tax receipts.

On a side note, private equity likes to say they only rehabilitate sick and dying businesses, but they also like to take up healthy organizations, or fully recovered entities, and load them up with debt, repeatedly. Take HCA for example or private equity's greatest failure to date, TXU. And to think of all those union and state employee retirement plans, which dump retirement money into private equity, which operates directly at cross-purposes with these same employees economic and political interests…? One wonders if these unions and state employees, and their leadership, will ever wise up?

But wait it gets better, because the *crème de la crème* of Silicon Valley also has a deep disdain for paying taxes, take Apple and Google as yet another example. Both companies exploit a tax scheme called a "double irish" or "dutch sandwich," whereby overseas earnings are sent to Ireland, then the Netherlands, and onto Bermuda. As reported by Bloomberg in 2010, the result is from 2007 to the date the article was written, Google paid less than a three percent tax rate, per annum, on offshore earnings. Tax arbitrage defined! Google's actual payroll and revenue generated from Ireland, the Netherlands, and Bermuda maybe negligible or non-existent, but international revenues and earnings are repatriated around the horn. All perfectly legal, and we wonder why the U.S., and assorted Western democracies – like Ireland, is running catastrophic and unsustainable fiscal deficits, and their respective citizens suffer fiscal austerity. Last I read, Facebook, America's favorite on line toy, was about to join the ranks of Apple and Google, by deploying the double irish tax dodge.

Meanwhile, Apple, America's – indeed the world's – largest market cap, or stock valuation, has more cash on hand than the U.S. Treasury – most of it safe and secure offshore.

And there is where it will lie until such time as the Republican Party breaks the spell of Mr. Norquist, and decides to stop mortgaging America's future with debt and deficit spending. Of course this blog has written extensively as to why the Republican Party favors deficit financing… all the better to allow the Wall Street Cartel to dictate fiscal and government policy.   And to think this is the party, or used to be, of rugged individualism and the "maverick" mentality. Today's Republican Party looks more like a flock of woolly mammals than proud and iconic mustangs I once knew it to be. It's only a matter of time before Republicans wake up and see Mr. Norquist for who he is.

Could you imagine if the middle class rose up and demanded to be paid by their employers, through stock manipulation and debt turned to dividends, at the capital gains rate? We'd all be a little richer, since our tax rate – like Candidate Romney's – would effectively be fifteen percent; but the government would come crashing down. The elimination of government, ultimately, maybe the goal of certain elements within the Republican Party, like Mr. Norquist and the billionaire Koch Brothers! Starve the beast of funds, and it will eventually parish, and along with it the social contract. Alas, greed makes the world go around.

PS:

And speaking of unmitigated greed… the present administration knows that rising fuel prices at the pump are not due to any short fall in supply (America in fact has stockpiles of oil in Cushing Oklahoma and more natural gas coming on line than this country knows what to do with); but rather excessive speculation in oil – brought about by central banks flooding the world with paper currency – is driving fuel costs ever higher. When zombie-banking institutions aren't hoarding the tsunami of central bank currency, they are speculating with it. And hence, Americans are being bent over the hoods of their cars at the pump, which is a direct threat to Mr. Obama's second term. To mitigate this greed and it's threat to the nascent economic recovery, either the state or federal government should purchase, or support the purchase of the Sunoco refinery in Philadelphia, presently up for sale, and operate it at maximum capacity. All the better to keep both Cartels worst tendencies in check, the American consumer protected, and help insure President Obama's second term. Heh, if you're going to operate a Cartel – the public and the Cartel should expect government intervention to protect the consumer and the economy from monopoly's worst tendencies.

Unleashing a flood of oil from the Strategic Reserve would also send a message to the speculators that it is no longer open season on the American consumer.

Doctor Feelbad

By JM Hamilton (3-31-12)

"Of course I'm respectable, I'm old. Politicians, ugly buildings, and whores all get respectable if they last long enough." **- John Huston (aka Noah Cross) from the movie Chinatown**

It would appear that Mr. Huston left doctors off the list of items that become more respectable with time. After all, the practice of medicine must be the second oldest profession (think about that – but only for a second). As my readers know this blog is fond of taking on both the sacred and the profane; and this week we lance that most sacred of boils, the medical profession. Aside from the almighty herself – there is perhaps no group of individuals or body of professionals, we hold in higher regard than doctors and the industries that support same. Perhaps it is because Americans place such a high value on life, and in particular our own, that we have a special fondness – call it near pagan idolatry – for the men and women wearing white coats.

How else can we explain why we would allow this industry/profession to run with double digit cost increases, perennially? There's no other industry like it. Medical inflation is destroying our Federal and State budgets, and my guess is probably the single biggest reason why corporations and business are reluctant to hire Americans.

And as much as JMH is a fan of President Obama and his administration, replete with it's many successes, one of its two greatest failures was the Democratic Party's complete waste of 111th Congress, with the passage of the Patient Care and Affordable Protection Act, otherwise known as the healthcare reform.

Why my disdain for this legislation? After all before it was derisively known as "Obamacare," it was called "Romneycare" and was originally thought up by a right-wing think tank, the Heritage Foundation. No, the goal of healthcare reform was perfectly acceptable: universal care via the private sector coupled with REFORM (read: cost containment). But the appalling outcome was the complete lack of reform. That is to say, in order to get this dog passed the Democratic leadership had to "suck up" to nearly every medical special interest known to man – but primarily Big Pharma, major corporate hospitals chains, and of course, doctors. Meanwhile, Rome burned, unemployment soared, and the banking industry (the architect of our destruction) grew bigger and more powerful.

Had the 111th passed true health care cost containment, the Democratic Party very well might have addressed the unemployment issue, simultaneously; because employers would not then be confronted with this run away inflationary train.

Next time you look at your ever shrinking paycheck with it's every shrinking purchasing power, don't blame your employer — blame ever escalating healthcare costs (and several other predatory monopolies and cartels I enjoy writing about). That's where your annual pay raise has gone: to pay for double-digit medical care increases. As we know real U.S. wages have been stagnant since the 90's.

What might true reform have looked like then, so that you might actually enjoy a future payroll increase going forward, that is if both political parties weren't so slavishly devoted to special interests and had the guts to take on same?

First and foremost fee for service (FFS), the primary payment arrangement for doctors in the U.S., should be abolished. Doctors should be placed on a salary – based upon what the market will afford, and incentivized based upon outcome, cost containment, and preventive care. In exchange for going to a salary, and committing to providing care within the U.S., doctors might be made immune from medical malpractice litigation and some percentage of their medical education paid for; in exchange for foregoing medical malpractice insurance, professional lapses/problems might be reviewed by a board made up of professional peers, *and patients*.

By placing doctors on salary, and eliminating medical malpractice costs for same, America would take one large step forward in controlling double digit medical cost increases, since doctors would no longer be incentivized to order superfluous tests and exams. And not to get nasty, but if doctors become like any other class of worker in America, we would expect their wages to "flat line." For as we learned in the last couple of years some captains of industry collude to contain payroll expense, prevent the bidding up of worker income, and eliminate employee poaching (witness the Justice Department settlement with Silicon Valley). Hey if nearly every other industry or business class in America colludes, directly or indirectly, to set the wages of their labor- why should doctors be exempt?

But controlling FFS and doctor wages is just the first step. America is probably the only Western Democracy that does not negotiate the price of medicine and drugs with major pharmaceutical companies (otherwise known as Big Pharma). As a consequence, American labor is uncompetitive, and the drug cartel makes obscene profits. The world, in turn, rides our coattails and benefits from the subsidy America pays Big Pharma. The **Washington Post** estimates the mark up maybe as high as 20%; and we have all read about contrived shortages of key medicines daily, which further hike profit margins. Right out of the monopoly play book. Big Pharma – with its seemingly never ending patented medicines – is just another monopoly preying upon ordinary Americans and the system; as such it presents an enormous economic drag (i.e. tax).

Profits in America, in turn, finance Big Pharms' dividends, stock buy backs, mergers and acquisition, with only a small percentage of Big Pharma profits going to finance R&D. As a result, America is going broke, and Big Pharma has grown larger, less efficient and more politically powerful.

America then has one of two solutions: either present a bill to the other Western democracies to pay their fair share of Big Pharma's mark up (not a likely scenario); or two, negotiate – annually – lower drug costs and margins, like every other country. As this Cartel has shown less productivity in recent years (with a slow down in new medicines), and diseconomies of scale, strong consideration should also be given to breaking up these companies to make them more competitive and more attuned to the free market principles the executives of Big Pharma subscribe to.

Finally, it appears that an absurd and disproportionate amount of annual medical costs are spent prolonging terminal patients last few months of life…. this clearly needs to change. That is, here's your morphine drip, go home, our prayers are with you, and we'll see you in heaven. Sound cruel? No, what's cruel is spending criminal amounts of money to keep Uncle Benny alive for the last three months of his existence, when that money could be spent on preventive care, or even education for our youth. Perish the thought.

Perhaps the one positive that came out of healthcare reform was data collection, and the mandate for electronic records, which could ultimately lead to Artificial Intelligence within the medical field. How many times in the last five years, have you logged onto Web MD and diagnosed your own health problem in advance of your doctor visit? And how often were you, or rather WebMD, found to be correct? Digital medical records, and the accumulation and analysis of medical data, may eventually solve escalating medical costs, w/out reform. The advent of digital medical records and computer diagnostics and diagnosis … may make doctors obsolete, if nothing else certainly general practitioners.

Let's hope that arrival of medical AI appears before Big Pharma and our white coated friends bankrupt our country and make U.S. employment untenable.

P.S.

Until that day arrives… I just want to go on record as stating that I love my doctor. She's a wonderful person.

As for politicians who sit in judgment on this law within the Supreme Court (as flawed as it maybe)… I can think of no greater reasons to re-elect our sitting President than to replace these conservative judges, as they retire or shuffle off their mortal coil. Republican governor Rick Perry of Texas did have at least one great idea, while on the campaign trail this year and last…. and that is Americans should not be held hostage by the political beliefs of the judges on the bench in perpetuity. As Noah Cross might have said, some of the older judges on the court have earned our respect, and like any good politician/"jurist," we wish them well in retirement.

http://blog.jmhamiltonpublishing.com/2012/03/12/the-price-of-medicine-.aspx

More Cowbell

By J.M. Hamilton (4-7-12)

"Guess what? I got a fever, and the only prescription is more cowbell!" -
Christopher Walken (aka Bruce Dickenson) Saturday Night Live 4-8-2000

One of the funniest sketches on **Saturday Night Live'** near forty year run was written and performed by Will Farrell, and starred Christopher Walken, as the music producer for the **Blue Oyster Cult** song *Don't Fear the Reaper.* Inexplicably, Mr. Walken continues to call for more cowbell during the recording of the song, and Mr. Farrell obliges with hilarious results. The skit was so popular that "cowbell" has become a popular culture metaphor for the often times crazed absurdity and futility of life.

As much as JMH enjoys watching Mr. Walken's artistic endeavors, I have greater admiration for Mr. Krugman at the **New York Times.** After all Mr. Krugman – a Nobel Laureate and first rate economist – was warning the world about the excesses of untrammeled free enterprise, when many of us were still smoking the fantasy of self- regulating markets. *Laissez Faire* capitalism is a pipedream the GOP, and Mr. Romney, just can't let go of, despite the ruin it has caused the nation and global markets.

Mr. Krugman is often right, and his concern for the general welfare of our society and this country are never in doubt. And if JMH disagrees with Mr. Krugman in any single area it is with his continual calls to wind up the printing presses at the Fed, yet again.

(And even here, if the debt to GDP ratio wasn't already so high as a result of excessive overspending and monetary profligacy brought about by successive Republican administrations, or if Mr. Bernanke was willing to dump money on the demand side of the curve, I believe Mr. Krugman's proposed solution would be spot on.)

But given that the U.S. has already been through two rounds of quantitative easing (QE), an on-going Operation Twist, and that QE has now been exported and adopted in Europe, with the same effect – a short term economic rush followed by a hangover and the realization that more liquidity is not the solution – continued calls for more monetary stimulus by many economist sound a lot like calls for more cowbell.

In fact, QE appears to be having a deleterious effect, in that:

A) It has provided cover for politicians (i.e. the Republican controlled Congress) to continue to do nothing (if the Fed lets interest rates rise naturally – the interest expense on the national debt would force politicians to deal with our fiscal nightmare and set spending and revenue priorities);
B) QE has run up headline inflation on commodities actually hurting the 99 percent, thus harming the very people it – supposedly – is intended to help; and
C) QE allowed the banks not to address the mortgage crisis— which has delayed restructuring and write downs, and most importantly, a healthy economic recovery.

And on this final point, Fed mandate aside, undoubtedly the true beneficiaries of QE and Twist have been the banks, and shadow banking, the very institutions that placed the world in economic crisis mode.

That said, Mr. Krugman at the **Times** might ultimately get his wish for additional QE, but possibly from a different corner of the world. My guess is the next round of quantitative easing will come from Europe, where it is referred to as LTRO. Spain has now moved to the forefront, as Europe's financial basket case, the sugar high of LTRO 1 is wearing off, and the sharks are circling with interest rates rising.

Troubled European banks are hoarding cash or buying more government debt, the economies are in the tank among the peripheral nations (often referred to by the acronym PIIGS); and my guess is the recent trend of European capital flight will continue, which should be good for short term holders of US Treasuries and holders of Treasury options to purchase same.

Goldman Sachs alum and EU bank president Mario Draghi is almost certainly talking with Mr. Bernanke, and assorted central bank heads, and deciding which central bank will stomp the printing press accelerator next. What we very well may be witnessing, through a veil of secrecy, is coordination among central banks. No surprise.

Since we live in one world with one global economy – whether the Fed punches the accelerator, or the ECB does first, is probably immaterial – the effect should be the same: temporary relief followed by more economic malaise (since the fundamental/structural problems remain). Mr. Bernanke probably is not so much concerned about the criticism of the Republican Party (after all should Mr. Romney enter the White House – Lord save us – I can't imagine a President Romney recommending a dramatically different tack in regards Fed policy); but rather, Mr. Bernanke is perhaps biding his time/ waiting for his turn to mash the accelerator yet again, Europe's problems being far greater than our own at the moment.

If the US economy stumbles (see Friday's unemployment figures) look for the Fed to punch it- sooner rather than later. After all this is an election year.

Denizens of the stock market take heart; another flood of liquidity is more than likely on the way.

Good for the asset class… Not so great for the 99 percent.

As with Mr. Krugman, I sincerely hope that President Obama returns for a second term; and some of the boldness, strength and courage that our President has shown as of late, in tackling special interests, is made even more manifest. Private investors will eventually return to the stock market, when they see that it is cleaned up and running fairly for all participants. A first term President Romney is likely to be less assertive in this regard, and a greater advocate for the policies and principles that placed this country in its present crisis.

Mr. Romney's plea in Wisconsin this week was most telling, as reported in the NY Times:

"This time we'll get it right."

Sounds like Mr. Romney is calling for more cowbell.

Dumbed Down Madness

By J.M. Hamilton (4-20-12)

"We have now sunk to a depth at which restatement of the obvious is the first duty of intelligent men. " - **George Orwell**

Question: When did the Republican Party begin to advocate "dumbing down" and turning off on higher education?

Answer: The GOP embraced this concept with the realization that those fortunate enough to enjoy a higher education were fleeing their Party, and migrating to the opposition by a considerable margin.

We get the following from the April 1ˢᵗ **New York Times,** in a story by Mr. Thomas Edsall, *The Politics of Going to College*:

"In 1984, <u>those with college and advanced degrees</u> made up 35.3 percent of the electorate. Reagan's strongest margins were among the college educated, who backed him over Walter F. Mondale by a crushing 62.7-36.9 margin. Among all those with both college and advanced degrees, Reagan won 58.7 percent, a landslide margin.

Jump <u>to 2008</u>. Even though those with college degrees <u>made up 27.9 percent of the population</u> that year, they cast 45 percent of the presidential vote. These voters register and go to the polls in substantially higher numbers than the less well educated.

By 2008, the Republican advantage of the early 1980s among voters with a college degree or higher had disappeared. Barack Obama carried this demographic with 54.1 percent. He beat McCain 50-48 among those with bachelor's degrees, and by a decisive 58-40 among the 17 percent of the 2008 electorate with post-graduate degrees."

But the bad news for Republicans doesn't stop there, women are amassing college degrees and embracing knowledge in greater numbers then men; and as we all know, per recent polls, women favor President Obama, over the presumed Republican nominee, by a double-digit margin.

The Republican Party is, of course, a two trick pony: But President Obama has shown the GOP how to conduct foreign policy and eliminate thugs and villains (with stealth and special forces; and not with Republican favored cost inefficient and amoral defense policies, such as: ready to use standing armies; invasion, occupation, nation building; and redundant budget breaking military departments and weapon systems). As for the economy (the Republican Party's second trick – and a really nasty one at that), it is possibly on the mend under a Democratic administration, despite enormous economic and fiscal head winds - see the "PS" below. With a monopoly constrained economy possibly perking up, the GOP – via Rick Santorum – trotted out the only issues that still divide Americans, forty to fifty year old social issues. And in the process this regressive may have fired up his base, but he ran off the majority of women voters and gave independents serious pause and second thoughts. No wonder the GOP, in recent weeks, had done everything in its power to shelve Mr. Santorum's campaign.

And what did the reactionary Mr. Santorum have up his sleeve next… the disenfranchisement of women, or perhaps he wanted to bring back the poll tax?

Americans, the educated and uneducated, Republican and Democrat, actually agree on a great deal. Americans, red and blue, all want a healthy economy, fiscally sound Federal and State governments, good roads and bridges, a responsible military *defense*, and last but certainly not least, an affordable and decent education for their children and grand children. And of course, there is America's love affair with entitlement spending. To which the astute and wise Barney Frank recently commented in **New York Magazine**: "Yeah, they want more from government, but they don't want to pay for it."

Today's Republican leadership isn't interested in what unites us, however. No, the GOP, in its present incarnation, is only interested in their core constituency, the one percent; and of course, amassing and maintaining power at your expense, trashing government (via "borrow and spend" policies), taking away private and public benefits and democratic power from the ninety-nine - to be redistributed to the one percent, and maintaining a dysfunctional tax system that benefits their core constituency. Of course, key to their success is maintaining their base within the ninety-nine percent – you see, there's that annoying thing for the GOP, and the plutocracy that pulls it strings, called democracy.

The economic ruin created by three decades of Republican Party's *laissez faire* ideology – if Japan is any example – will take decades to heal. But as mentioned in our last editorial, the presumptive GOP nominee, "Mr. Severe," wants to continue this failed doctrine, so that his buddies in Private Equity can continue to raid and loot businesses and short their tax payments, globally. Again, at your expense.

To continue their failed policies the GOP will continue to push fear, specious declamation, and disinformation; but in order for this to work it must prey upon an under-educated electorate. *Ipso facto*, with educated citizens fleeing the Party in droves, the Republican's core has become, in some instances: the cerebrally enfeebled, the frightened, and under educated Americans. All of which might explain the dearth of fresh ideas, and the uniformity of opinions coming out of the Party.

Of course, going back to the Greeks, the whole premise supporting democracy, as a form of government, is that an educated and informed public will make up the constituency.

No wonder Mr. Santorum, and Mr. Severe, do not want you to enjoy a higher education…. Because, gosh darn it, you just might begin to engage in some critical thinking and analysis on your own, instead of buying into the GOP's failed fables and fear.
As noted in the aforementioned **Times** piece:

"President Obama once said he wants everybody in America to go to college. What a snob," Santorum <u>told a Tea Party meeting in Troy, Mich.,</u> on Feb. 25. "I understand why he wants you to go to college. He wants to remake you in his image."

What both GOP candidates fail to mention at the same time they are trashing higher education is that they themselves, both Messrs. Romney and Santorum, are products of higher education and in possession of rather distinguished degrees. My guess is neither of these men would have made it quite as far in life without their education; that is to say, neither appears overly gifted with natural talent, mental or physical. Nor has either candidate mentioned the general but often direct correlation between a higher education and income.

And only somebody with fiscally and morally bankrupt economic and foreign policies would resort to sophistry, and equate education with snobbery. Those affected by snobbery are everywhere these days, including demagogues, the religiously and socially intolerant, and the under-educated (call it reverse snobbery if you will, but it's all the same, it stems from pride).

But that's what today's Republican Party has become, a toxic, bile filled bag, spewing anger, animosity, and discord (just observe the Senate minority leadership). For the good of the nation, let's hope this current brand of GOP leadership stays in the minority.

And the truly sad part in all this? This nation needs a strong, rationale, and dare I say it - highly educated - Republican Party to keep the Democratic Party's worst impulses in check.

But for the moment, if you happen to be highly educated – or just like to keep up on current events, engage in learning for your own betterment, or even perhaps like to think for one's self (shucks, maybe your just curious) – then per the GOP, you are defective, obviously an elitist, and quite possibly a threat to the Republican Party's hopes to retake the White House.

We should heed well Mr. Santorum's advice and continue to let him and the plutocracy call the shots, after all look what it has yielded: their enrichment and our enslavement.

(What's that? Doubt you're enslaved? Look at the never ending rounds of bank bailouts at taxpayer expense - both front and back door; rising gas prices at the pump – when this nation has all but achieved energy independence under the Obama administration; and the declining purchasing power of the dollar. These are all examples of taxes upon your wallet that you have little or no say over, but must contend with and navigate daily. But unlike the President, the Congress or the Senate, you can't vote for the CEO – or the CEO's pay package – at Goldman Sachs, Exxon, or Citi…not even if you're a stockholder.)

It is so much better to deny learning, keep your blinders on, and embrace ignorance and bliss, so that you can be more easily exploited by the plutocracy that has hijacked the GOP, and thanks to the Supreme Court, the democratic process itself.

P.S.
"During times of universal deceit, telling the truth becomes a revolutionary act."
—   George Orwell

Interesting how yesterday's toxic assets, CDO's and MBS, have earned renewed cache from their creators the banks, as well as hedge funds, mutual funds, private equity, and wealthy investors. The fix must be in…

therefore, don't count on seeing any universally restructured mortgages, debt forgiveness on same, or a spirited economic recovery anytime soon. This same cadre - populated and managed as often as not by GOP heavy hitters – has done everything in its power to run President Obama out of power, via capital strike, commodity speculation and manipulation (read: inflation), and with a little help from Big Oil, sending gas prices at the pump ever higher. A President Romney would only encourage this group, and embrace the very policies that trashed this nation and Europe in 2008 to the present day.

A special nod to Mr. Blow in this week's Times, who offered up the following observations:

http://blog.jmhamiltonpublishing.com/2012/04/19/barack-obama-and-mitt-romney-the-democrats-and-republicans-have-radically-divergent-views-about-the-direction-of-the-country-one-is-progressive-the-other-is-regressive.aspx

"L" is for Leverage

By J.M. Hamilton (5-5-2012)

"Those who control the present, control the past and those who control the past, control the future." - George Orwell

Orwell wrote of it in his book **1984**, and I clearly remember it actually being practiced by the former Soviet Union as described in the pages of **National Review**. Revisionism, or the re-writing of history for political purposes, has traditionally been associated with totalitarian regimes; but to actually see it practiced by Western democracies is something entirely different. One can tune into **Bloomberg Surveillance** hosted by Ken Prewitt and Tom Keene, quite possibly the most balanced and informative radio program ever produced, and hear any number of prominent Western economist blame the current economic crisis on euro-socialism and government profligacy. These same economist won't mention *laissez faire* dogma or an altogether different brand of socialism, corporate welfare in the form of endless bank bailouts, as the reason so many European governments are now considering default and rebooting their pre-euro currencies.

For many a struggling government hitting the fiscal and monetary reset button is a rational alternative to economic nuclear winter, besides there's the matter of an angry populace to contend with.

One might gather from some of my scribbling that JMH is a heartless fiscal hawk, but I'm no austerity freak. If anything, JMH has argued that Keynesian policy, which has been driving modern economic thought and Western economies since the 1930's Great Depression, has hit the wall, and due to sustained political abuse has reached its limits. Having reached the denouement of Keynesian fiscal and monetary policy, this leaves structural reform, default and reorganization, view our editorial, **Thinking the Unthinkable** (link below). Unfortunately debt reorganization and kick starting old currencies can be just as nasty of a cure as fiscal austerity, except the people, and their democratically elected leaders, have some feelings of control over their destiny and sovereignty (as opposed to having the IMF or the E.U. Central Bank install a banker as head of state, as happened in Greece and Italy).

So JMH has written about re-org but what might "government structural reform" look like? What many economists refer to as "structural reform," often involves free market initiatives, such as deregulation, privatization, and other measures that allow businesses to compete and prosper. But the kind of structural reform to be described in today's editorial, involves reforming government spending and containing globalization's worst traits; and with approximately 40% of the U.S. economy driven by public spending, and globalization sucking the wind out of Western democracies (read: regulatory, labor and tax arbitrage) - these are very large issues. But it is rarely if ever discussed. Instead politicians like to talk and act upon the federal budget with macro increases and reductions in government spending, or supply side cuts or increases in taxation.

Of course macro solutions mask one of the real issues, which is a colossal amount of government waste.

Government has grown so huge and so big that there is a tremendous amount of government mismanagement and fraud, stemming from the policies of both political parties.

The Republicans like to, when they can, pay for their largesse to big business via tax breaks; this way their spending is *sub rosa*, and starves the beast (borrow and spend). Democrats, authors of the New Deal and Great Society programs, traditionally believe in entitlement spending directed at the middle class and the poor or the 99% (and embrace tax and spend policies). JMH has also argued both parties are engaged in the redistribution of resources for the benefit of their respective political base.

The crime then is not necessarily in the redistribution of resources, which Hayek and rocked ribbed conservatives often bemoan. Both parties by now are neck deep into socialism. Redistribution of resources is the central tenet of government. It's what government does. It's been with us since a Monarch's tax collectors rode up and demanded tribute from the peasants and serfs mucking about upon the King's land.

The problem is this: Every time the nation overspends on a V-22 Osprey (a classic DOD boon doggle), or the government hands too much money out to Big Pharma (because we are the only Western Democracy who doesn't negotiate a cap on drug costs) etc, etc..... We are shorting this generation and our children, and we are shorting the economy and American business. Deficit spending, and eventually higher taxes to pay down same, takes money out the economy and all too often redistributes it to monopolies and cartels, which provide government goods and services, often at an extraordinary profit. To grease the wheels some of this excess ends up in political action committees and re-election campaigns, which explains why politicians never get around to addressing the problem.

So how is this wrong corrected? By running government to some degree like a business. That is to say, by using the power of leverage. Not the kind of financial leverage that drove this nation to her knees in 2008, which is responsible for our on-going financial crisis. No, I'm talking about deploying the awesome leveraging power of the state to make sure vendors offer the most competitive deals to the taxpayer imaginable, squeezing profit margins, windfall profits taxes on government contracts leading to "unexpected" rich rewards, audits, cost overruns picked up by the government contractor - instead of the taxpayer, and an independent government bureau responsible for executing this cost savings, and rewarded for same.

The savings for this venture could in turn be re-allocated back to government programs for those most in need, children, pairing down the costs of higher education, or paying down the national debt.

This means government vendors must be squeezed. If you're lucky enough to have a government contract be thankful and move along--- it's not a license to steal. **(Please excuse the generalization: None of this is say that all government vendors are robbing the country blind.)**

Politicians are great at redistributing money, what they are, clearly, not good at is demanding value for the nation and the taxpayer, once those resources have been deployed. And unfortunately, this is why our democracy is in need of an autonomous government ministry, whose mandate is to insure efficiency, financial rectitude, and maximum economies of scale.

Not unlike private equity coming into a private enterprise and chewing away at waste and mismanagement, federal and state government could utilize these same principles; but instead of the resulting savings going to a few private equity execs at the top, the returns accrue to the public, the taxpayer, and those most in need. Bring back Quadrangle Executive and former "Car Czar," Mr. Steven Rattner to work out on government vendors, like Big Pharma, to ensure that *res publica's* interests are being represented and are receiving the best deal possible. Lord knows Congress won't do it.

What follows are just a few examples of where leverage can be applied

for the betterment of the American people, and assorted random thoughts:

Using the power of the state to demand a fair and equitable deal can also be applied to manufacturing multi-nationals. These multi-nationals, in many instances, have become like sovereigns of old, that is to say free to extract wealth and resources from the land, and the masses; but also entirely free of any and all responsibility to societies they operate within (think of both Apple and Google sitting upon mountains of cash, while pulling out all the stops, via offshore tax dodges, to pay no taxes). Whenever a manufacturer fails to pay their fair share, it leads to deficit spending and/or higher tax burden on those who cannot escape paying taxes, typically the already squeezed middle and upper income tax brackets.

Indeed, Multinationals stride across the globe seemingly acting as mini-kingdoms or demi-states. Think of Mr. Rex Tillerson, chairmen and CEO of Exxon, and a head of state in his own right, very recently sitting down with Russian premiere to carve up the Arctic for drilling. Interesting how Mr. Tillerson's first name is also latin for the word "King." At least Mr. Tillerson is honest, as noted by **Alan Abelson in Barron's** recently, who acknowledged Mr. Tillerson's comment that speculation adds a 50% mark up to a barrel of oil. Mr. Tillerson would know. Speculation in oil results in a tax born by the public at the pump, and represents a serious gouge upon discretionary income for many citizens. Perhaps someone should pass the word on to Mr. Duffy, head of CME Group, the commodities exchange responsible for $1.6 Billion in missing client money from the MF Global disaster. Mr. Duffy has the nerve to chastise President Obama for his recent comments on speculation, and the drag/tax it places on the economy. Mr. Duffy, like so many Republicans, apparently lives in a world of denial, just ask Mr. Tillerson. But I digress.

Perhaps government leverage of an entirely different sort can be brought to bear upon commodity speculators; speculators apparently aren't subject to many of the same insider trading laws that govern stock exchanges. Now there's a start right there.

The Wall Street banking cartel is yet another global leviathan that is accountable to no one, not even themselves, as they are backed by the full faith and credit of the U.S. government. So why are we discussing student loans? And why is the U.S. government/taxpayer picking up the interest on same? Why isn't the government's leverage or the *quid pro quo* as follows:

Dear Banking Cartel... you want to run your operations as TBTF institutions, reinsured by the Fed and the Treasury, well some of the "quid" is you will offer student loans at a fixed rate of 3%. Consider it a cost of doing business, and your contribution to the society you all too often prey upon, and depend upon as a financial backstop.

Since TBTF banking institutions are backed by the full faith and credit of the American people (in many instances their financial rating depends upon it), and therefore, Americans, at any one time, may be the *defacto* owners and creditors and reinsurers of these businesses... shouldn't the American public, unlike ordinary stockholders, have some say in the composition of management and the board of directors? If the *vox populi* had state mandated voting rights within the Banking Cartel, how quickly would management, boards and stockholders break up these institutions, themselves, to a more prudent and financially rewarding size - to just below the TBTF threshold?

The answer: So fast that it would make your head spin.

Or perhaps citizens should demand premium or a risk charge for providing financial insurance for the casino that has become Wall Street and CME Group?

Answer: I think we tried that once but didn't Treasury or the Fed fold under the withering and blinding heat of bank lobbyist?

Moving along... NAFTA and assorted so-called "free trade" agreements sent millions of jobs offshore, along with it the U.S. tax base. How about bringing some of those jobs back? America's primacy as a global market it greatly diminished by the growth in emerging markets (yet another aspect of globalization), but the U.S. still amounts to roughly 25% of global GDP. There's a leverage opportunity right there. Okay, going forward if you want to sell products and services in America shouldn't your corporation hire Americans proportionately? That is to say, if America makes up 35% of global sales should not at least 35% of your labor force be American? Ditto a proportionate minimum corporate tax, based upon U.S. sales.

These are just a hand full of examples where through the power of leverage the state can exact the best deals possible, just like any responsible business person would, on behalf of the U.S. economy, American business, and the American public. The state, by abdicating responsibility to *laissez faire* ideology, got us into this mess and the state will have to get us out, or fail trying.

What would it take to make some of these dreams a reality? Just a few laws from a few civic-minded politicians. Our ongoing fiscal and economic crisis, accompanied by a myriad of problems, would appear to demand many solutions, among them tried and true business practices, like the *quid pro quo.* I've made the case before, just as it took a Republican president to embrace Communist China, and drive a wedge between Soviet-Sino relations; it took Democratic administration to roll back the welfare state. (In short a Democrat could have never embraced Red China, just as a Republican could never get away with rolling back the welfare state; and in fact, Republican administrations have often extended and expanded Great Society and New Deal programs).

But with Congress and the Senate failing the American public by the second with internecine and guerrilla political warfare, what the nation needs now more than ever is a return to the imperial presidency and the presidential power of impoundment.

Alas, if only the original "outside the box" thinker, and flaming liberal, Richard Nixon, was around to get us out of this jam.

The closest thing we have to Mr. Nixon on the political landscape at the moment is President Obama, and President Obama is far, far to the right of number Thirty-seven.

P.S.

Which brings us back full circle to history. And it appears that this weekend both the French and Greek citizens will be making some of their own history. France appears to be on the verge of electing their first Socialist Head of State in 30 years. And the Greeks - holding elections of their own - are inching ever closer to abandoning the euro, and the bankocracy which demands austerity. The PIIGS, Central banks and world governments watch with bated breath.

Of course, in a couple of my editorials, some of them well over a year old, JMH predicted the rise of the 99% over the existing banking order. JMH forecast that government's may fall, and banks may fail, but that the people would ultimately prevail. Looks like a revolution against the global leviathan may be beginning around the Southern edges of Europe and France. Perhaps its time to check your insurance policies for any exclusions against rebellion and revolution, at least for the summer home in the South of France.

But don't blame me... I just study and chronicle a little bit of history. As I have said before, if this blog is too upsetting for you - nobody is forcing you to read it.

Pull away and go play. Besides the pending revolution will have corporate sponsors, and can be watched later on YouTube or Hulu.

http://blog.jmhamiltonpublishing.com/2010/07/05/thinking-the-unthinkable.aspx

http://blog.jmhamiltonpublishing.com/2010/12/25/a-posthumous-nobel-award-for-dr-suess-in-economics.aspx

http://blog.jmhamiltonpublishing.com/2011/10/23/the-good-the-bad-and-the-ugly.aspx

http://www.bloomberg.com/radio/

Binary Party

By J.M. Hamilton (5-18-12)

"Power tends to corrupt, and absolute power corrupts absolutely. Great men are almost always bad men." – Baron Acton

Far too many years to count now, or maybe its just vanity that prohibits me from counting, a boss called me into his office.

He pointed his finger at me, and half serious, half in jest, said in a stentorian tone:

"Mr. Hamilton, are you and your job of any intrinsic or extrinsic value to society?"

It had the feel of a "Dickensonian" moment: "I pay my taxes, sir. I try."

And of course, I believe that my job adds value to society and I am fortunate enough to work for a company that provides a meaningful and valuable service, particularly in times of want and need.

Which is a lot more than I can say for your typical Wall Street Bank.

Wall Street Banks gamble, bet, and speculate (i.e. "make markets") for the possible enrichment of a few and to the detriment of the many. Sometimes there's a crash, and at other times there's merely a bailout, but the path always leads to what the one percent like to refer to as "creative destruction."

For the ninety-nine "creative destruction" is code for another round of socialism and redistribution of wealth from the many to the few, a wrecked economy, unemployment, inflation, and our government – and at least one political party – becoming more binary and extreme to rationalize, justify and prop up a failed financial elite.

Their products are the products of any casino, binary bets: derivatives, synthetic derivatives, repos, collateralized debt, and in most instances are highly illiquid.

One wonders if the financial elite that rule us will ever swear off boom and bust cycles, in favor of a more mundane glide path to economic harmony and prosperity?

It can be done, but at the expense of the wolves.

But is Mr. Dimon listening?

That is to say, many of JP Morgan's services and products are of no intrinsic or extrinsic worth to society. And the only product banking does provide that is esteemed by society (the ninety-nine), JP Morgan largely abandoned sometime ago…. Ordinary lending at non-usurious rates, where the bank actually underwrites the prospect, and retains the loan on its books. How quaint. Or put another way, how did society function for the last two millennium without CDO's, MBS, and derivatives and swaps, which are reinsured and underwritten by the American taxpayer?

What will we ever do without financial products that lever up the riches, and entitlements, for the one percent, but enslave the ninety-nine in a never-ending stream of ruinous bank bailouts?

If Wall Street doesn't get the message this time, perhaps it time to elect officials who will nationalize, smash, and sell off the leviathan: as non-threatening commercial banks (non-speculative – backed by the Fed and the Treasury); and investment houses (free to gamble with theirs and their clients money, and not reinsured by the American people). These reconfigured institutions might be retained by the government, particularly staid commercial banking, or released back into the wilds of the free market.

As it stands, Wall Street is a threat to the American people and to our national security.

I know… quite radical stuff, right?

I'm going to hazard a guess. Everything is relative, even the extrinsic and intrinsic values of society and her politics. And while JMH may sound left of center today, say in ten to twenty years, if the nation and her elite continue upon its present course, this blog may, possibly, read like the notes of a reactionary right winger, and a slave to the bourgeoisie.

Newton's third law of motion is that for every action there's a reaction.

The Republican Party and the Chicago School of Economics, and their *laissez faire* ideology (both owned and manipulated by the financial elite), have ruled this country for more than three decades, and their hegemony over political and economic discourse has – one would hope – reached its zenith. Enter

Baron Acton, above, and his famous quote. And enter a few famous Republicans and their quotes:

"I would remind you, extremism in the defense of Liberty is no vice." – Mr. Barry Goldwater.

"Either you are with us, or you are with the terrorist." – Mr. George W. Bush

"I fought against long odds in a deep blue state, but I was a severely conservative Republican governor." – Mr. Romney

Nothing but the extreme here. No room for polite discourse here? No nuance or shades of grey here? Ronald Reagan and Richard Nixon need not apply to today's – shoot from the hip – kill you now, check the facts later – Republican Party.

Besides thinking requires energy, and darn it… thought and time.

It's so much easier to keep doing what we are doing, except the speculative bubbles, crashes and financial hangovers are occurring with greater and greater frequency, and the public is beginning to wake up and take notice. The crashes are no longer isolated but global in nature…. Indeed, the world is very small.

And finally the true right wing extremist in today's Republican Party are unleashing, as Mr. Newton forecast, a virulent and no longer dormant response from the true Left. A socialist head of state in France, resurgent communist and fascist political parties in Europe, and elected officials in Greece that are perhaps willing to tell both the IMF and the E.U. central bank to "go to hell." Potentially setting off contagion and the euro's collapse, a veritable masochist's party.

So please allow me to let you in on a little secret. Come closer because I want to whisper this in your ear:

"The Republican Party, with it's severe economic and financial ideology, just might want to tone it down a little and rejoin the human race; because you're a breeding ground for revolution, the poster child of anarchy, and your extremism is unleashing forces beyond your control."

The GOP would be terribly naïve to think their policies do not have global impact.

Check out the Arab Spring, and please — by all means — check out Europe. It's not too late.

And above all, don't shoot the messenger. Please.

P.S.

A business model that is based upon unmitigated greed, rabid speculation, and offers no redeeming product or service to society, and in fact is detrimental and dangerous to society, must be relegated to the dustbin of history. Just ask Mr. Jamie Dimon. And so must politicians who support same. Monolithic banking institutions, gambling and earning lousy returns on equity, are failed monuments to the egos that manage them.

Not so ironically, the Tea Bag movement has already been co-opted and absorbed by the Robber Barons — moreover, the mainstream media has reported that the militants within the party have accepted large sums of money from the Cartel they were elected to end.

"If a free society cannot help the many who are poor, it cannot save the few who are rich." — President John F. Kennedy 1-20-1961

Private Equity Nation

"This relationship feels a bit one-way to me." Jamie Dimon, CEO JP Morgan Chase, as reported in the 2-28-10 New York Times piece, *For Buyout Kingpins, the TXU Utility Deal Gets Tricky*

By J.M. Hamilton 6-2-12

That must have been some dinner conversation between Mr. Dimon, known Master of the Universe, and Mr. Henry Kravis, Private Equity founder at KKR. Very few people have put one over on Mr. Dimon (save possibly Bruno Iksil aka the London Whale); and yet to this day, there appears to be a great deal of remorse surrounding the TXU deal (rechristened Energy Future Holdings), private equity's largest ever recorded deal and subsequently, private equity's largest failure. The genesis of the deal was pre-2008 financial crash, and has been tanking ever since with the decline in natural gas prices.

But fear not for the bankers and private equity, there was still fees and front loaded riches to be had for the insiders, while the bondholders that financed the majority of the $48 billion dollar leveraged buyout suffered substantial loss. Ms. Anderson and Ms. Creswell noted as much in the aforementioned **Times** piece:

"Despite such internecine brawls, the TXU deal was lucrative for many behind it. The utility's former chief executive, Mr. Wilder, walked away with a payday of $226 million, according to the research firm Equilar. The Wall Street banks divvied up fees totaling nearly $1.1 billion. And the private equity firms paid themselves $300 million in fees for arranging their own deal. (The buyout group receives an extra $35 million each year in management fees.)"

And that's how Private Equity (PE) operates. Like the banking Cartel that finances them, PE proprietors often make money coming and going, while investors and clients all too often get left holding the bag; and the communities, government, local business and vendors that host and support private equity owned and operated businesses take another hit in the form of lost business, layoffs, and a diminished tax base.

Our last editorial, **Binary Party**, was about the political extremism of the radical right in this country, more commonly known as the Republican Party. Today's editorial is about financial and economic extremism, and there is no other business sector within the economy more radical or extreme than private equity. Not even the Wall Street banking cartel can match the shear rapaciousness of private equity (PE), whose defenders – the plutocracy – say that to attack PE is to attack capitalism.

If Wall Street banking is the vampire squid sucking on the face of humanity, then PE is an economic black plague. At a loss for a legitimate and valid defense for PE's activities, its defenders often resort to ad hominem attacks, like Governor Chris Christie on a profanity-laced tirade. Words like "socialist" and "communist" often get thrown around and directed at anybody who has the audacity to say an unkind word about PE; but if you look at how private equity operates – and examine the largess and subsidies provided by government in the form of advantageous tax and monetary policies– it can easily be said the true socialist are PE owners and operators. Make no mistake about it, the private equity model is directly dependent upon Federal Reserve generosity, and charitable donations courtesy of the U.S. tax code. Without these government benefits, PE would have not have spread like a virus, or the plague, across U.S. and global economies.

Before we demonstrate the socialist component of private equity, lets run down some interesting PE facts and information. Shall we?

$$$First of all, private equity is on trial in a Federal court, presently, for allegedly fixing bids and collusion. Mr. Romney, and the gang, would like to keep this under raps, but this four year running legal battle just might go viral in the coming weeks and months leading up to the election. As reported in the **Washington Post (Private equity industry in the crosshairs 1-26-12)**, the antitrust lawsuit alleges that PE colluded to bid down the prices on some of the largest deals in history, among them TXU. The **Post** goes on to note: *"The lawsuit, filed in 2007, charged that the firms illegally colluded on nine deals. The judge has since allowed evidence to be gathered on 18 others."*

$$$Alleged price fixing and collusion? It is alleged that it maybe all in a day's pay for PE execs, in these so call "club deals." The **Post**, again, from the same article: *"In this conspiracy, the winners and losers are clear," the plaintiffs wrote in their complaint. "The winners are the private-equity firms, management and the investment banks. . . . The losers are the shareholders, whose equity defendants acquired deceptively and on the cheap."*

$$$PE stockholders getting burned… seems like a familiar theme, among investors of shadow banking, private equity, and the Wall Street Cartel. JMH already noted the lousy returns on equity produced by the Leviathan, and I read this week that Goldman Sachs attempted to defend its ROE to shareholders. If we take a look at the numerous private equity IPO's that have transpired over the last decade, we can easily see that shareholders have been burned repeatedly: Carlyle; Apollo; and the largest and darkest star, Blackstone. Need we name more? Check out the initial offering price on any private equity IPO and see where that stock's price sits today (just be prepared to get out the Visine before you do so, and if you per chance own the stock have a fist full of valium on hand). Bondholders or stockholder, its all the same…. There's a distinct possibility of losing serious money when you invest in PE, particularly in these precarious economic times.

$$$What's that – PE makes money? For the insiders and the principles of the organization absolutely, but if you're a stockholder…. Who really knows? First of all, it's commonly known that PE financials do not always conform to GAAP. Moreover, is some of these sweetheart deals, so called "club deals," some of the key PE actors will have differing valuations on the very same investment. How exactly does that happen? And between the multiple funds and all that money sloshing around, and with some of the deals heading south, who's to say PE isn't – in some instances – just another Madoff Ponzi scheme? Heh, as long as investor money continues to roll in, who says it isn't a cash flow business? Just don't get caught asking for a redemption, when the music stops playing and the economy enters a downward spiral.

$$$Of course to secure profits and provide insurance for all that junk debt financing PE deals, who is to say the Wall Street banks aren't betting against their own issuance, through hybrid derivatives and swaps? And if another PE investment fails, and the stockholders and the bondholders get burned, what does the bank care if they're investments and speculative bets are insured through an opaque swaps/derivatives market? It's called "market making." PE and the Cartel make the market, and investors get played.

$$$But JMH you're awfully cynical, everyone knows investors get rich if they invest in PE. That's probably true to some extent, except, as reported recently, one in five PE mangers bites the dust. It's also true as long as the stock market remains upright, so that PE can dump its debt-laden investments off on unsuspecting rubes in the stock market, via IPOs. And as long as the Fed chairmen keeps his foot firmly on the accelerator of the printing presses, PE

generally makes out. True, a bull market plus easy money, plus favored tax status, often does equal private equity success.

$$$There's just one problem. As anyone has observed as of late, the bubbles are coming with greater and greater frequency, accompanied by crash and recession. The stock market often turns bearish, and the capital and liquidity markets seize up, because no bank can trust the other banks financials. Which leads to this **(as reported by Ms. Julie Creswell for the NY Times, October-9-2009, Profits for Buyout Firms as Company Debt Soared):** *"More than half the roughly 220 companies that have defaulted on their debt in some form this year were either owned at one time or are still controlled by private equity firms, according to analysts at Standard & Poor's."*

$$$What's that? Ms. Creswell's information is so 2009? Walk with me, and check this out as reported by **Bloomberg (Europe Leveraged Loan Defaults May Rise to 25%, Moody's Says: 5-29-12):** *"At least 25 percent of the unrated European leverage buyout companies with debt due by 2015 may default as the economy worsens and private-equity owners refuse to inject capital, according to Moody's Investors Service."* Looks like history is about to repeat once again.

Did anyone notice how the U.S. stock market performed this week?

$$$It's not just PE's financial statements, or its "get rich quick" mantra – at the expense of society, clients and world governments, or even the catastrophic falls in PE stock prices post IPO…. Private equity is moral hazard defined, very much like the Wall Street Cartel. But don't rely on my word… just remember what Mr. Dimon had to say: **"This relationship feels a bit one-way to me."**

Indeed, Mr. Dimon.

$$$Before we touch on the socialism component, lets take a brief second to examine some PE investments over the last couple of years:

PE investing in life insurance policies, the quicker you die, the quicker PE gets rich: Check.

PE investing in mortgage foreclosure mills, only to get burned by the robo-signing scandal: Check again.

PE investing in CDOs and MBS, the very financial instruments that took the national economy down… well now that the fix is in, and there will be no widespread refinancing or debt forgiveness for one in five residential mortgage holders who are underwater… who really can blame PE.   It's good money. Check.

PE's Bain Capital, Mr. Romney's old stomping grounds, sells surveillance equipment to China, so that the commies can better oppress their people. Why not just sell mom, and apple pie to the red bastards? Check.

And PE wonders why it's earned the epithet from some members of the GOP, Vulture Capitalist.

One more quick thought, next time you check in to a hospital, or have dental work done from a national chain, it may be in the best interests of your health to find out if there is private equity ownership.

$$$Lest we forget and as JMH has noted in prior blogs, PE plays a singular role in globalization or simply put: labor, tax and regulatory arbitrage.   Which means PE goes offshore to manufacture goods and employ its labor, and dumps these products back on U.S. shores for our bankrupted and unemployed population to purchase. And we wonder why the national debt is stratospheric.   But don't take my word for it, let's hear it from none other than **Mr. and Ms. Jack and Suzy Welch from this week's Reuters:** *"Thus private equity firms often goad their acquisitions into the borderless world, which explains why most successful PE leaders tend to have global mindsets about business, regulation, growth and geopolitics."*

$$$So without all the government giveaways and socialism (carried interest, the tax deductibility of debt, easy money courtesy of the Fed, and a stock market pumped on steroids), where does that leave private equity?   Answer: It leaves PE on the same playing field as nearly any other American business. You see, it's really not hard to burn down and strip businesses, when the government supports you at less than half the going tax rate (carried interest), or tax policy supports debt over equity, and the Cartel that supports and participates in PE is bailed out repeatedly by the U.S. taxpayer.

Destroying business, jobs, and the U.S. tax base is not hard.

What's difficult is investing blood, sweat and equity in startups, and creating new business, jobs, and opportunity.

Something PE increasingly doesn't have the stomach for.

All the proceeding really goes to show is just how decadent and depraved the GOP has become, especially when their nominee is the king daddy of private equity himself, Mr. Severe. Who's to say what Mr. Romney actually is, however, since we have the breathing and living embodiment of the duality of man right before our eyes. On one hand we have a liberal Massachusetts governor and author of Romneycare; and on the other hand we have the fire breathing corporate raider and a founding member of the economic plague.

What we do know is that Mr. Romney and the plutocracy want to buy the presidency very badly, so that they can continue to do pretty much as they damn well please under their extremist – *laissez faire* – ideology.

Perhaps past is prologue, here again, it terms of divining what a Romney administration would look like. What have prior Republican administrations done, from Reagan forward, but start up unnecessary wars, run up huge deficits, cut taxes for the rich, borrow and spend, and let private equity export jobs and the tax base offshore, all in the name of free trade and capitalism. Meanwhile America crumbles under ruinous debt, and her citizens suffer thanks to private equity's unmitigated greed.

My guess is some Republicans, presently, are gloating that the economy is listing, and further hoping that it sinks altogether, so that they can usher in their candidate. These same Republicans should mind what they wish for and be careful not to gloat… because as the economy and stock market goes, so goes private equity, her investors, and if properly linked, Mr. Romney's chances in the fall.

But don't say a word against private equity, otherwise you're a commie and… and … a freedom hater. Yeah! And a "socialist" too, as another famous and now deceased Republican demagogue once stated, right down to Representative Helen Douglas' pretty pink panties.

There's nothing wrong with profits or profit taking, as long as you don't deploy an economic plague, or burn down a nation, in the process of making those profits. Make no mistake about it, private equity is an industry in dire need of serious regulation.

P.S. This week I have four quick words of investment advice, for bondholders and stockholders. They are: Sell Private Equity Short!

Establishment

By J.M. Hamilton 6-14-12

I never will, by any word or act, bow to the shrine of intolerance or admit a right of inquiry into the religious opinions of others. — Thomas Jefferson

A conservative at the **NY Times**, Mr. David Brooks, was complaining about the lack of respect accorded by the general population to the "establishment" this week, and I couldn't help but find myself amused and relieved. For here Mr. Brooks offered up a political counterpoint to an editorial written by Mr. Luigi Zingales (of Chicago School of Economics fame). Both editorials, please see links below, make perfect bookends to this week's JMH editorial. Mr. Brooks laments the lack of good "followers" in America today; and Mr. Zingales — a bit of a conservative in his own right, and certainly a libertarian with strong capitalist credentials, fears the corruption of the political and business establishment culminating, or metastasizing, into crony capitalism. Mr. Zingales holds up Italy's corrupted economy and government by way of comparison, and the path he asserts the U.S. is headed down, if we are not careful.

JMH, of course, has argued for some time that we are already there. Witness the idolatry and blind deference U.S. Senate members accorded Mr. Dimon this week.

Now none of this is to say Mr. Brooks is not a great guy and a worthy polemicist… Shucks, about six years ago and for nearly all of my adult life — starting at the age of two- I would have agreed with nearly everything Mr. Brooks puts down on paper.

But something happened in 2007 and 2008 that called into question my entire belief system, and apparently the belief systems of many U.S. Citizens (99%), or what Mr. Brook's refers to as "followers," who are having a exceptionally hard time buying what the "establishment" is now laying down as gospel.

What could have awoken the masses from their apathy and slumber, and motivated the "followers" to turn against their master, the establishment? Was it, as Mr. Brooks asserts, that our own personal "vanity" has made Tea Partiers and disenfranchised libertarians and liberals jaded, or was it something else that turned us off on the ruling economic and political elite?

Was it the fact that for the last thirty years the establishment underwrote the greatest Keynesian raid heretofore known to man, whereby the one percent/establishment crushed democracy and redistributed wealth and expropriated political powers for themselves?

Perhaps it's the intergenerational wealth larceny that has become today's FED policy, again all in the interest of keeping the rescued Cartel/establishment afloat, at the expense of savers and retirees.

Or maybe it was the toxic assets that have been transferred from the Cartel's/establishment's balance sheet and onto the public sectors balance sheets at list price, only to be sold back, selectively, to the Cartel and shadow banking at a discount.

Was it the fact that the political establishment just could never say "no" to big business or the Chamber of Commerce, and allowed them under the rubric of free trade and capitalism to transfer jobs, tax base, and the U.S. manufacturing economy offshore?

Was it the fact that the establishment showed us the true meaning of socialism with endless bank bailouts – running into the trillions- while hypocritically attempting to light a match to the social contract, and seeking significant reductions/privatization in Medicare, Medicaid, and social spending?

Was it the insider trading cases and the manifestation of a two-tiered stock market: one for the insiders/establishment, and the other for the followers.

Perhaps it's the two tiered justice system: where white collar criminals/the establishment are rarely if ever convicted, and then there's the justice system for the rest of us — the "followers" facing the criminal justice industrial complex and corporations profiting from the incarceration of individuals for victimless crimes (so that the U S has the highest incarceration rate among western democracies). If we are to believe the numbers, the U.S. incarceration rate, per Wikipedia, is 39% higher than Russia's and several hundred percent higher than China's….. What's wrong with this picture?

Or perhaps it's our beloved supreme court, which like our Republican lead congress, suffers from very low follower opinion polls; and why should followers be upset when this very same court tells us that corporations/establishment are people too, who may and will collectively purchase our government under a Citizens United decision.

Perhaps it's the abuse the establishment has heaped upon our fighting men and women with endless wars, so that the U.S. solider suicide rate now exceeds our monthly casualty rate. But heh, those solider/followers volunteered for it, so that makes it all okay.

Just maybe as Mr. Zingales notes, from the freshwater school of economics no less, that the U.S. establishment has abandoned meritocracy, industriousness, and capitalism…. for cronyism, speculation/private equity schemes, and monopoly.

Maybe its the real unemployment and underemployment rate in this country, and for much of Europe, is in the high teens— or in some instances in the neighborhood of twenty percent or more; as noted in the **Times** this week many U.S. citizens have watched their net worth crumble to 1990 levels in the span of four years.

Thank you, Establishment!

Mr. Brooks went on to note: "To have good leaders you have to have good followers— able to recognize just authority, admire it, be grateful for it and emulate it."

To which JMH responds, which part would you like us to emulate Mr. Brooks?

Democracy is a wonderful thing. It makes people feel empowered, no matter how distorted the representative reality from the ideal. Take that away, or the ability to protest, or form new political parties, or rebel against the established order of things…. And we find ourselves living in another elitist dictatorship, or government by the establishment. The very things are founding fathers fought against.

Americans of all stripes understand human failings in the economic and political establishment; what the followers cannot understand – even if made legitimate under the laws of the state – is blatant political corruption, economic theft leading to lost decades and lives, and the death of opportunity – strangled by the corporatist and monopolist. Hence, the rise in America and Europe of extremist political parties, like Occupiers, the Tea Party, and in Europe — Socialist, Anarchist and Communist.

When the establishment abandons the 99%/followers, the followers look for solutions outside mainstream political parties.

P.S.

To his credit, Mr. Brooks wrote admiringly of Mr. Jefferson, whom he referred to – longingly – as a "graceful aristocratic democrat."

Remarkably, Mr. Jefferson wrote the defining document of the American Revolution and provided the ultimate act of rebellion against the established British aristocracy, with the Declaration of Independence. One wonders what are third U.S. president would have had to say about what the Wall Street Cartel/establishment has done with his Agrarian Dream, or additional thoughts Mr. Jefferson may have had on the establishment of his day?

We need not wonder, here are a few quotes from Mr. Jefferson on the establishment of his day:

"All tyranny needs to gain a foothold is for people to remain silent."

"In every country and every age, the priest has been hostile to Liberty."

"Experience demands that man is the only animal which devours his own kind, for I can apply no milder term to the general prey of the rich upon the poor."

His thoughts on globalism? *"Merchants have no country. The mere spot that they stand on does not constitute so strong an attachment as that from which they draw their gains."*

"The tree of liberty must be refreshed from time to time with the blood of patriots and tyrants."

"Experience hath shewn, that even under the best forms of government those entrusted with power have, in time, and by slow operations, perverted into tyranny."

"Friendship is but another name for an alliance with the follies and misfortunes of others. Our own share of miseries is sufficient: why enter then as volunteers into those of another."

"I hope we shall crush in its birth the aristocracy of our monied corporations which dare already to challenge our government to a trial of strength, and bid defiance to the laws of this country."

"I believe banking institutions are more dangerous than standing armies."

"A Bill of Rights is what the people are entitled to against any government, and what no just government should refuse, or rest in inference."

Given our nation's current predicament, I wonder if Mr. Jefferson would have been in favor of an economic bill of rights?

A Rusting City

By J.M. Hamilton 6-30-12

"I've spoken of the shining city all my political life, but I don't know if I ever quite communicated what I saw when I said it. But in my mind it was a tall, proud city built on rocks stronger than oceans, windswept, God-blessed, and teeming with people of all kinds living in harmony and peace; a city with free ports that hummed with commerce and creativity. And if there had to be city walls, the walls had doors and the doors were open to anyone with the will and the heart to get here. That's how I saw it, and see it still. And how stands the city on this winter night? More prosperous, more secure and happier than it was eight years ago…. And she's still a beacon, still a magnet for all who must have freedom…" — **Farewell Address to the Nation, January 11, 1989**

It was a dark and stormy night. No, let's start over.

Once upon a time, a very eloquent leader came to be elected to run a tarnished and rusting city. The city had fallen into disrepair and faced double-digit unemployment, inflation, and interest rates (mostly because the city had been taken off the gold standard by a prior administrator, and the printing presses had been maxed out to gain a mayoral second term). An index was even created to measure just how bad things had become for the citizens, a "misery index." Times were indeed difficult. The leader was a gifted orator and roused his tribe/Party against government; he talked down government programs, oppressive taxation, and government regulation; and he spoke proudly of the private sector, capitalism, and privatization.

But the wise ruler also was smart enough to remember the great depression, and at one time had actually been a democrat. Oh my!

A Democrat in Wolf's Clothing?

And yet, there seemed to be a wide divergence between the mayor's rhetoric and his actual policies. For despite his strong anti-government language, the leader didn't have the heart to cut government programs for the elderly. In fact government spending and entitlements expanded and grew, as did deficit spending; he also protected the city's workers and jobs from the free trade policy he advocated, with tariffs and barriers to trade; and the renown mayor of the city raised taxes no less than eleven times during his two terms, and yet, the deficits – government spending versus tax revenue – grew and grew. The top tax rate for the largest wage earners was 50% for much of the great communicator's terms in office.

Despite the mayor's policies, the city – possibly by shear force of his charm and persuasion – prospered. While others saw through the leader's verbal skills and recognized that he had merely adopted liberal economic policy – held widely in disrepute within the mayor's Party, commonly known as Keynesian Economics; the leader claimed that the free market, tax cuts, and deregulation had brought the city back and made her shiny again, while failing to acknowledge government's role (both fiscal and monetary policy) in his and the city's success. After eight long years, the mayor retired for well-earned rest and relaxation. Indeed, he seemingly had done very well.

Except the mayor's words appeared to have cast an enchanted spell.

The leader was remembered very fondly, and over time his political Party/tribe built a cult of personality around him and his ideology. The Party remembered with great relish the great communicator's words, all the while ignoring or wishing away his actions and deeds. Or attributing the continuing problems of the city — rampant fiscal profligacy and deficit spending — to a failure to cut revenue/taxes. The Party, which prided itself on its tremendous business acumen, seemingly believed that while no business could spend indefinitely without raising revenue/increasing sales, apparently believed that government was magical and that it could continue to grow and spend indefinitely without raising revenue/taxes. By sorcery, the Laffer Curve, and supply side economics, the Party of the great leader wished away the government's deficits but did nothing to stop its "borrow and spend policies."

What Big Teeth You Have…Grandma

What's worse the Party ignored their leaders practice – and track record – to avoid foreign entanglements and wars. Instead, the Party began to fight in foreign lands seemingly endless wars, or battles to protect oil rich cities, all to the great benefit of: trade routes, "managed" energy production, commercial and sovereign interests, and two of the Party's greatest benefactors, the military industrial complex and Big Oil. However, these wars cost the city greatly in terms of blood and treasure, and while they caused a short-term boom in her economy, they often left the shiny city winded financially, morally, and martially (for taxes had been not raised to pay for city's foreign adventures — indeed, they had been cut). Denizens of the world often wondered why the shiny city, often fought in resource rich lands, protecting the interest's of dictators and despots, while contrary to the City's ideal, she often ignored human rights atrocities committed by dictators in lands that were not resource rich or had minimal links to the city's economy or business interests. Worse still, when the city was at the apogee of her power, she failed to spread democracy and stability globally; but rather, continued to support military and authoritarian regimes, an opportunity squandered.

And I'll Huff and I'll Puff and I'll Blow Your House Down...

But worst of all, the great communicator's Party – having completely abandoned the financial rules and regulations put in place after the great depression, such as Glass-Steagall – allowed the city's banks to gamble and engage in idle speculation, at the expense of the city's economy and the banks traditional role of lending to the fair city's citizens and businesses. A tremendous bubble ensued, and the city's real estate market came crashing down, and with it a lifetime of accumulated wealth, and the livelihood of a great many of the city's businesses and inhabitants. Worse still, it turned out that the city's banks had bet against the city and her people, and some of the banks very own products, and the banks reaped significant financial reward for their wickedness in the city lead bailout. Separately the tax code had been turned to Swiss cheese; the Party having been lobbied to create loopholes for the rich and the powerful – and having accepted large political campaign contributions – acquiesced to many demands. The city's budget was now ruinous, and she could no longer provide basic services for her people or make good on her financial commitments. The city's central banker took to printing money to pay for the city's massive debts and tax cuts for the rich, the Party had so favored.

In the end, the Party's and the leader's free enterprise and anti-government language had become such a cornerstone of their beliefs that businesses and entire sectors of the city's economy were given free reign and allowed to merge and denigrate into mere monopoly. The cartels often worked directly at cross-purposes with the city's consumers, the city's labor force, her financial health, and the city's once great markets. Contrary to the great leader's policies and actions that helped and aided the city's workers and her markets, trade barriers were taken down, "free trade" agreements ratified, and many of the city's jobs were sent offshore – which only made the city's fiscal crisis worse, so diminished now was the city's tax base.

Yes, inexpensive products were exported back to the shiny city and her once great markets, but who could afford them, with such high unemployment rates, depressed wage levels, and monopolies preying upon the citizenry for limited discretionary income?

The shiny city and the Party listened to the great communicators words, and ignored his actions at their own peril, and the city fell into disrepair, was over extended fiscally, and the need to print money to pay her bills, and for additional bank bailouts, grew greater. Over the span of time, and contrary to the Party's and the leader's speeches, the shiny city had adopted the liberal economist Keynes' policies *almost* to the letter. Moreover, redistributed wealth was not shared equally for a just and fair society; but rather, it went to the wealthy, often in the form of tax cuts, bailouts, special regulations, inflationary monetary policy, and accounting magic and subsidies.

The city soon grew rusty again, along with her infrastructure, and she was ill prepared for the next calamity to come, because she had squandered her treasure and credit line.

In a final irony, the great leader, along with his city, counted among their many successes their signature achievement – the dismantling of a withering crony empire. Ultimately, in many ways the shiny city was rapidly becoming the very thing she and her citizens had fought a great cold war against, an empire that was overextended economically, militarily, financially and intellectually.

After a thirty-year reign, the Party and many of the leader's words became little more than a fairy tale.

For while the free market and capitalism are great producers of wealth, the free market works best when partnered with a strong and healthy government to ameliorate private enterprises worst attributes: that of monopoly, concentration of wealth and power, cronyism, and government and regulatory capture.

The great communicator knew this, and his actions revealed as much, but his rhetoric, almost spell like, had been twisted to a very bad end, indeed.

And the moral of the story: Watch both the words and actions of actors turned politician. For while actions speak louder than words, sometimes a leader's words, unintentionally, may have damaging consequences for future generations.

P.S.

And the mayor's lasting legacy? The mayor showed us that when the debt to GDP ratio is low, anyone – even a public relations man from General Electric – can kick start an economy by adopting Keynesian fiscal and monetary policy; what takes discipline, foresight and good stewardship is raising taxes during prosperous times.

Ultimately, the mayor's lasting legacy was his dark words against government turned a generation off on public service, so that the city – all too often – became led by easily manipulated second-string hacks, extremist, and political opportunist. Malaise and lost decades ensued.

The End.

Malum in se

By J.M. Hamilton 7-14-12

"He is calm in the face of a storm, and he sees the world as it is, not how we'd like it to be."

-Treasury Secretary Geithner, as quoted in Bloomberg 7-2-12

"Some men see things as they are and say, 'Why?' I dream things that never were and say, 'Why not?'"

- Robert Fitzgerald Kennedy, U.S. Attorney General; U.S. Senator

This essay may, for some, get a little crude this week, so for those with virgin eyes, you may not want to read further.

Who am I kidding? It's going to be crude!

You can almost taste it. One can certainly feel it, and read about it. It's invasive. And it has metastasized throughout the body politic. It's called **cynicism**, or by any other words: "an attitude of scornful, jaded, negativity."

I remember the first time I encountered it. It was 1990. We were still basking in the warm Republican glow of Reaganomics. In Texas, the Republican Party had put forth a businessman named "Claytie" Williams, to run against then State Treasurer, Ann Richards.

d̲emocrat!

And, Mr. Williams was about to politically stomp Ms. Richards, big time. He had a twenty-point lead.

Republicans were feeling real good.

Mr. Williams was about to become the second Republican governor in the State of Texas, since the Civil War's Reconstruction. Yup. A carpetbagger was about to enter the governor's mansion, but at least he was one of ours.

And then something happened like a bolt out of the blue…
revelations! Turned out Claytie's tongue would be his undoing; turned out Mr.

Williams had a fondness for cynical, dark humor. Poof, his lead went up in smoke. He was quoted as saying amongst the "boys," the following joke:

"Rape is just like the weather... it's inevitable, just relax and enjoy it."

Ms. Richards never looked back and won the governorship. Republican's shrieked and howled and chewed on their own body parts. Damn, I was sore.

Now, you have to remember Mr. Williams comment was Pre-Hillary and Pre-P.C. (politically correct), but it displayed – even if in jest – the dark side of American politics and of human nature. Many of us have watched political cynicism grow and grow ever since, if not at the state level then certainly at the national level.

Today, the author of our economic recovery, and our economic messiah, if you believe his P.R., Mr. Geithner, was recently quoted in **Bloomberg** as praising Mr. Draghi, E.U. Central Bank President, and Goldman Sachs Alum, with the aforementioned quote.

Mr. Draghi gets it, per Mr. Geithner, not how the world ought to be, but how it is.

According to Mr. Geithner, one might infer, how the world should and will be is with Bank Presidents running the planet, impervious to their own malign actions, backed by the full faith and credit on the American taxpayer, and never, ever sanctioned or held accountable for their outrageous behavior; that is to say, no matter how economically debilitating banker fraud to the global economy; the amount of debt the bank bailouts piled upon the taxpayer; and no matter how many bank created hardships face the ever growing ranks of the unemployed.

Per Mr. Geithner, that's just the way it is:

Libor scandals, impacting hundreds of trillions in banking instruments and investments;

Derivative and swaps scandals in London, *a la* Mr. Dimon and "the London Whale;"

Alleged Energy market manipulation in California by J.P. Morgan;

Accounting shenanigans and off balance sheet transactions;

Money laundering;

Offshore accounts;

Taxpayer funded Banks gambling in Private Equity;

Another Futures Dealer vanishes with hundreds of million in client money gone missing (and the banks and the regulators are unaware?);

Tax evasion; and

Accounts for drug dealers.

What have I missed? These are just the Headlines for the last thirty days. This list doesn't begin to account for the 2008 Banking Armageddon, even though many of these events are redundant. Recidivism is the hallmark of this crisis.

And the proceeding list is a direct result of the 2008 actions of the Gang of Four: Messrs. Bush, Paulson, Bernanke, and Geithner! This nation should have led the way for the world, and never bailed out the banks, or certainly not without nationalization, penalty and a change in management.

Lost Japanese decades, stagnation, and malaise… this is what Mr. Geithner, the Bank Presidents, and SCOTUS have delivered.

Somebody should explain to Mr. Geithner that cynicism is not what government is about.

What Government is about is doing the impossible. As Mr. Kennedy so eloquently said above, it's about dreaming things that never were, and saying, "why not." It's about:

Another Texan, President L.B.J., signing Civil Rights legislation;

It's about President John F. Kennedy setting the nation's sites on the moon;

President Roosevelt's efforts and success in defeating National Socialism in Europe;

It's about President Truman establishing the policy of Communist containment, which allowed President Reagan to ultimately defeat the Soviets;

It's about President Lincoln signing the emancipation proclamation, and

President Obama demonstrating vision and attempting to steer this country away from the Bankocracy that rules us all, despite the "ball and chain" that is Mr. Geithner.

That's what government can be about. It should not be about a personal bailout fund for the Cartel.

By the way, notice how the dreamers and doers above are all Democrats? Okay, Lincoln would be a Democrat by today's standards, as the underwriter of the first Federal income tax. Even Reagan was a Democrat before joining the Republican Party.

In the last four years, the U.S. and Europe have suffered a withering shit storm of deception and greed perpetrated upon us all by the banks, and public officials in the banker's pockets. As Mr. Geithner cynically alludes to, the more things change the more they stay the same. But Americans and Europeans, by now, know the difference between *Malum in se,* and *Malum prohibitum.* And just because banking atrocities have not been made illegal, because politicians conveniently abdicate responsibility, or feckless regulators refuse to act, doesn't mean what the bankers are doing to humanity isn't inherently evil, or enjoys public consent.

Until what the **Economist** refers to as "banksters" are held accountable, lost careers and prison time, this storm will continue.

At the end of the day, Americans refuse to take Mr. Clayton Williams advice. We will not sit back and enjoy the rape perpetrated upon us all by the international banking cartel.

P.S.

Mr. Geithner, how much longer do you think the banking dictatorship, and *your* **world and "the way it is" will last???**

"Every dictatorship has ultimately strangled in a web of repression it wove for its people, making mistakes that could not be corrected because criticism was prohibited."

- Robert Fitzgerald Kennedy, U.S. Attorney General; U.S. Senato

Uncertainty

By J.M. Hamilton 7-28-12

"In this world nothing can be said to be certain, except death and taxes."
– Benjamin Franklin

"We have met the enemy and he is us." – Walt Kelly – Pogo

I think it was my father who got me hooked on the Sunday morning political talk shows… if memory serves one was *This Week*, with David Brinkley. Loved that guy: urbane, sharp as a razor, and did not suffer fools gladly. *Face the Nation* fell in there somewhere and then I usually turned over to **PBS** and *Firing Line*. Hosted by God's gift to the Republican Party, William F. Buckley, *Firing Line* was my favorite. Alas, Buckley and *Firing Line* are no more.

If we tune into these shows now, perhaps as it always was, the discussion is on the topical and heated political issues of the day. However, what one notices almost immediately is that there is barely any mention of the financial connections to our elected leaders and their corporate sponsors. Most of the major networks, of course, are run by huge corporate conglomerates, and the owners and sponsors of these shows are all safely ensconced in the Corporate Hall of Fame.

Nothing wrong with any of this, but one can't help wonder does all that corporate money put a crimp in the Sunday morning dialogue, and cloud where this country's locus of power truly lies? The talking heads give lofty declamation about Washington D.C., but you hear nary a word about Cupertino, CA and even less so about Fairfield, CT or Decatur, IL. And none of the pundits mentions the Caymans or Luxembourg.

Why is that?

Republicans have been waging war against the Obama administration ever since the President came into office, saying that his brand of rule creates too "uncertain" an environment for America's business leaders, and as if on cue, the Chamber of Commerce echoes those sentiments frequently and often (or is it the other way around?). Many Captains of Industry have seen their balance sheets rise with expanding cash holdings, enjoyed highly inexpensive debt financing courtesy of the Federal Reserve, and a stock market recovery — all under this administration. Moreover, taxes have not increased under the Obama administration, and in fact, government nationally has shrank.

All of which probably makes this presidency either the most pro-business Democratic administration ever to enter the White House, or the President has merely switched parties and forgotten to tell the American people.

To read more on the political conservatism of the current administration read, *The Ultimate GOP Candidate has yet to Step Forward*:

http://blog.jmhamiltonpublishing.com/2012/01/08/the-ultimate-gop-candidate-has-yet-to-step-forward.aspx

So what exactly is there to be uncertain about? It's as if the *enfant terrible*, with its sextillions flowing in from Wall Street banks and corporate donors, had its "lolly" taken away (after calling the shots since President Reagan's inauguration, nearly a thirty-plus year GOP run).

Might it be time for the Party to "man up" a little bit? Might it be time for the Republican controlled House to stop the temper tantrum and assume some responsibility for governing? How many times can the house GOP engage in political masturbation and vote down President Obama's healthcare legislation?

As Mr. Franklin told us long ago, wisely and sagely, the only thing certain in this world is death and taxes. However, I guess if you're like a handful of CEOs, and Republicans have been sucking on your knee caps for the last thirty years, and you have been told by the Party that your every utterance is a divine right, well then this Administration might appear scary.

Of course, it's the Republican Party, and some of their sponsors, who: led the charge over the last thirty years in dismantling capitalism's rules and regulations; allowed jobs – and American corporate top line growth – to be exported off shore, via free trade agreements; and as the political voice of the Wall Street banks – directly contributed to the uncertainty created for all, businesses and citizens alike, with the past, present and future financial crisis.

Read a recent piece, *Malum in se*, to learn just how much uncertainty the Republican Party and the Banks have created:

The uncertainty isn't created by this administration, but rather, it is created by an elite cadre of monopolist, banking, and shadow banking interests, often with interlocking boards — and the politicians and the Republican Party who are sponsored by same. We've seen, daily, that when the Cartel pursues their inalienable right to the profit motive, it has far reaching consequences for America and the world. Seemingly, these monolithic interests can no longer play in the house without smashing ma's furniture.

Once again, many of the oligarchy sponsor, own, or own stock in the organizations that control the Sunday morning talk shows and the major news organizations. Might that be impacting the Sunday morning message? After all, it would not be good to hear the Sunday pundits discussing the nexus between the real economic and political power in this country, and the law making men and women who reside in the nation's capital. That might prove upsetting to many, and fly in the face, to some degree, with the belief that the power in this country rests with people and less so with the plutocracy.

And can you blame the one percent?

After all, life and business are uncertain enough without having Aunt Bessie, in Beaverton, Oregon, attempting to contact Mr. Lloyd Blankfein because her cat is up the tree.

Still, one can wish for the day when *This Week* is hosted by Mr. Tom Keene, and at the roundtable sits the CEOs, Messrs. Dimon, Cook, and Immelt, and of course, Ms. Woertz. As informed citizens we should know a great deal more about what the Titans are thinking. Should we not?

P.S.

The GOP has been intransigent for some time now, and one might argue learned their favorite political tactic from none other than the NRA. Yes, the NRA – who perfected in the modern era the political strategy of "scorched earth" or absolutism. That is one must never yield any ground to the opposition and must continuously move forward on the offensive, no matter how detrimental to society at large.

The NRA didn't create "scorched earth tactics," they just reinvented and honed them to a sharp point. "Scorched earth" has been around for centuries, and as often as not, it is the preferred tool of despots and dictators the world over.

The strategy has its pitfalls... witness the recent number of dictators who have had a falling out with their citizens, and have seen their kingdoms turned up side down.

If only they had opened up the dialogue, allowed the safety valve of descent and freedom of speech?

If only they had on occasion compromised? If only they had abandoned absolutism in favor of democratic reform!

They still might be in power.

As of late, the catalyst, the spark, for many a dictator's fall was rising food prices.

Power to the Market!

By J.M. Hamilton (8-11-12)

"Because the free market system is so weak politically, the forms of capitalism that are experienced in many countries are very far from the ideal. They are corrupted (diluted) versions, in which powerful interests prevent competition from playing its natural, healthy role…." – Luigi Zingales – The University of Chicago Booth School of Business

The Moral imperative of capitalism is its incredible ability, when fully functioning, to create goods and services on a spectacular scale. And service a large number of people, the market, with quality goods and services. Its ability to foster ancillary jobs and innovation are well known phenomenon.

It is the competitive feature of capitalism, and the government when fully functioning in its supportive role, that protects the market (the people) from the merchant's/proprietor's worst impulses, which are greed, the quest for unlimited market share and profits, and the elimination of competition.

The bastard child of competition and of capitalism, indeed what Mr. Adam Smith warned us against, is crony capitalism. As crony capitalism is produced, fostered and sanctioned by the state, it is perhaps the most debilitating economic feature of our time that we have the means to control: crony capitalism ultimately leads to monopoly and an unprecedented concentration of wealth and power. Possibly more insidious than communism itself because it wraps itself in the cloak of free enterprise, crony capitalism is the "anti-capitalism," and as such, it leaves a debilitating stain upon the most productive economic system known to man.

More frightening still, because of the link between crony capitalism (monopoly) and true capitalism (competition on the supply side of the curve), capitalism is under attack like never before, so that record numbers of people are turning to the state for assistance.

Monopoly begets monopoly: At a micro level, monopoly in one market, say big oil, inevitably leads to monopoly in other markets, say cellular service, as one market provider attempts to duplicate the profit taking success of another market governed by a monopoly or cartel; separately, because at any given time discretionary income for a nation is fixed, if a monopolistic supplier preys upon a market with inelastic demand, say energy or big oil, this results in diminished demand for other goods and services, as capped discretionary income is eroded by monopolistic profits/taxation. This in turn leads suppliers of other competitive markets to seek out combination, as a means to shore up reduced earnings, sales and income.

Politicians under the dogma of *laissez faire* capitalism have allowed combination *ad nauseum* to the detriment of the worker, corporate top line growth, tax revenue, and most importantly the market. Why? Simply put because monopolistic profits, lead to monopoly sized campaign contributions, and intellectual and political hegemony over the body politic. Bottom line, monopolistic profits are the mother's milk of American politics, like a fist inside a velvet glove or muppet. Some of the largest GOP and DNC campaign contributors come from markets dominated by cartels, oligopoly, or monopoly.

Government, fiscal and monetary policy, can provide a short term fix to problems created by crony capitalism and monopoly; but they are not a long term substitute for structural reform (i.e. the breakup of these organizations)

Of course monopolistic profits and predatory pricing ultimately are anti-market, crush the welfare of the people, savage competitive markets and top line growth, and lead to the collapse of markets. Witness the record profits made by big oil leading up to the 2007-2008 economic collapse. Witness the individual investor flight out of the stock market, due to the flash crash, rigged stock markets, problematic IPOs, program trading, insider trading, and opaque markets, like dark pools.

"Anti-Capitalism" causes instability across the globe, observe the Egyptian military's vast control over broad swaths of the Egyptian economy, ditto Iran's Revolutionary Guard and its extensive ownership and control over that economy. Ultimately, if enough markets are dominated by cartels and monopolies, the cabal at the top can collude to chart a nation's political future, and manipulate a macro economy via capital strike and finance.

By breaking up the concentration of wealth, power, and some of these monolithic institutions, we actually create more opportunity and a larger number of jobs, not just among the rank and file but also among management and the executive class. Specifically in regards Wall Street banks – stock valuations demand it, the dearth of the return on equity demands it, and the market demands the break up of these banking institutions.

Diseconomies of scale, failed management, and egregious risk management insist upon it.

(Don't get me wrong, I am not writing against the scale and size of business, as long as big business operates, side by side, with competitors, and government provides effective "rules of the road" or regulation to protect said market.)

As often as not, the excuse for these catastrophic combinations, provided by management, is that it is "in the interest of the stockholder;" however, when the break up value of these monstrosities is greater than the stock valuation by a wide margin– seemingly and conveniently, the interests of management always trumps stockholder value. Observe Wall Street's reaction to Mr. Sandy Weill's embrace of the proposed return of Glass Steagall.

Just as politicians created the monopolies and cartels- it can aid the market (i.e. the American people) and the economy by breaking up these statist monstrosities, which often can only exists by state backstop and support.

Possible solutions to our economic crisis are simple: support the interests of the market, or the demand side of the curve, and economic recovery will follow. Here are a few simple thoughts and ideas:

1) Leverage the great American market! Insist that if business sells in America – they produce the goods and services sold in this country with American labor. If a business doesn't hire American, that's fine but then access to the American market would be cut off. Since this rule would apply across the board to all domestic and foreign companies selling in the US, no one could complain that they were unfairly treated or at a competitive disadvantage.

2) Close all tax loopholes and dodges, which would allow for a lower corporate tax rate— since it would be a requirement that US labor be utilized for goods and services sold in the US, there would be no opportunity for tax and labor arbitrage for domestically produced goods and services. If larger business begins paying taxes at a lower effective tax rate (in lieu of paying little or no taxes at all), the consumer could theoretically, enjoy a lower tax rate since they are no longer subsidizing businesses that have the skills and the means to engage in tax avoidance. This too would help stimulate the economy by increasing consumer/market discretionary income.

Eliminate the American tax for goods and services sold overseas by American companies, as long as they employ Americans for goods and services sold in this country, with one exception- some percentage of the cost of the US military industrial complex (MIC) should be carried by all foreign governments and multinationals based upon their respective contribution to global GDP and global international sales, respectively. The US military protects and provides stability for global markets, and the beneficiaries of that protection should pay their fair share. If this in turn relieves additional tax burden on the American consumer/market, it means more income and opportunity flowing into our economy, and less consumer/market money flowing into the MIC, via the government.

That's another half trillion dollars the US taxpayer (businesses and individuals) would no longer be burdened with that could flow directly into our economy, or be allocated to deficit reduction.

3.) Cap the election season, so that politicians may only run for office the three months proceeding the election, in lieu of the two year – continuous period presently allotted; and cap the amount of campaign contributions taken in per politician, so as to end the financial/contribution arms race that is core to the modern day election cycle. By capping both the duration of the election cycle and campaign contributions, we put a huge dent in the power of cartels and monopolies to control political candidates. In this manner elections become about ideas, and not who has the biggest wad of cash.

4) Break up cartels and monopolies.

Power to the market!

Ten

By J.M. Hamilton 8-24-12

"Illegitimati non carborundum" - WWII General Stilwell's Motto

Strike the match. Apply the flame to the pipe, inhale deeply. It's harsh, indeed. Eyes burning… hold it in. Exhale a little, inhale deeper. Hold it. Thoughts drift. Sit down quickly before you fall. Feeling light headed, near bursting, lungs spasm …. that's it… **exhale the politics.** Head rush. It happens every four years for us political junkies, a presidential election year. The heady euphoria, the high, the heated debate, the gladiatorial combat… for some, the ultimate blood sport is better than sex. And you think this cycle is nasty, can you imagine when we have two female candidates for the highest office going at it, hammer and tong? Look the freak out.

But this year it's not quite the same… there's a feeling in some circles that the outcome, no matter who wins, will be quite similar. A president, Democrat or Republican, hamstrung by a losing hand from day one: a debt to GDP ratio that is untenable; a feuding, bickering, do nothing congress; a Federal Reserve that has all but exhausted its bag of tricks; an economy on tenterhooks; and exceptionally nasty gale force economic headwinds coming out of both Europe and the Pacific Rim. Withering. Whomever wins, or perhaps this year whomever simultaneously wins and ultimately loses a crown made of thorns, will have an exceptionally hard time of it; and the "change" that many had "hoped" for, welcome or unwelcome, may overtake us all like a thief in the night.

Let's hope its welcome.

But enough of the dark stuff… because hope does spring eternal, and those who are reading this piece are above ground, and we live again to fight another day. Besides there's another democracy in play every day of our lives, and your power to affect real change is so much more potent in this arena, the free market, than the quadrennial vote within the political arena for the duopoly that, at the risk of sounding cynical, is often mere management for the plutocracy that rules us all. That's right, you vote daily without even realizing it. You vote with your credit card, your debit card, and with cash, when you spend and even when you choose not to spend, you are voting… economic democracy in action. And although you may not know it, collectively, as a nation, as a market, we have the ability to bring about tremendous change, by the corporations we choose to support and not to support, daily, as we vote with our dollars. If only as a market, as a people, we could pull it together to exact real change and let our dollars do the voting.

Real change could happen within a corporate quarterly financial statement. I kid you not.

Maybe some day. And this topic, economic democracy, we'll save for another day. So lets get down to it… today's topic, political democracy and the choice before us, and in particular, next week's Republican convention. **And my top ten list of things you will not hear from the GOP this coming week.** You see, as a life long Republican who fled the party in 2008, I feel uniquely qualified to write on this topic. Many of the Party's core principles still make sense; it's just that the GOP all too often pays lip service to these principles and has largely abandoned them. So lets go. I've rambled on long enough. And, as they say, let's do this.

1) We the GOP are wedded to our Judeo-Christian heritage, the central tenant of which is, "we will love our neighbors as ourselves." To clarify, we will love all our neighbors the world over, irregardless of race, color, creed, religious affiliation – or not, and sexual orientation. As we were taught, we will judge not, and remain tolerant, and only when third parties attack us, will we bring the hammer of the goddesses, the U.S. armed forces.

2) The truly great general and Republican President, Eisenhower, in his farewell address to the nation, warned us against the military industrial complex. Let us heed his words, and respect, appreciate, but contain, this cherished industry for the benefit of America and her markets:

This conjunction of an immense military establishment and a large arms industry is new in the American experience. The total influence – economic, political, even spiritual – is felt in every city, every Statehouse, every office of the Federal government. We recognize the imperative need for this development. Yet we must not fail to comprehend its grave implications. Our toil, resources and livelihood are all involved; so is the very structure of our society.

In the councils of government, we must guard against the acquisition of unwarranted influence, whether sought or unsought, by the military-industrial complex. The potential for the disastrous rise of misplaced power exists and will persist.

We must never let the weight of this combination endanger our liberties or democratic processes. We should take nothing for granted. Only an alert and knowledgeable citizenry can compel the proper meshing of the huge industrial and military machinery of defense with our peaceful methods and goals, so that security and liberty may prosper together.

The war in Afghanistan has become an abomination, OBL is long dead, the GOP supports immediate withdrawal of our armed forces. Ditto the war on drugs!

3) We believe in the free market, and we do not believe that government should be in the business of serving oligarchies, or creating oligarchies, to the detriment of the citizenry, national security, the federal budget, and the nation's economy. The GOP has a tremendous affinity for the power of capitalism and the power of markets. We believe monopolies and cartels are antithetical to these ideals, and we will seek to break them up, namely, the Wall Street banks.

4) The GOP will request that Chairmen Bernanke, who has provided political cover for the both political parties, stop flooding the market with easy money, and instead we will reach across the aisle to make the prudent and tough decisions that lay ahead for the good of the nation, by charting a firm course for U.S. tax, fiscal, and healthcare policy.

5) The Republican Party has tried tax cuts and redistribution of governmental resources for the wealthy for over thirty years, and our government budget is now in shambles as a result. Therefore, we will now try a new approach with an equal distribution of the tax burden across all classes of society, and the closure of all tax loopholes, dodges, and accounting trickery. Flat tax anyone?

6) We, the Republican Party, believe in the power of the market, but the market, the people and the workers, can only function optimally when we keep jobs here at home. Therefore, we will support the market by mandating that companies who sell in America, domestic and foreign, hire Americans in direct proportion to their U.S. to Foreign sales ratio. What these same companies do outside our borders, as long as it is not detrimental to U.S. interests, they are free to pursue.

7) The Republican Party promises not to legislate morality, and we pledge to stop fighting 40 year old social policy, so that we can partner with the Democrats to place our Federal government in order, promote jobs and growth, and project stability to the business community and the free market!

8) We believe Republican Governor Rick Perry, from the great state of Texas, was onto something, when he recommended judicial term limits for the members of the Supreme Court. Power corrupts, and in some instances, Supreme Court justices corrupt absolutely. Lets give others a chance to serve, and not burden successive generations with the same cabal of tenured lawyers wearing black robes.

10) And finally, the Republican Party believes the greatest gift given this nation was our democratic ideals. While we recognize money is naturally inherent to the political process, we also recognize that money can distort our ideals, our political party, and can influence legislation in unhealthy ways. Therefore, the Republican Party, the party of integrity, will place a voluntary limit on campaign spending, by political race, not to exceed the amount of money spent by our Democratic competitor, with the balance of the money taken in going to charitable organizations. We believe in the importance of the citizen-politician, as opposed to the career-politician, and we will ask our elected members to sign a pact agreeing not to serve more than two terms, per office. Thus, setting an example for the Democratic Party.

10.5) The GOP recognizes that FHFA Director DeMarco meant well, but he has single-handedly hindered our economic recovery, by obstructing the restructuring and forgiveness of residential mortgage debt; and we will join the President in asking him to step down immediately. The banks received assistance, and now it's time to begin our economic recovery in earnest, by offering assistance to home owners, the housing market, and establishing a floor underneath home prices from which will spring our economic recovery.

10.7) To enhance Party credibility and in order to appeal to our nation's youth and educated swing voter, we will ask all nuts, freaks, cuckoos and whackos to exit the Party immediately. Michele, darling… Ms. Bachmann, please don't let the door hit you on the a$$ on the way out. Ditto, Mr. Akin!

10.9) We love our guns, but we love our children more… therefore, we will call upon all members of the GOP to destroy and boycott all automatic weapons.

God Bless!

P.S.

Much was made this week of Mr. Buffet's move against muni investing, what did Mr. Buffet see that the market has not seen yet.

1)   Ms. Meredith Whitney was correct, only two to three years ahead of schedule.

2)   The rating agencies imprimatur is nearly worthless.

3)   The U.S. economy is possibly headed for recession, and the fiscal cliff is on the horizon.

4)   Economic headwinds out of Europe will likely magnify, post-November elections, when Germany likely decides the fate of the Euro.

5)   The economies of the Pacific Rim are spent.

6)   Any credible replacement for the LIBOR, again post November elections, will likely lead to higher interest rates, and possibly higher adjusted interest payments for municipalities.

7)   The stigma of default is gone.

Cue the Gas Spike

"And they're off."

By J.M. Hamilton 9-8-12

With the pleasantries of their respective conventions out of the way, we now get down to business, and the final drive to the finish. If my powers of observation are accurate, and I sometimes get it right, this may prove to be the ugliest presidential election in history.

The stakes are high for the nation's future, and both Parties have pretty much labeled each other: Mr. Obama, per the GOP, is a "comsymp," and if we are to believe the Dems, Mr. Romney is a robber baron. I have to give this one to the Democrats, simply because the wealthy – including private equity, Bain Capital and Mr. Romney – have faired so well under this administration. In fact, I'm somewhat surprised that Mr. Romney isn't lending his capital and political support to this administration (being a Massachusetts liberal, who offered up the blue print, Romneycare). My guess is Mr. Obama is a capitalist with a heart. But that's neither here nor there, because the gloves are coming off, and the Republicans have come to play hard ball, and they – like it or not – know how to play.

By way of example, I remember a time back in 2003. The Democratic presidential candidates were just coming out the shoot, when the first Secretary of Homeland Security, Mr. Tom Ridge's office, began to beat the Homeland Security Advisory System (HSAS) like a gong. You remember the Homeland Security Advisory System, don't you? That's the now defunct color-coded system that warned you of impending terror alerts and terror attacks. As we all know, up until President Obama showed the Republicans how to track down the world's most wanted man, and how to wipe out Al Qaeda leadership with relatively inexpensive drone strikes (versus highly expensive Republican lead standing armies, surges, and attempts at nation building), the Democrats were perceived to be – on defense matters and foreign policy issues – a group of weak kneed sissies and thumb suckers. Coming on the heals of 9-11, foreign policy was the hot button going into the 2004 election. The Republicans were, possibly, leaving very little to chance. What better way to remind a cowed and corralled electorate about the Republican's foreign policy and martial credibility, and 9-11 itself, than to set off the Security Advisory System… repeatedly.

You think I jest? Well, lets review. In 2002, per the DHS. gov web site, the HSAS was introduced, and changed two times; in 2003, when Democrats were warming up to take on President Bush, the HSAS was changed seven times; in 2004, the HSAS was only changed three times, for a grand total of ten times during the election season. Then, starting in 2005 and 2006, there was only two changes per year, and no changes at all for 2007, 2008, 2009 and 2010. Zero.

Now, I'm not suggesting that the HSAS, and the American public, were manipulated for political purposes, or maybe I am, but that's quite a spike in activity. Coincidence? The spike in HSAS activity came, conveniently, during an election cycle, when: national security was the hot button; Mr. Kerry was being "swift-boated;" and the U.S. was fighting two wars with a credit card. Hundreds of billions, indeed trillions, were at stake for the American defense contractors and the banks, who finance war (plus those generous tax cuts for the wealthy). Play with the terror alert button? Nah! Never happened.

You may love them; you may hate them, but the Republicans come to play. And they have the money. So with less than two months away until D-Day, what tricks might the Republican's, and their allies the *uber* wealthy and the global banking cabal, throw at the Democratic Party to push this election over the edge? Keep in mind our friendly central bankers – Messrs. Draghi and Bernanke – appear to be priming the pump for a spike in…. you guessed it… commodity, fuel, and stock prices, once again. Escalating fuel prices helped push the economy over the edge back in 2008, just as the perfect storm of a financial crisis took the global economy out.

Quantitative Easing, LITRO… call it what you will (many call it printing money), the banks and the asset classes love it. Stocks rise, commodity prices (read: food and gas prices) rise, and the consumer/99% get hit in the wallet, and the economy stalls after the brief sugar rush. So with the economy struggling to produce jobs, the FED is strongly considering playing into the GOP's hands once again. The FED's normally strong magic isn't working because the banks are on strike, and will either hang onto the money, park it with a friendly central banker, or send it offshore into the carry trade, or into stocks and commodities. (This may explain, to some degree, why Mr. Draghi plans on "sterilizing" his latest offering.) Big Oil, too, no fan of Dems, will almost assuredly play their part in the coming weeks and days. The liquidity trap is in full bloom.

So what's Mr. Obama to do? We are in hurricane season. And President Bush (W) did release the Strategic Petroleum Reserve during Hurricane Katrina, and his father tapped same during the first Iraq war. Yes, a gusher of oil to allay stoppages caused by the next hurricane just might put a damper on price spikes at the pumps, and thwart Republican and allied efforts to slow down the economy further for political gain and the White House throne.

The Dems know how to play hardball too, and are far from innocent, but you get the feeling that they have to at least think about it; whereas with the Republicans and the plutocracy, it is reflexive, innate, and hardwired into their DNA.

Capital strike by the banks, spiking commodity prices, a Citizens United decision by the Supreme Court, an obstructionist Republican congress, and the FHFA Director, Mr. Demarco, withholding support for residential mortgage restructuring and debt forgiveness (all on an unprecedented banking collapse): why it's absolutely amazing – and a testament to the virility of the American economy and this administration that President Obama has done as well as he has. And on foreign policy, clearly Mr. Romney is no match for the President.

The plutocracy has no reservations about playing with the American economy and our lives. They have the wealth and they can bide their time, but the 99% don't have the luxury, which puts incredible pressure on a Democratic administration that is attempting to turn the Titanic around on a dime. Tax reform, hopefully, will quite possibly be the primary issue addressed by the next administration/congress. For this reason, and often prayed for Supreme Court retirements, we need to put this President back in the White House.

The President, clearly, needs more time. After all, and in an oft repeated but highly accurate line, we don't want to hand the keys to the White House back to the same tribe that put us here, do we?

Now if Mr. Bernanke could figure out of way to put QE3 on the demand side of the curve, versus into the hands of the bankers – supply… the economy would mend, and this election would be sewn up for President Obama.

P.S. None of this is take away from Mr. Romney… he has a place in government too. Just like former car czar, Mr. Steven Rattner, the former Bain Capital CEO would do an excellent job, working out on fraud, waste, graft and corruption associated with government Healthcare providers, Big Pharma, and over at DOD. Think of the billions Mr.

Romney could save the American taxpayer, by deploying private equity management and tactics to government vendors (with the windfall accruing to this country and our children.) Private equity is not always bad, and can be quite useful when deployed correctly, for the good of the American people and as venture capitalist investing in new business and start ups.

Party of Fear

By J.M. Hamilton (9-21-12)

The only thing we have to fear is ignorance.

"It's what people know about themselves inside that makes them afraid." - Clint Eastwood – High Plains Drifter

I kept thinking about Candidate Romney this week, and his staff. This is a man who gave up being a private equity billionaire, so that he could help us all, or at least 53% of us, by becoming President. Mr. Romney has been running for the nation's highest office for years, the opportunity costs for this candidate are enormous. And yet, Mr. Romney's defeat hangs in the air, like Napoleon fleeing Russia at the onset of winter, and leaving behind his *Grand Armee*. Ravenous Russian wolves in pursuit of the emperor's sleigh, snapping at the trace horses for miles upon miles in a desolate winter scape. Maddening. Or for Mr. Romney's team is it like Hitler, and staff, spending final moments with his bride, with U.S and Russian soldiers closing in, a mighty German nation ruined. Feelings of despair and of what might have been – dashed hopes and dreams – deep down in the bunker. Valhalla beckons.

Mr. Romney's fall, like Napoleon's and Hitler's, is largely self-inflicted.

Granted the candidate is no megalomaniac; but if the video that *Mother Jone's* offered up this week is any indication, Mr. Romney does appear to be suffering from an acute form of socio-economic prejudice, having written off nearly half the nation (only to tell us this week, it was all a mistake and he loves 100%of us, after all). Of course, many of those Mr. Romney wrote off as parasitic are the Republican faithful, including tax dodging U.S. soldiers (as noted by Mr. Kristof in the **Times**). The very people who lay their lives down for us, the plutocracy, and the DOD. But we can't blame this all on Mr. Romney; he's just the most recent incarnation of a long line of Republican Party leaders, who have suspended rational thinking for a failed ideology, with ruinous results for the country.

Mr. Romney is rich and his party represents the wealthy, and those who wish to be. Today's GOP is quite possibly more reactionary than ever, and it refuses to change, even at the risk of extinction. This is a party that preys upon your fear, and has no reservation about prevarication or stretching the truth, witness Mr.

Ryan's GOP convention speech (which even his own Party assailed). The antidote for fear is knowledge and education, and as GOP Candidate Santorum conveyed earlier in the Republican campaign, education is no good. You see, education and knowledge gets in the in way of your exploitation, and makes things harder on the ruling oligarchs. The only question that remains this election season is will Mr. Sheldon Adelson and the Koch brothers double-down? How much money is the plutocracy willing to spend in support of a failed candidacy and an attempt to purchase the White House? My guess is a lot more. Cost-Benefit analysis would suggest upping the ante.

Contained is this week's *New Yorker* is an extraordinary piece on the very first political consulting firm, Campaign Inc. The piece is entitled the **Lie Factory**, and was written by Jill Lepore. Needless to say it is outstanding and, among other things, draws the connection between political consulting and advertising campaigns. Both enterprises are selling something.

Among the tried and true principles of Campaign Inc. were: make it personal; candidates are easier to sell than issues; attack, attack, attack; never underestimate the opposition; never explain anything; fan flames (embrace and win controversy); simplify, simplify, simplify.

Said Mr. Whitaker, a partner in Campaign Inc. (CI), which was formed in the 1930's, "A wall goes up when you try to make Mr. and Mrs. Average American Citizen work or think. The average American doesn't want to be educated."

Today, political consulting is big business. Campaign Inc.'s principals are on full display this election season, and they have been a key part of most successful campaigns for the last eighty years. Perhaps by no coincidence, CI's primary clients were big business and the GOP.

If we think long and hard about it, one could easily argue that nearly a century of political consulting has brought the country to where it is today. Where glib one-liners and sound bites are not only used to gain political advantage, and admission to political office, but become public policy itself. It's much easier to trot out negative advertising, than to explain a highly complex problem, and the detailed solution to that problem (and the reality is few candidates have the skills to pull it off, and many have lost office trying). Many of our problems today are so complex that the quick lie or one liner can no longer stand up to scrutiny, and so as we have seen in this election cycle, the candidates don't even try. Again, observe the GOP's criticism of the Romney/Ryan tickets refusal to fill in the blanks on their proposed fiscal and tax policies. And they are the experts?

Or witness both candidates, Messrs. Romney and Obama, failure to address the financial crisis, and the resulting mortgage debacle, four years on-going, and the cornerstone of the nation's economic problems.

Other key examples where the quick fix, or simple solution, have failed the nation are:

Endless rounds of quantitative easing, which is nothing more than code for back door bank bailouts. The Cartel is so powerful now that it appears to be dictating Fed policy. The Fed has become the go to market for MBS and CDO's, the liabilities and moral hazard for bank excess have been transferred from private sector balance sheets and onto the public's. And the result of the Fed's efforts: Stagflation in commodity prices, and Stagdeflation in home prices. Central banks around the world have swaddled zombie banks in a cocoon of soothing liquidity, so that the inevitable write-downs can be postponed at taxpayer, market, worker and business expense. Contagion is spreading and sound healthy currencies and economies are being dragged down with the bad, all so that we can prop up banks. The "lost Japanese decade" scenario is with us to stay now. One can gather from Mr. Romney's reticence on the matter that he would have done nothing different than the President's team, Messrs. Geithner, Summers and Bernanke. *Banking uber alles!*

Check out Mr. Romney's criticism of this administration and its handling of the Middle East. The GOP's solution to every problem involving an Arab country is to subcontract out foreign policy to the state of Israel, play the fear card, and reach for the DOD. That's right, order two air strikes and call me in the AM. That sound bite, the Arabs are the problem, and Islam is the issue, entirely misses the boat. Some in-depth analysis might conclude that there is extreme poverty throughout much of the Middle-East, brought about by wide disparities in economic opportunity and education, and concentrated wealth and power into too few hands. Successive authoritarian regimes, with the economic and military support of Western democracies, have amassed fantastic wealth, at the expense of Arab citizens. Poverty stricken, these Arab citizens have turned to all that they have left, religion and the Prophet Mohammad. In some instances these citizens have been radicalized by poverty, and are all too easily manipulated by their religious and political leaders. The antidote for Arab radicalism is democracy, education, and greater economic opportunity; but that solution will take patience and time, indeed generations, with many problems for U.S. companies operating in the region along the way. This scenario doesn't fit into Big Oil's or the DOD's agenda, so don't look for Candidate Romney to trot that out any time soon. Besides the proceeding doesn't fit into a neat power point presentation, or a Campaign Inc. style sound bite, so forget about it.

Better to sound bellicose and rattle the saber, it plays nicely into many American's fears and prejudice. Campaign Inc. would advise a candidate, and a political party, to have an enemy at all times, and if one can't be found then create one!

And finally, Mr. Romney appears to have an issue with the 47%, who receive some sort of government benefit, many of whom are Republican. The Campaign Inc. sound bite is that these folks are moochers, the state is growing, and the solution is more tax cuts for the wealthy. What doesn't fit neatly into this paradigm is the fact that economist after economist will tell you that concentrated wealth and power (like that which has occurred in this country over the last 35 years, with ever declining upper income tax rates) correlates into lost educational and economic opportunities, and therefore, greater reliance upon the state for solutions. Democratic power abhors a vacuum: and if U.S. entrepreneurs and major corporations are no longer going to hire American, pay a living wage, or provide retirement benefits, then these free market institutions are ceding authority and power to the state, and building an ever growing Democratic base.

America needs an industrial policy that includes favorable policies for business, the market, and the worker. However, industrial policy might also include telling CEO's something that they haven't heard from the GOP in several decades, that is the *laissez faire* fairy tale is dead, markets do not have perfect knowledge and are not self-regulating; hence the need for a new industrial policy.

But that's not very "Campaign Inc." Much better to stick to playing the fear card, campaign on ignorance, and continue to let things slide into crisis.

Channel Your Inner Rahm

By J.M. Hamilton (10-6-12)

On the heels of the debate J.M.H. asked, why did the President bring a rhetorical knife to a ~~gunfight~~ debate? Now, admittedly the President didn't sound bad, but it certainly wasn't his A-game. His body language and non-verbal cues were lethargic. And because the President was in a defensive mode all evening, Mr. Romney, who was positively glowing, never felt any pressure and had absolutely nothing to lose, even if some of his answers were at odds with the GOP platform and his own campaign. To his credit, we saw how Mr. Romney is likely to perform under extreme pressure. Mr. Romney came across as both moderate and empathetic, that is to say, diametrically opposed to his Republican base.

For the President, it was an opportunity squandered. By not finishing off Mr. Romney, he breathed air into his campaign and gave Republicans something very dangerous to the President's second term goal…. hope.

Mr. Romney performed very well, which is ultimately good for democracy because more viewers are likely to tune into the next debate – which gives both Party leaders yet another chance to discuss the issues that really ail the nation. President Obama has campaigned on many of these issues, and these debates present both a challenge and an opportunity to educate the American public. Presently, the debate is government-centric and focused (nothing wrong with that because the government is part of the problem and the solution), but the private sector is not without its ills, inefficiencies, and fraudulent practices, too.

Here then are a handful of questions that the next moderator might ask, but is not likely to. And if the moderator won't ask them, what's to prevent Mr. Romney or the President from turning the question or dialogue to address these issues:

1)   Many of America's recessions in recent decades, starting in the seventies, have been precipitated by oil price shocks. Meanwhile Exxon and the oil cartel report record profits. What would you do as president, or in your second term, to rein in the economic and political power of the domestic oil cartel?

2)   Energy independence is staring America in the face, and yet, Big Oil wants to build a pipeline in Alaska to export natural gas/energy independence to

China and the pacific-rim. All the better to keep prices higher here in the U.S. Do American companies have an obligation and duty to look after America and her markets, first and foremost? And what would you do as President to make sure American interest always come before *government protected private interests*, like that of the cartel?

3) FHFA director Demarco has stood in the way of our economic recovery by denying Freddie and Fannie the ability to restructure and writing down home loans, allegedly, among other reasons, because FHFA made outsized financial bets against restructuring? Now the FHFA is backing away from competing against the banking cartel in initiating mortgages? What should be done with Mr. Demarco?

4) And speaking of cartels, the U.S. protects its citizens in some markets dominated by monopolies, such as power producers and utilities. Government allows these utilities to make a capped or reasonable profit but not monopolistic profits. Would either candidate like to speak to how we can rein in the banking, and oil cartels, and seemingly their unlimited ability to prey upon the American consumer?

5) Would either candidate favor a windfall profits tax on cartels, and/or regulation prohibiting activities that our detrimental to America's economy and national security?

6) America spends more on national security than the G-20 combined… there are obvious inefficiencies in the system, and yet, neither party addresses these issues. U.S. companies also possess more than a 50% market share in the global weapons trade. Is this something America, the champion of democracy, wants to be known for? Please discuss.

7) **Mr. Romney is against trickle down government and Mr. Obama is against trickle down private sector economics…. Would either candidate like to speak to the Federal Reserve's policy of trickle down monetary policy?**

8) Private Equity makes unseemly profits by maxing out an acquisition's credit line, paying themselves a rich reward, down sizing workers and exporting jobs off shore. Should there be any restrictions on these activities?

9) Many private equity acquisitions, encumbered by debt, ultimately end up bankrupt. This in turn puts undue pressure on the government, as unemployed

workers seek government assistance. Question: Should government limit these activities; place limits on the amount of debt /leverage applied to PE deals; and install claw back provisions in PE pay packages, capital gains, and dividends, whereby, if an acquisition fails, the government/citizens will seek redress by impounding profits made in said acquisition/deal?

10) What would either candidate do to stop the revolving door between government regulatory agencies and the private interests they regulate? And more telling still, do government regulators service the industries they regulate, or do they protect America, her markets and the consumer?

11) This one for candidate Romney: Sir, you recently spoke of the 47%... would you like to comment on the 53% and the various forms of government assistance they receive, via the tax code to name just one?

12) And President Obama: The "free trade" movement has benefited the one percent immensely at the expense of American workers, and a more polarized and economically unjust society. Opportunity in America has diminished with globalization and free trade. Your administration passed several Bush era free trade agreements. Would this nation benefit from a more U.S. centric industrial policy? Why or why not?

And there you have it. Questions and much needed responses we are not likely to hear. Nevertheless, both Republicans and Democrats campaigned on some of these same issues, particularly private equity.

President Obama has an opportunity to win in the next debate, and cement his hold on power for another four years. Time to channel your inner Rahm Emanuel, Mr. President.

P.S.

This week former G.E. CEO Mr. Jack Welch took the government to task for allegedly cooking the books. Mr. Welch believes that the unemployment figure is bogus and minted, all in an effort to aid President Obama.

To which J.M.H. responds, what technical expertise does Mr. Welch possess in fraudulent accounting, and image burnishing by numbers?

Be on the look out for my new book coming soon on Amazon.com and Kindle

Dallas Texas - Circa 1992

By J.M. Hamilton (10-12-12)

Obama led by 56 percent to 38 percent among women in a survey of likely voters released yesterday by Quinnipiac University. Romney led among men, 52 percent to 42 percent. – **Bloomberg News 10-3-12**

Young men are full of piss and vinegar, and enough testosterone to fuel a football team or a thermo-nuclear war. It's why we ask them to join the military and protect our markets, fight to preserve the interests of the plutocracy, and lay their lives down in our nation's wars. Many of them our dirt poor, what candidate Romney would call the 47%. When called upon, male youth can be extremely focused, and completely convinced that they know it all.

"Pssst....Jay?"

The sales manager had come up from behind me, and I turned quickly.

"Jay, I hear you are a Republican?" He whispered.

The man was twenty years my senior. I was still in my twenties.

"Yes," I responded.

Decked out in pin stripes and a navy blue suit, he motioned furtively for me to follow him. It was mid-day, during the work week. I was playing hooky or going on a field trip with the boss.

I got in the car. The manager, wordlessly, turned on the ignition and drove out from the under-ground parking. It was a bright day... we drove about fifteen minutes to a rally. Parking, if I recall, was brutal.

We walked into a small hall, and immediately, I felt as if I was suffocating. The air and oxygen were literally sucked out of the room. There was a man at the podium that I could barely see... we were late, and he was well into his speech. Everybody in the room was standing, and howling, feverishly. I could not hear the speaker, but I eventually got into a position where I could see his face.

His hair was black and disheveled, and his white face shined. His eyes burned; he was in his glory. These were his people. And the Texans, or insurgency, was drowning out his every remark with whoops and hollers, and yells of rapturous praise. I only heard snatches of his speech that day. The crowd consisted almost entirely of young men, with a sprinkling of those in their middle years.

Bush (HW) had failed us, and before that Reagan had let us all down, and had compromised with the enemy, the democratic party. And we were not going to take it anymore. The "read my lips - no new taxes pledge" broken, we had enough and we were very angry. We were going to cross the line and vote for the Proto-Tea Party candidate. And if you think about it... he was the man, the original Tea-Partier. The only other politician, that I think now, might make equal claim was Newt Gingrich.

That day.... in that hall.... you could have thrown a side of beef into the crowd and it would have evaporated before it even had a chance to hit the floor. The energy in that room was fierce... more like a rock concert mixed in with a martial arts cage match, than a political rally.

And I remember thinking, if this is how it could always be. If somehow God would bless our nation and we could have a republican party that would stand on principle, that would not yield in its commitment and campaign promises. A man who would not falter under the democratic party's onslaught, who would not cave as Reagan and Bush had, and in a craven manner compromised.   In '92, in Dallas Texas, our heroes had become such a disappointment.

After awhile the rally ended, we returned to the car.   I think we were in shock. We drove back to the office in virtual silence.

Pat Buchanan had rocked our world.   I voted for him in the Texas primary.

Today, now that I'm older, I can see that one has to be careful what one wishes for.   Today, I wish we had two political parties that were willing to talk to each other, work together, and like Messrs. Reagan and Bush (HW) be willing to compromise with the other side, for the good of the nation.

Lesson learned.

The Last Temptation of President Obama

Angel: *"He tested you, and he's happy with you."*

By J.M. Hamilton (10-14-12)

The best Scorsese film ever made is not the film many would think…. I would argue it is **the Last Temptation of Christ**. When the film was released in 1988, many within the Bible Belt were offended. Born-again, Evangelicals, Southern Baptist, many stood outside movie theaters protesting the movie's release. I lived in Dallas at the time and walked across a picket line to see the movie. My guess is many who boycotted the movie did so because their pastor or the religious oligarchy had condemned the movie, not because they themselves had viewed the movie and were offended.

What's so startling about the movie is its literal interpretation of Christ's life, if we believe the paradigm. Namely, that Christ was both man and God, and it was the human component of Christ that made his sacrifice complete. The movie depicts Christ as being sorely tempted by what appears to be a beautiful angel, who tells him that he does not have to die on the cross. If he follows this "angel's" counsel, Christ must know that God loves him, he can have a normal and full life, and all that this entails, including a wife and family. Come down, she beckons.

In the end the angel, as depicted in the movie, is something entirely different, and Christ fulfills his destiny, and dies upon the cross. Christ did not succumb to temptation, and salvation ensues.

President Obama is obviously not Christ, but now more than ever he, too, must be sorely tempted.

Upon entering the White House, the President inherited a situation, an economy and a foreign policy, that was thirty years in the making. And the Republican Party had, by and large, had their way, politically, in shaping the country, the world, and the economy that the President inherited. The shape of the economy was perhaps something that had not been seen or endured by the United States, since the great depression.

Among the economic and social characteristics of what the GOP gifted the President, were:

Two endless wars and failed nation building exercises;
Budget deficits as far as the eye could see, starting with Mr. Reagan and blown out further by Mr. Bush (W);
A sense of privilege and entitlement among the plutocracy, Wall Street, and the business elite that President Eisenhower would have not recognized; Private equity firms preying upon American business to the detriment of the country, the tax base, markets and labor;
A government that had been co-opted by the wealthy and the plutocracy, via the governments/private sectors revolving door, lobbyist, corruption and unlimited campaign contributions;
A country, having been failed by the political elite, that was on full boil, and metastasizing into bi-polar political extremes;
Free -trade agreements and globalization, conducted under the guise of capitalism, that were nothing more than a license to commit tax, regulation, and labor arbitrage… at the expense of the United States;
Unregulated monopolies and cartels, in Big Oil, Banking, and Big Pharma, which create a tremendous tax/drag on the economy; and
A stock market, banking system, and housing market addicted to the easy money policies of the Fed, and who fight, diminish, and co-opt regulators and regulatory bodies at every turn.

To name just a few…

How tempted must the President be?

If he hands the reins back to Candidate Romney, the GOP can continue with their borrow and spend policies, and preside over a government on the fiscal brink, and a struggling economy. The plutocracy can continue down their present path unhindered, to the detriment of the U.S., her markets, and the American people. What a fitting end for the GOP.

If President Obama stays on for a second term, he will have to wrestle with a Republican congress and a government in stalemate. He'll likely receive no economic help from either China or Europe, and the various cartels will fight the President at every turn. The debt to GDP ratio is untenable, but not of Mr. Obama's making. The consumer is tapped out, and not likely to receive any relief from the banking cartel, after it has been bailed out – repeatedly – at taxpayer expense. Public owned GSE's, Fannie and Freddie, are also unlikely to provide little in the way of relief for American consumers and homeowners. Wages and labor opportunities maybe improving but are tenuous. If the President fails during his second term, Americans will blame him and the Democratic Party, and likely forget the thirty year GOP reign and policies that caused the aforementioned events the President inherited.

Many economist will tell you that there might be year or greater lag between when economic and political policy is implemented and the people and the economy see their impact or results. Just ask the first President Bush (H.W.), whose failed re-election bid fell just a couple of months ahead of an economic recovery of his making. Could it be the same for President Obama?

Just how tempted must this President be to throw Tuesday night's debate?

He can retire without a second-term, wealthy, famous, and knowing that he had done his very best for the nation in his first term (accomplishing a great many things, where others have failed).

How great the burden?

We'll all find out just how tempted the President is with Tuesday night's debate.

P.S.

My book is done, complete with never before seen editorials. The title of the book is Playbook. Look for it on Amazon in the next week or two.

Chairmen Bernanke and Trickle Down Monetary Policy

"It's pretty clear that the stock market is the most important transmission mechanism of monetary policy right now," said <u>Peter Hooper</u>, *chief economist at Deutsche Bank AG in New York.* **Bloomberg (10-3-12), Bernanke Seeks Gain for Stocks in Push for Jobs: Economy**

By J.M. Hamilton (10-17-12)

How bad is it when, within the last sixty days, nearly every central bank in the world has added monetary stimulus to the global economy, or intimated that they are about to pop the clutch on the printing presses once again? Answer: Pretty bad.

We are into year four of this crisis, and the politicians have largely abdicated responsibility, and instead relied upon central bankers to lead the way. As J.M.H. has written before, monetary policy is a crude instrument to conduct the affairs of state; and some would argue, myself included, that central banks have only aggravated the situation, with economic contagion spreading. Those European governments that are acting to address fiscal policy and structural reform are doing so under duress, at the expense of those citizens who can least afford the hardship. Moreover, these states are addressing these problems at the point of a financial gun; that is, the threat of having the next ECB or IMF subsidy/bailout withheld. Even left of center governments, elected because the populace it tired of choking on bank mandated austerity, find that once they are in power – they still have to answer to the banks (granted many southern periphery nations are already under bank management).

Meanwhile the 99% suffer, and the one percent prosper.

Any reasonable leader would suggest that it is in Greece's or Spain's best interest to let the banks go under, and reboot their sovereign pre-euro currency. Iceland defaulted, let their banks fail, and today they are economically as right as rain. German politicians, opposed to bailing out their southern neighbors, are beginning to advocate that the PIIGS leave the euro. Apparently, not all Germans are enthralled with Ms. Merkel's commitment to the banks, I mean Euro, and bailing out their neighboring states. But its not that simple, and no leader, even left of center politicians, wants to be responsible for breaking clear of the Euro, or declaring bankruptcy; because to do so would constitute a credit event, and more than likely set off economic Armageddon, via a web of credit default swaps (CDS).

CDS, of course, are insurance products issued by banks that are used to insure government bonds against default, and are also speculative instruments used to bet upon sovereign debt and against sovereign nations. It is these instruments that caused the global crisis in 2008, and it is these very instruments that prevent the world from clearing the decks, and breaking free from the economic malaise that binds most Western democracies to the banking cartel. And as of this date, reform of these CDS instruments, including clearing houses, putting up collateral to back these instruments (an impossibility because who has tens of trillion in security to support a gambling addiction), and transparency, has yet to transpire. It is these instruments that prohibit governments from restructuring, or rebooting old or creating new currencies. Why? Because the banks call the shots and the banks own the governments and the politicians, and again, nobody wants to responsible for setting off a global doomsday scenario.

The symbiotic relationship between banks and governments works like this: the banks screw up in another speculative frenzy; tapped out governments bailout the banks at taxpayer expense; governments borrow to bailout the banks harming their credit rating; interest rates rise; and central and national banks invest in what is by now rapidly becoming junk sovereign debt (witness Spain's credit rating). Hence, creating another bubble, a very un-virtuous cycle, indeed. The politicians fail to rein in the banks, because politicians are owned by them. Meanwhile, the banks and the right-wingers say the problem is not the bank bailouts, but social policies and social spending of the various governments – which leads to calls for austerity. However, in many countries the social spending is but a fraction of the money and welfare spent on the banking cartel.

The great enabler in all this are the central banks. The Fed's stated mandate of course, is maximum employment and price stability, but their real master is the banking cartel, who is calling the shots.

Take the U.S. housing market for instance, which has laid like a dead dog in the street for four to fives years now. The engine of economic growth, the arbiter of Main Street health, and the storehouse of the public's wealth – I write of course of the residential housing market - has languished, losing in some markets as much as thirty percent of it's value. Why? Because nobody has untangled the mess that the bank created: MBS and CDO products, and the MERS registry system.

The banks, of course, don't want engage in traditional lending (preferring instead speculation in securities, commodities, private equity/hedge funds, and public debt), and so have held the economy and the nation's housing market hostage, by insisting that the collateralized mortgage market – or debt securitization - be reinvigorated, so that they can generate huge fees, w/out maintaining any underwriting responsibility for their loans or tying up bank capital.

Whew!

Entre Fed and Chairmen Bernanke, once again: and rather than announce QE4, QE5, etc, etc, etc… the Fed has said it will continue to purchase MBS from the banks in perpetuity to the tune of 40 billion per month, at taxpayer expense.

Gee, do you see another housing bubble on the horizon, with the taxpayer holding the bag yet again? Instead, however, when this blows, the banks will be able to point their collective fingers at the Fed, and blame the public sector once again. Much of the MBS undoubtedly ends up with the GSEs, Freddie and Fannie, which is a favorite whipping boy of the GOP.

With the Fed buying MBS, this frees the banks to pump up a stock market that no rational or sane adult will invest in, because the stock market is now about as safe as a crack den in a very bad part of town.

Mr. Jamie Dimon, on the heals of Chairmen Bernanke's announcement of unlimited MBS purchases, states that the housing recovery is now underway. His bank and the cartel got their way, a reinvigorated collateralized debt market, and now the taxpayer sponsored lending can begin in earnest. There's just two problems: one in five mortgage owners is underwater, and there are still millions of unsold homes in the inventory, many of which are kept conveniently on the sidelines so that home prices can begin to reflate.

Meanwhile, the consumer – the engine of economic growth - is tapped out, mired in debt, and in many instances upside down or underwater on their home loan. The banks refuse to write down the home loans, and do not have to because of the Fed's easy money policies and interest rate suppression. The consumers only means of getting out from under their debt is wage inflation, but wages in this country are suppressed by unemployment and free trade and globalization -which SURPRISE benefit the one percent and the banks. As evidenced by Japan, both the banks and the politicians are willing to wait a generation or more until a real recovery ensues, and home prices reflate; as they control the Fed and global central banks, and as they are wrapped in a cocoon of liquidity – the cartel feels little pain.

In short, Keynesian policy is working very well for the one percent, and has shielded the banks from their responsibility in this crisis. However, Keynesian policy is doing very little for the rest of the nation, because the Cartel is not lending the money out, and it is having little stimulative impact upon the economy.

They say the definition of insanity is doing the same thing over repeatedly, and getting the same negative outcome; but nobody has the *cojones* to call Fed policy insane. The savers in this country are being robbed, via interest rate suppression, so that the folks who put this nation into the tank can prosper in the stock market and with alternative speculative investments, like commodities and fuel (which again, give the 99% the shaft).

Having failed in their endeavor to rescue the American economy, the Fed's monetary policy now appears to be trickle down, at best. That is, the reflation of asset prices, like stocks and commodities, in the hopes that the rich and the elites will spend more, and the breadcrumbs will come floating down to the 99%. This is the very policy that Democrats decry, when Republican reverse engineer taxation in favor of the wealthy. There's just two problems with trickle down policies, whether they be tax or monetary policy: wealth has become increasingly concentrated into too few hands, and the consumer is tapped out… both of which leads to a decreased economic demand.

In short, trickle down monetary policy does not work. And QE3, et al., only prolongs the very painful deleveraging process.

An alternative path? Having failed in its endeavor, and because Keynesian monetary policy is now facing the roadblock of a very nasty cartel, the Fed could consider an alternative solution, which is to raise interest rates, like Mr. Volker did in the late seventies and early eighties. This will force banks to write down asset prices, and offer to restructure or forgive debt on home loans. This will allow housing to bottom and recover. Higher interest rates would stop commodity inflation. It will put interest income back into the hands of savers and the consumer who have fled the stock market for good reason, and spread the wealth of monetary policy throughout all saving classes of society – instead of into the hands of a few. And it would help get this country on its feet again, as savers began to spend. This in turn will generate growth and opportunity, and an expand the tax base and reinvigorate the economy. Higher interest rates would also force politicians to finally put their fiscal house in order, as well as reform the stock market, since capital would flow to bonds and money market funds. Outlawing CDS until this crisis is over, and unwinding these bets, means that the bank's financial gun held to our collective head simply disappears. It's one thing to ask taxpayers to bailout a nation, it's another thing, entirely, for the public support those who bet and gambled against a nation and her people, in the first place. Telling FHFA director DeMarco to move forward and compete against the cartel is also the appropriate thing to do, since lending rates have not fallen as rapidly as the banks borrowing costs.

Of course, there could be short-term side affects to increasing interest rates… some banks might fail, some governments might default, and some of the one percent might get burned betting against nation states and their economies. In the short run, their would undoubtedly be economic hardship and dislocation, but for a finite period of time. The alternative, however, and the path we are presently on, is a stagnant economy, sub par growth, a more polarized society, higher headline inflation, and a Federal Reserve/GSEs loaded up with MBS and CDOs. Not to a mention the ticking time bomb of a disorderly default scenario.

And yet, another housing bubble on the horizon, instigated by the Fed.

Isn't it time for the Fed to reconsider its bank-centric economic policies, and failed trickle down monetary policy?